Twitter
Second Edition

Digital Media and Society Series

Twitter

Social Communication in the Twitter Age

Second Edition

Dhiraj Murthy

The right of Dhiraj Murthy to be identified as Author of this Work has been asserted in accordance with the UK Copyright, Designs and Patents Act 1988.

First edition published in 2013 by Polity Press
This second edition first published in 2018 by Polity Press

Polity Press
65 Bridge Street
Cambridge CB2 1UR, UK

Polity Press
101 Station Landing, Suite 300
Medford, MA 02155, USA

ISBN-13: 978-1-5095-1249-2
ISBN-13: 978-1-5095-1250-8(pb)

A catalogue record for this book is available from the British Library.

Library of Congress Cataloging-in-Publication Data

Names: Murthy, Dhiraj, author.
Title: Twitter : social communication in the twitter age / Dhiraj Murthy.
Description: Second Edition. | Medford, MA : Polity Press, [2017] | Series: Digital media and society | Revised edition of the author's Twitter, 2013. | Includes bibliographical references and index.
Identifiers: LCCN 2017031442 (print) | LCCN 2017031887 (ebook) | ISBN 9781509512539 (Epub) | ISBN 9781509512492 (hardback) | ISBN 9781509512508 (pbk.)
Subjects: LCSH: Twitter. | Online social networks.
Classification: LCC HM743.T95 (ebook) | LCC HM743.T95 M87 2017 (print) | DDC 006.7/54--dc23
LC record available at https://lccn.loc.gov/2017031442

Typeset in 10.25 on 13 pt Scala
by Servis Filmsetting Ltd, Stockport, Cheshire

For Kalpana, Deya Anjali, and Akash
Dedicated in loving memory of Nagavenamma and
Venkatachala Shetty

You're not reducing face-to-face time . . . You don't choose to stay in and do Twitter. It's like those spare moments on the Web when I'm doing another task I switch over to Twitter for literally 15 seconds. There is no fewer face-to-face, no fewer phone calls, there's more awareness of other people in my life and maybe that even leads to further conversation with some people.

Evan Williams, co-founder of Twitter
(cited in Niedzviecki 2009: 132)

Contents

Figures and Tables

FIGURES

Table

Preface and Acknowledgments

"What Hath God Wrought" – Samuel Morse's first message, on May 24, 1844, on the newly completed telegraph wire linking Baltimore and Washington – was a mere 21 characters long. Alexander Graham Bell's first message on the telephone to his lab assistant on March 10, 1876, "Mr Watson – come here – I want to see you," was more liberal: 42 characters long. And 95 years later, Ray Tomlinson sent the first email, with the message "QWERTYUIOP," from one computer in Cambridge, Massachusetts, to another computer sitting beside it. Tomlinson's message: a spartan 10 characters.

In the past, technology determined the length and duration of the message. In the internet age of today, our ability to communicate is seemingly limitless. But the computer has ushered in a new era of brevity. Twitter is a digital throwback to the analog succinctness of telegrams. Yet what is the significance of this electronically diminished turn to terseness? Does it signal the dumbing down of society, the victory of short attention spans, or the rise of new virtual "me" cultures? Are we saying more with less, or just saying less? Or perhaps we are saying more about less. This position is well illustrated by "status updates," short one- or two-line messages on the popular social networking platform Facebook. Though these short messages are often trivially banal (e.g., "mustard dripping out of my bagel sandwich"), they are elevated to "news," which Facebook automatically distributes to your group of "friends," selected individuals who have access to your Facebook "profile," that is, your personalized web page on the site. Once the update percolates to your friends, they have the opportunity to comment on your update, generating a rash of discussion about dripping mustard, and so on. A photo of the offending bagel sandwich might be included as well. Platforms such as Snapchat and Instagram prioritize the role of images, but brief comments remain very important to these media.

This form of curt social exchange has become the norm with messages on Twitter, the popular social media website where individuals respond to the question "What's happening?" with a maximum of 140 characters. These messages, known as "tweets," can be sent through the internet, mobile devices such as smartphones and tablets, and text messages. But, unlike status updates, their strict limit of 140 characters produces at best eloquently terse responses and at worst heavily truncated speech. Tweets such as "gonna see flm tonite!" or "jimmy wil be fired l8r 2day" are reflective of the latter. The first tweet on the site, "just setting up my twttr"[1] (24 characters), by Jack Dorsey, the creator of Twitter, on March 21, 2006, perhaps led by example. This book emphasizes that Dorsey's message, like that of Morse, was brief and, like that of Bell, was unremarkable – setting up one's Twitter and asking the recipient to return.

After 11 years of 140-character tweets, Twitter decided to double this to 280 characters from November 2017. Before rolling the change out to the general public, Twitter began trialing this "feature" with a select group of users (Watson 2017), though initial testing suggested that only 5 per cent of the group opted to use over 140 characters in their tweets (Newton 2017). Critics (e.g., Silver 2017) argue that this will drown out Twitter timelines, compromising the platform's uniquely succinct form of social communication.

Our contemporary use of Twitter – in part a social, political, and economic information network – has evolved over more than a decade. So it may be some years before the impact of the 280-character expansion can be evaluated. Given that our behaviors on all social media platforms are interlinked, it may be that Twitter is answering a call for individuals to express themselves more fully, though in the context of these platforms more broadly, 280 characters is still relatively terse.

By drawing this line between the telegraph and telephone to Twitter, this book makes its central argument – that the rise of these messages does not signal the death of meaningful communication. Rather, Twitter has the potential to increase our awareness of others and to augment our spheres of knowledge, tapping us into a global network of individuals who are passionately giving us instant updates on topics and areas in which they are knowledgeable or participating in real-time. In doing so, however, the depth of our engagements with this global network of people and ideas can also, sometimes, become more superficial. For example, policymaking by elected officials on Twitter may not only be superficial due to brevity, but also potentially dangerous due to a lack of context for foreign policymakers reading these tweets. Of course, the opposite can be true too where brief, superficial tweets are positive, serving as public evidence of continued political engagement.

Many of us would be worried if Twitter replaced "traditional" media or the longer-length media of blogs, message boards, and email lists. The likelihood of this is, of course, minimal. However, Twitter is also mediating access to these types of content for many. For example, Twitter's "Moments" feature presents a selection of trending "news" for users to be able to easily navigate. Though aspects of Twitter such as this may be reducing information diversity or dumbing down what we consume (and this potentially has real effects on politics, economics, and society), this book concludes with the suggestion that there is something profoundly remarkable in us being able to follow minute-by-minute commentary in the aftermath of an earthquake, or even the breakup of a celebrity couple. This book is distinctive in not only having Twitter as its main subject, but also its approach of theorizing the site as a collection of communities of knowledge, ad hoc groups where individual voices are aggregated into flows of dialog and information (whether it be the election of Donald Trump or the death of Prince). The first edition of this book in 2013 was instrumental in starting this conversation, and this second edition continues the important work of thinking critically about Twitter.

Ultimately, Twitter affords a unique opportunity to re-evaluate how communication and culture can be individualistic and communal simultaneously. I also describe how these changes in communication are not restricted exclusively to the West, as any mobile phone, even the most basic model, is compatible with Twitter. Tweets can be quickly and easily sent, a fact that has led to the growth of its base to 313 million monthly active users with 79 percent of accounts outside of the USA (Twitter.com 2016a). This has been useful in communicating information about disasters (e.g., the 2016 Kaikoura earthquake in New Zealand) and social movements (e.g., #BlackLivesMatter). At an individual level, tweets have reported everything from someone's cancer diagnosis to unlawful arrests. For example, in April 2008, James Karl Buck, a graduate student at the University of California, Berkeley, was arrested photographing an anti-government labor protest in Mahalla, Egypt. He quickly sent a one-word tweet from his phone, "arrested," which caught the attention of Buck's Twitter "followers," those who subscribe to his tweets. His one-word tweet led to Berkeley hiring a lawyer and Buck's eventual release. There are, of course, many distinctions to be made between the tweets sent by Buck, or those sent during the Mumbai bomb blasts, and the more unremarkable, everyday tweets. Contrast the tweet Prasad Naik sent moments after the Mumbai bomb blasts, "Firing happening at the Oberoi hotel where my sister works. Faaak!" with Biz Stone's third tweet, "wishing I had another sammich."[2] Though an intentionally striking and loaded comparison, it is just this absurdity that happens daily, hourly, and by the minute on Twitter. This combination of banal/profound, combined with the one-to-many – explicitly – public broadcasting of tweets, differentiates Twitter from Facebook and text messages.

Rather than selectively condemning Twitter (e.g., as a threat to democracy) or, on the other hand, praising it (e.g., a bringer of democracy), the book poses important questions to explore the possibilities and pitfalls of this new communications medium. Although I examine the practice of social media through specific Twitter-mediated events, this book's emphasis is both explanatory and theoretical. Specifically, my prime aim is to better understand the meanings behind Twitter and similar social media through concise yet sophisticated interpretations of theories of media and communication, drawing upon a diverse array of scholars, from Marshall McLuhan to Erving Goffman and Gilles Deleuze to Martin Heidegger. Though this network of thinkers and scholars crosses several disciplines, their work sheds light on a problem of communication faced since the dawn of the modern age: unraveling the connections, to paraphrase McLuhan, between the medium and the message. The chapters present analyses of the shifts in which we communicate by exploring the role of Twitter in discourses of new media forms, communication, social formations, and digitally mediated communities. Early chapters introduce Twitter, historically contextualize it, and present theoretical frames to analyze the medium. Comparisons between historical media forms are made to highlight the fact that new media forms are not all that "new" in many of the ways in which they organize our social lives. For example, when the telephone began to get a critical mass in US households, there were similar feelings of anxiety that the "public" would erode the "private," as anyone could call your house as you were having an intimate family dinner or in deep conversation with a visiting friend. The middle chapters include specific discussions of Twitter and its relationship to journalism, disasters, social activism, health, and celebrities/branding. The book then brings together theory and practice to make conclusions on the medium itself and its role in social communication within an "update culture," a culture in which society has placed importance on updating friends, family, peers, colleagues, and the general public. The question of whether this pattern signifies "me-centric" rather than "society-centric" cultures is explored in the conclusion. At the start of each chapter, I single out an individual tweet to frame the forthcoming chapter.

Since writing the first edition of this book in 2011–13, the arguments I had made in terms of Twitter being a place to update the world about one's experiences, thoughts, and reflections have now become part of mainstream understandings/engagements about the medium. Pop culture has often interrogated why Twitter has become part of our daily lives. The Comedy Central television show *South Park* compares leaving Twitter to suicide (T. Parker 2016) and the celebrity Alec Baldwin makes a cameo appearance as a social media addict who posts compulsively on Twitter, ultimately opting to have antenna implants in his head in order to broadcast his thoughts without even typing (T. Parker 2013). Their parody highlights serious public concerns over the seamless broadcasting of what people are thinking (what Mark Zuckerberg termed "frictionless sharing" (Payne 2014), and such practices may be crossing over into the line of what is colloquially referred to as "Too Much Information" (TMI).

This is an important aspect of public perceptions of Twitter and what role it plays in society. Some argue that the medium has blurred the private and public too much and that the private needs to be more ring-fenced. Others argue that this blurring of public and private is a net positive in the context of Twitter. For example, the medium could potentially be changing citizen activism in countries with no freedom of the press, or providing women with a public sphere to discuss intimate partner violence (IPV) (Cravens, Whiting, and Aamar 2015). Twitter has become the subject of very large social questions and the medium has been placed right in the middle of many prominent debates.

What is noteworthy is that privacy cuts both ways as some argue that they do not want to know what someone had for breakfast a particular day, but at the same time want individuals to be broadcasting live updates during disasters, activist events/social crises, celebrity breakups, and presidential elections. This is tricky terrain. The case of Lisa Bonchek Adams, a mother of three who had terminal cancer and tweeted over 176,000 times, is a good example. With many intimate tweets that explicitly conveyed to her followers her experiences with cancer, she mostly drew support, but also condemnation. On the one side, the argument was that individuals such as Adams should be encouraged to use Twitter in these ways as often patients of chronic illnesses such as terminal cancer need high levels of support and Twitter enables new ways to support these types of individuals both by other cancer patients and survivors, as well as by the public at large (Murthy and Eldredge 2016). Others, such as the journalists Emma and Bill Keller, publicly argued against her approach (Elliott 2014). This case provoked a sharp controversy about the public and the private, and what role Twitter should play in our lives. In an age where some perceive that everything is posted on social media, this case highlights how boundaries are being negotiated and redrawn all the time. And my book too had to be rewritten!

My work on this book has been shaped by generous input and encouragement from family, friends, colleagues, and scholars. I am very grateful for their involvement in the development of this book. Students in my classes over the years have been taught material from early versions of chapters, and offered engaging and highly useful feedback. I am also indebted to my students for providing me with a treasure trove of examples of interesting Twitter users and tweets. Thank you to my former research fellow, Macgill Eldredge, who imported the data sources in chapter 7 into a standardized format and produced the spike data histogram, and my graduate students – Kyser Lough for shooting the image used in figure 1.1 and Jordon Brown for proofreading assistance. The reference librarians at the British Library patiently helped me navigate archives regarding the telegraph, material which fundamentally shaped the historical context of the book. I have greatly benefited from input from my colleagues at Bowdoin College, Goldsmiths (University of London), and The University of Texas at Austin. I would also like to thank Andrea Drugan, Ellen MacDonald-Kramer, Mary Savigar, and the rest of the Polity team for their invaluable support in making this project a reality. Screenshots of tweets are used where possible to provide a fuller context.[3]

Text Acknowledgments

Parts of chapter 3 have previously appeared in "Towards a sociological understanding of social media: theorizing Twitter," *Sociology* 46(6) (2012): 1059–73, and parts of chapter 4 have previously appeared in "Twitter: microphone for the masses?," *Media, Culture & Society* 33(5) (2011): 779–89. Parts of chapter 7 have previously appeared in "Who tweets about cancer? An analysis of cancer-related tweets in the USA," *Digital Health* 2 (2016).

 **L O S T B O Y**
@Truebluеian753

 Follow ˅

Facebook is my Image. Twitter is my mouth.
Instagram is my eyes and Spotify is my Ears.

4:38 AM - 24 Nov 2016

The tweet above compares four popular online social spaces. For those unfamiliar with Twitter, the following chapter explores what the medium is, how it is structured, and how people use it. Twitter may not be a mouthpiece but it is seen that way by many. Others see the medium as facilitating support communities and some have used it for speed dating. The following chapter provides a basic introduction to Twitter as a communications medium.

CHAPTER ONE

What is Twitter?

> It's funny because I actually started drinking late in life, at like twenty-two or so. So my parents who live in St. Louis never really knew that I started drinking. I was with Ev and we were drinking whiskey and I decided to Twitter about it. And my mom was like, "I knew you drink cider sometimes, but whiskey?" (Jack Dorsey, talking with Evan Williams, Twitter co-founder, cited in Niedzviecki 2009: 130)

Blair (1915), in his popular twentieth-century stage song, "I hear a little Twitter and a Song," was, of course, referring to birdsong. However, so ubiquitous has the social media platform become, that for most internet-using adults, to hear a twitter today refers to one of the largest and most popular social media websites.[1] Twitter allows users to maintain a public web-based asynchronous "conversation" through the use of 140-character messages (the length of text messages) sent from mobile phones and mobile devices, including tablets and watches, or through its website. Twitter's aim is for users to respond to the question "What's happening?" in 140 characters or fewer.[2] These messages on Twitter (termed "tweets") are automatically posted and are publicly accessible on the user's profile page on the Twitter website. Tweets are a public version of the types of updates found on popular social media platforms such as Facebook, WhatsApp, and Telegram. One important distinction is that tweets are fully public, rather than being restricted to one's friends. And like these other platforms, tweets can include emoticons and emojis as well as embedded hyperlinks, images, animated gifs, and/or video. The dialogue between Twitter users occurs through the at-sign (e.g., a user can direct tweets to another user by prefixing a post with an at-sign before the target user's name). Anyone can post a tweet directed to @KimKardashian, @real DonaldTrump, or @BrunoMars, and many do. Additionally, anyone can instantly see a tweet and respond to it.[3] One does not even need to "know" the other user or have their permission to direct a tweet at them. Around 4.8 percent of users make their tweets "protected," a status by which only approved "followers" of their tweets have access to them.[4]

According to Lüfkens (2016), there are "793 Twitter accounts belonging to heads of state and government in 173 countries, representing 90 percent of all UN member states." Twitter has 313 million monthly active users with 79 percent of accounts outside of the USA (Twitter.com 2016a). Though it is unclear how many of these users' tweets ever get read, the fact is people are sending tweets and consider them to be meaningful. Twitter co-founders Jack Dorsey and Evan Williams[5] believe that the medium's appeal is due to "its ease of use, its instant accessibility, [and] its short bursts of seemingly unimportant chatter" (Niedzviecki 2009: 129). As these founders of Twitter highlight, one factor that has facilitated the popularity of the medium is its ease of use. Anyone with a mobile phone – and 63 percent of people in the world now have one, while 151 countries have 4G networks (GSMA Intelligence 2016) – can quickly fire off a tweet. And because sending a text message has become a banal activity in scores of countries around the world (Kohut et al. 2011), the learning curve for using Twitter is relatively low for individuals familiar with "texting." The ubiquity of the platform has contributed to this accessibility. As even the most basic mobile phone can be used, the technology is potentially accessible even in impoverished countries, as Twitter allows users to tweet via text in scores of countries, including sub-Saharan Africa (Twitter.com 2016b). This is an important distinction of the medium from Facebook and other emergent social technologies. One does not need broadband internet access or even a computer to regularly use Twitter (this is not to say that Twitter's uptake crosses traditional social boundaries and inequalities). Additionally, the time commitment required to post a tweet is minimal in comparison to posting a blog or publishing other material on the internet. As Twitter creator and co-founder Dorsey (cited in Niedzviecki 2009: 129) puts it, Twitter's attraction is premised on "connection with very low expectation." Indeed, the contribution itself can be of "low expectation."

Though restricted to 140 characters, Twitter has simple yet powerful methods of connecting tweets to larger themes, specific people, and groups. This is a unique aspect of the medium. Specifically, tweets can be categorized by a "hashtag." Any word(s) preceded by a hash sign "#" are used in Twitter to note a subject, event, or association. Hashtags are an integral part of Twitter's ability to link the conversations of strangers together. For example, people during the 2016 FIFA World Cup soccer tournament tweeted with both the #worldcup hashtag as well as tags to indicate teams (e.g., #eng for England and #ned for the Netherlands). Similarly, tweets pertaining to the 2011 Occupy Wall Street movement generally used #occupywallstreet and #ows. By including a hashtag in one's tweet, it becomes included into a larger "conversation" consisting of all tweets with the hashtag. The structure of communication via hashtags facilitates impromptu interactions of individuals (often strangers) into these conversations. It is for this reason that Twitter has been considered useful in social movements like Occupy Wall Street and Black Lives Matter (see chapter 6 for more detail). Because hashtags represent an aggregation of tagged tweets, conversations are created more organically. Just because people are tweeting under the same hashtag, this does not mean they are conversing with each other in the traditional sense. Rather, the discourse is not structured around directed communication between identified interactants. It is more of a stream, which is composed of a polyphony of voices all chiming in. Group chats in other, private, social media platforms such as WhatsApp and Facebook can have some similarities to Twitter feeds. Older technologies that most parallel Twitter in this way are internet chat rooms and telephone party lines. In the case of the "Black Lives Matter" hashtag, it was a confluence of diverse #BlackLivesMatter tweets that contributed to engagement by individuals. Either serendipitously or by reading through scores of tweets appearing second by second, individuals and groups interacted with each other after seeing relevant tweets.

Because tweets can also be directed to specific individual(s), even if she/he is a stranger or a celebrity, Twitter is unique in facilitating interactions across discrete social networks. For example, individuals can and do tweet @KatyPerry, the American pop singer and most followed Twitter user (with over 100 million followers). This form of directed interaction is powerful in that all discourse is public and its audience is not limited to the explicitly specified interactants. Often, individuals tweeting are putting on a show for others. Or there is no show at all. Rather, the ease of interaction offers a platform to voice a concern. For example, referring to the November 2016 shootings at Ohio State University in the USA, @lauriehandler tweets: "It speaks VOLUMES that @realDonaldTrump spent the whole day having a tantrum and never once acknowledged the tragic events at @OhioState."[6] Not only does this tweet emphasize the direct communication of the medium, but also its real-time nature.

A user's profile page, known on Twitter as a timeline (see figure 1.1), includes all tweets (whether or not they are directed to another user). This shapes Twitter because anyone can "lurk" (i.e., observe profiles without their target knowing of this lurking). Not only does this encourage the theatrical aspect of profiles, but it also presents a different picture of consumers of a profile. Specifically, it facilitates new forms of consumption of a user's feed. Because anyone can see anyone else's tweeting history (from music tastes to the fact that one forgot to do the laundry), it not only presents a different view of users, but also allows consumers of a profile to follow "leads" they find to be interesting (e.g., a tweet about a charitable event or a band). On the other hand, this also presents issues of privacy (Murthy 2012). The barriers between public and private become extremely blurred as anyone can see very specific conversations between individuals, which are many times intended to be private but are tweeted nonetheless (given the medium's ability to foster this (see chapter 3)).

The function of following users in some ways mimics a television guide, where you can see a list of channels with some limited information of what is being broadcast on the channel at that moment. If the channel piques your curiosity, you can stay tuned in. On Twitter, one can tune into the timelines of particular Twitter users who can be people you are interested in (from A-list celebrities to your neighbor), a professional organization, a magazine/journal, a company, and so on. The relationship of following and followed within Twitter shapes the consumption of tweets and user profiles. It has become

Figure 1.1   Twitter feed; reproduced with permission of Kyser Lough

commonplace to be "friends" with others on various websites. "Friendship" tends to indicate some level of familiarity with that person. However, on Twitter, one does not need to be on a first-name basis or even "know" the user to follow them. This relational structure leads to Twitter users following popular users (often celebrities or news organizations). Recall the television channel analogy; these popular Twitter users are followed because people would like to tune into these channels (regularly or at least once in a while).

This structure of channels and consumers of channels of information draws from notions of broadcasting (Allen 1992). Specifically, Twitter has been designed to facilitate interactive multicasting (i.e., the broadcasting of many to many). Television and radio are both one-to-many models where a station broadcasts to many consumers. Twitter encourages a many-to-many model through both hashtags and retweets. A "retweet" (commonly abbreviated as "RT") allows people to "forward" tweets to their followers and is a key way in which Twitter attempts to facilitate the (re)distribution of tweets outside of one's immediate, more "bounded" network to broader, more unknown audiences. It is also one of the central mechanisms by which tweets become noticed by others on Twitter. Specifically, if a tweet is retweeted often enough or by the right person(s), it gathers momentum that can emulate a snowball effect. This is all part of interactive multicasting, wherein many users are vying for the eyes and ears of many users. Again, this is in distinction from the more limited set of broadcasters in traditional broadcast media. Additionally, interactive multicasting blurs the role of consumers on Twitter as these consumers simultaneously become producers when they add a phrase and retweet a news story they find interesting. Even if they do not modify the original tweets, a retweet rebroadcasts the tweets to their many followers – though not production, it is broadcasting. Hashtags themselves are emblematic of interactive multicasting in that many users are broadcasting to many users on the topic. The "interactive" part refers to the multimedia content embedded in tweets (including hyperlinks, photographs, and videos). Recipients do not inherently passively consume these tweets. Rather, they can actively navigate this content or they can cross the blurred boundary and become content producers if they comment on the original content or tweet back to the original tweeting user (i.e., the original broadcaster).

Twitter and Social Media

Twitter is often compared to Facebook and sometimes considered as a public version of the popular social networking site. This comparison has some truth to it. Both media are social, tend to elicit regular contributions that are not verbose, and are highly interactive. However, the two media are unique in many important ways. The number of Twitter's daily active users is dwarfed by Facebook's count of more than a billion (Molla 2016). Their business models also differ hugely, with Twitter sticking to light forms of sponsored advertising, compared with Facebook's highly targeted method of not only increasing time spent within the platform, but also tailoring ads based on sophisticated models of their users. This resulted in Twitter's stock price plummeting, a bevy of takeover rumors, and a general bashing of the company on Wall Street. This has led to it being called a "pinata" (Molla 2016). From the perspective of social relations, Facebook involves bidirectional relations. When a friend request is accepted, the friendship is mutual. On Twitter, one can unidirectionally follow someone (which is exemplified in the case of following celebrities). Next, what you post on Twitter has a certain expectation of being public. Barring public Facebook groups, there is a certain level of expected privacy on Facebook timelines. This is not to say that Facebook content is fully private, but there is some general level of expected privacy, however minimal. (The same is true of the popular Instant Messaging platforms WhatsApp and Telegram.)

Twitter is a social media platform. Social media have been broadly defined to refer to "the many relatively inexpensive and widely accessible electronic tools that enable anyone to publish and access information, collaborate on a common effort, or build relationships" (Jue et al. 2010: 4). Social media tend to be publishing-oriented media and the "social" part of social media refers to its distinction from "traditional" media (Murthy 2011). Though Facebook and other social networking sites do multicast, this is not their emphasis per se. Rather, the intention is to foster friend connections through social sharing in a way that is designed to keep ties between users active and strong. Social media's emphasis is broadcast-based and encourages the accumulation of more and more followers who are aware of a user's published content (e.g., tweets).

In other words, Twitter is markedly distinct from Facebook's friend-centered social network model. Twitter, in many ways, shares similarities with blogs, albeit the posts on Twitter are considerably shorter. However, once one's tweets are aggregated, a new structure emerges. This is not merely a technical consideration, but rather the organization of communication as a series of short communiqués is qualitatively different from examining tweets individually. As a corpus, they begin to resemble a more coherent text. Granted, the corpus is disjointed, but narratives can and do emerge. For this reason, Twitter is best considered as a "microblog," a "blog" that consists of short messages rather than long ones (Java et al. 2007). It is considered the most popular microblogging service, though others such as FriendFeed,[7] Jaiku, Tumblr, Plurk, Sina Weibo (Chinese-language), and Squeelr (an anonymous microblogging service) also experienced exponential growth shortly after their launches. Microblogs differ from blogs in terms of the length of posts (a factor which also influences the frequency of posts in the two media). Ebner and Schiefner (2008) usefully compare this relationship between blogs and microblogs to that between email and text messages. In their study of blogs and microblogs, respondents saw the former as a tool for "knowledge saving, coherent statements and discourse," while the latter was most used for "writing about their thoughts and quick reflections" (Ebner and Schiefner 2008). However, the length of microblog posts should not be viewed as inherently deterministic of their communicative function. A key difference between blogs and microblogs is their social organization. Twitter, for example, implements a complex social structure which tweets support and foster. Tweets as "quick reflections" help keep social networks active on Twitter, whereas blogs are inherently more egocentric in focus.

The ways in which microblogs organize social communication may feel new. However, Twitter uses technology developed from earlier internet media such as text-based gaming in Multi-User Dungeons (MUDs), Instant Messenger (IM), and Internet Relay Chat (IRC). IRC and MUDs were early synchronous precursors to Twitter. A difference between these earlier technologies and Twitter is that the latter is almost always in the public domain,[8] whereas many MUDs and some chat rooms had restricted access. This is an important distinction. Twitter has similarities to both blogs and chat rooms,[9] but its emphasis on accessible dialogic communication in the public domain is unique.

Understandably, one may find the differences between microblogging, social networks, and social media difficult to discern. Indeed, the boundaries are often blurry. However, it is important to draw some lines between these categories. At the simplest level, social networks are friend-based networks where maintaining and developing friendship ties are critical (Facebook and WhatsApp are prominent examples of this). Social media are designated as broadcast media, whose intention is to publish content to networks known and unknown to the author (Twitter and Instagram are prominent examples of this).[10] There are different types of social media such as image-and-video-oriented social media. Twitter is one example of a microblogging-based social medium. For the sake of clarity, I define microblogging as an internet-based service in which: (1) users have a public profile where they broadcast short public messages/updates whether they are directed to specific user(s) or not; (2) messages become publicly aggregated together across users; and (3) users can decide whose messages they wish to receive, but not necessarily who can receive their messages; this is in distinction from most social networks where following each other is bidirectional (i.e., mutual). The boundaries of public and private are critical to understanding microblogging as well as its predecessor technologies. Rosenthal (2008: 159) helps make this distinction by observing that "[n]ewsletters by e-mail are still newsletters, but blogs bring personalized and interpersonal communication into the public domain." Microblogs like Twitter follow a similar logic in that they consist of very short updates that can be read at the individual update level (i.e., at the level of the tweet) or as an aggregation of tweets.

Like blogs, microblog entries can be on anything of interest to the author (from interpreting current events to daily trivialities). Microblogs, as a medium, depend on the regularity of content contribution. Niedzviecki (2009: 130) argues that Twitter "works because of its constancy and consistency, [factors which lead you to . . .] stop thinking about what you're revealing and who's on the other end, reading about your mundane life." Microblog services group lists of users together based on interests, and their microblogs throughout the day are able to sustain discernible conversations. As DeVoe (2009) succinctly argues, "successful microblogging depends on having an audience." And tweets have an audience – whether followers of the tweet's author, or strangers. Dorsey (cited in Niedzviecki 2009: 130) believes that Twitter users feel as if they are "writing to a wall" and they feel that "there's not much of an audience with Twitter." However, as Niedzviecki (2009: 130–1) highlights, this is purely a perception and, even if the audience is not "obvious or apparent," that does not translate to an absence of an audience with tweets disappearing into the ether. Rather, like any response-based medium, users would discontinue using the medium if they felt that they were not receiving the level of response they deemed important to them. Additionally, exceptional tweets are regularly highlighted in the media.[11]

Users of social media often consume media produced by people they are not acquainted with, but have found of interest. This is especially true of retweets and trending topics on Twitter. This can lead to interactions with strangers and, albeit more rarely, celebrities. In my research on new media and Muslim youth subculture (Murthy 2010), a respondent of mine recounted how he posted a tweet disparaging Deepak Chopra, only to find that Chopra himself responded and invited my respondent to have a meal with him (an offer which was taken up).[12]

Though instances like this one involving Chopra are the exception rather than the rule, they appear side by side with the hordes of more "normal" tweets. Of course, social network sites can include the banal and profound together (e.g., a Facebook user posts about their breakfast and later announces they are pregnant). However, a key difference here between social media and social network sites is the design of the former to be explicitly public and geared towards interactive multicasting. Combine the two – as Twitter does – and you have real-time public, many-to-many broadcasting to as wide a network as the content is propagated by its users. Though the tweets are aggregated into a microblog stream and constitute a corpus as a whole, they are still individual units. Tweets are analogous to bees in that they exist both as individuals and as part of a collectively built whole (i.e., the hive). And, like bees, a single tweet is a self-functioning unit in and of itself. Indeed, a single tweet can also pack a powerful sting! Ultimately, if an individual tweet is perceived as important to other users, it can travel far and wide, crossing many networks in the process. This is particularly true of tweets in social activism (see chapter 6).

Conclusion

This chapter has introduced what Twitter is and how it functions as a type of social media. A key aspect of this chapter has been to define differences between social network sites such as Facebook and social media such as Twitter. Additionally, Twitter has been explained as a microblogging technology which is specifically designed to broadcast short but regular bursts of content to particularly large audiences well beyond a user's direct social network. This chapter has highlighted how Twitter is structured to increase awareness of others (whether they are "friends" of yours or not). This awareness has been highlighted by Twitter's ability to broadcast the experiences of ordinary people during social movements and natural disasters.

Twitter has not just made the headlines through presidential tweets and breaking events. Rather, Twitter often pervades both the professional and personal lives of its users. For example, Twitter is seen by some as providing an alternative to dating apps (The List 2016). And, in Los Angeles, the Kogi Korean BBQ-To-Go van, which sells Korean-Mexican fusion tacos, sends tweets to its followers letting them know when and where the van will next be stopping and, over six years, amassed over 135,000 followers, and credits Twitter for its expansion to several trucks (Brindley 2015). Twitter has also become an increasingly popular medium for support networks. For example, Lisa Bonchek Adams, a breast cancer patient, tweeted over 176,000 times with many of those tweets about her own cancer experience. Adams's cancer eventually spread to her bones and the mother of three from Connecticut died in April 2015. Her tweets intimately chronicled her cancer experience (e.g., on January 4, 2014: "Very rough day here. Dizziness, weakness, pain. Need the tumours to shrink for relief. That will take time: chemo and radiation") (Murthy and Eldredge 2016). For Adams and many others like her, Twitter functions as a potentially highly engaged support network (see chapter 7 for a fuller discussion of Twitter in health contexts).

Additionally, Twitter has, in some ways, redefined existing cultural practices such as diary-keeping, news consumption, and job searching, to name a few. Indeed, as Clapperton (2009) remarks, it has redefined the way in which consumers complain. As he observes, big companies such as Jaguar trawl social media websites, looking for complaints, and then publicly respond to customers, offering help. And when companies treat customers badly, tweets can and do go viral. When United Airlines forcibly removed Dr David Dao from Flight 3411 on April 10, 2017, @JayseDavid (an everyday user with approximately 600 followers) tweeted "@United overbook #flight3411 and decided to force random passengers off the plane. Here's how they did it," embedding a 52-second video of the incident which became a worldwide news story.[13]

In Twitter's infancy, the platform was viewed as a potential threat to intellectual discourse, ultimately dumbing down communication. However, as the medium has matured, the debate has shifted somewhat to a question of whether Twitter is threatening freedom of the press and democracy. Such an accusation was quite unimaginable in the early years of Twitter. Indeed, in 2013 when the first edition of this book was published, it was more likely that observers of Twitter's fast growth viewed this as part of the ability of everyday people to communicate and have their voices heard. Of course, this is very much part of Twitter's social communication function today. As the sharing of the video of Dr David Dao being dragged off United Airlines Flight 3411 indicates, the ability of everyday users to "report" on what is happening around them remains a highly important aspect of the medium for citizen journalism and democratic engagement.

However, on the flipside, the maturity of Twitter as a way for everyday people to communicate with other everyday people has also made the platform an ideal one for politicians who wish to bypass the press and create their own "direct" accounts of issues. Donald Trump perhaps most effectively did this by labeling all media as purveyors of fake news and a threat to democracy (Borchers 2017). Trump's use of Twitter perhaps provides him with a unique ability to directly communicate with the public. McTernan (2016) argues that it is Twitter's "short, fast, immediate and above all direct and unmediated" nature that has attracted Trump to the platform. Twitter, like many other Silicon Valley-based social media platforms, follows the American notion of free speech. As such, hate speech, as well as extreme political positions, has been able to thrive on the platform. Movements such as the Alt-Right in the USA leverage Twitter through sustained use, leading Luke (2017: 287) to argue that "minimally credible political impossibilities became maximally acceptable rhetorical implausibilities to be tweeted, retweeted, and rehashed in 140 characters millions of times over."

This is partially attributable to the echo-chamber aspect of Twitter wherein liberal voices were not necessarily party to these discussions on Twitter, which were generally being preached to the sender's own choir. It is tempting to label Twitter as a threat to democracy in this vein. Indeed, Twitter is likely to face increasing pressure, especially by European governments, in regards to curbing hate speech, bullying, and extreme views on the platform. However, it is also the "anything goes" pioneering ethos of Twitter that has both retained the platform's uniqueness and plagued the company's profitability. Companies such as Facebook have been much quicker to adapt, customizing their experience to the regulations and requirements of specific countries.

This chapter has not sought to singularly reduce the diversity or complexities of Twitter, but rather to outline some of its functions and uses for those with little or no background of the medium. The following chapters will build upon the structural and definitional frameworks developed in this chapter. However, before doing so, the next chapter will specifically contextualize Twitter within "modern" forms of communications technology.

CHAPTER TWO

Contextualizing Twitter

The first twitter of Spring, How melodious its ring
The first twitter of Spring, How melodious its ring,
its ring,
[. . .]
O'er the down and the dell [. . .]
song birds that flit, Singing cheerily twit, twitter
twit, tra la la, tra la.

(Callcott 1863: 1–7)

In his late eighteenth-century play titled *The Telegraph, or, A New Way of Knowing Things* (1795), John Dent satirizes the effect of the telegraph at the time. As performed at the Theatre Royal in London, its protagonist, Sir Peter Curious, is dead set on getting a telegraph of his own so he can spy on his family and check if his wife, Lady Curious, is being unfaithful. Sir Peter describes the telegraph by saying it is "an apparatus, by which you may find out what's doing in one's family, let it be ever so far off" (Dent 1795: 9). The telegraph's ability to combine the immediacy of messages with interlocutors at great distances fascinates Sir Peter, leading him to add, "if you say in Basinghall Street, 'How d'ye do?' they'll answer you in five minutes, 'Pretty well I thank you' in the blue mountains" (Dent 1795: 9). Sir Peter, particularly keen to spy on his family, claims that the arrival of a telegraph of his own means that "I [Sir Peter] shall know to a certainty, what my Lady is about at Sydenham, and be convinced, whether I have any cause, or not, to suspect her of infidelity" (Dent 1795: 9–10). This notion that the telegraph will blur the boundaries of public and private culminates in a scene in which the coachman, gardener, butler, and housekeeper begin confessing impro-prieties (including the butler's theft of over a dozen bottles of champagne). They know that the days of raiding their boss's liquor cabinet are numbered as Sir Peter will, of course, find out about everything in the future through the telegraph (Dent 1795: 20–21).

Though Dent's play was written over 200 years ago, it is striking just how resonant it is with the contemporary recep-tion to new media technologies which similarly seek to compress time/space (Harvey 1989) as well as shrink/blur the boundaries between private and public. Modern-day Sir Peters snoop on loved ones or children through new app-based technologies, including social media platforms (such as Facebook, Twitter, Snapchat, WhatsApp, and Instagram). Dent's play also highlights the issues of privacy and time/space compression (i.e., shrinking the limits of geography and time). The relevance of his play is, however, much deeper in that the telegraph, his object of interest, has many paral-lels to Twitter. Like the telegraph, it is used to send short messages quickly and, like the telegraph, it is a controver-sial technology. In the eighteenth and indeed nineteenth centuries, most lauded the telegraph (with *The Times* (1796) calling it an "ingenious and useful contrivance" and *Scientific American* heralding it as the bringer of a "kinship of human-ity" (cited in Fischer 1992: 2)). Others at the time viewed it as a means to dumb down society and the harbinger of letter writing's death. Indeed, even in the early twentieth century, discussions of the telegraph's impact on letter writing contin-ued (e.g., *The Times* 1900). Although these early critics saw the telegraph's immediacy and brevity as a threat to letter writing, ironically, the telegraph highlighted the permanence of letter writing in that it remained an important medium. Similarly, when the telephone was seen as potentially replac-ing telegrams, the permanence of the telegram became highlighted; as Peggy Olson in her ad campaign during an episode of the television series *Mad Men* remarks, "You can't frame a phone call. A telegram is forever." Indeed, the Queen of England continues to send telegrams to Britons who become centenarians. Critics of Twitter such as Keen (2010) view social media as threatening blogging and other longer-length electronic media. But will the efficiency, immediacy, and brevity of Twitter, on the other hand, give permanence to earlier, less efficient, and longer-length electronic media? Additionally, as tweets are being archived by the American Library of Congress, will the next communicative technology give permanence to tweets?

Though these broad historical arguments reveal similarities between Twitter and older communication technologies, what makes the medium distinct is also the result of its departures from the telegraph. Specifically, it is free to use, public (or perhaps semi-public), multicast (i.e., many to many), multimedia, interactive, and networked. A multitude of tweets also instantaneously go "down the wire" rather than the one-by-one output of the telegraph messages. The power of Twitter and other social media is also that they are designed to provoke and call forth regular updates from their users. Telegraph messages were often unidirectional dicta or updates. Twitter's interactions are not only more interactive than the telegraph, but the more important point is that these interactions all occur publicly. Highlighting these differences is key to a critical yet balanced understanding of the potential uniqueness of Twitter.

Contextualizing Twitter

Sir Peter, the character in the play mentioned at the start of this chapter, believes that once he gets hold of a telegraph, he "shall then be acquainted with every thing, and find [his] Lady Curious out in all her tricks, and [his] servants too" (Dent 1795: 10–11). Though not "tricks," Twitter has enabled its users to become more aware of certain everyday aspects of fellow users' lives. For example, when someone follows the tweets of people met at conferences, she/he will most likely be exposed to some combination of their daily music listening habits, sports interests, current location, and shopping wish lists, amongst other things. Many see this as a means to get to know people at a more multidimensional level. Additionally, they see aspects of people's lives which are normally not in public view, what Erving Goffman (1959) refers to as the "backstage" of people's lives (see chapter 3 for a fuller discussion). Granted, the boundaries of public and private communication have shifted remarkably in modernity (Murdock 1993). However, speaking in the context of the telegraph and telephone, various emergent communication technologies have had the same effect historically. The question is, to what extent has Twitter further shifted these boundaries? Rather than view Twitter as "the fate of our age," another potential approach is to consider the power of Twitter to democratize media consumption. Does Twitter give consumers greater choice through more inclusive broadcasting? From this standpoint, Twitter users are individual consumers who make reflective decisions on what information they desire in their Twitter feeds. They can choose from a variety of sources: traditional media, individual commentators, friends, leaders in an occupational field, and so on. The hegemony of traditional media sources may be eroded in this case, as whoever is considered to be an expert or simply worthy of being listened to is potentially determined by consumers rather than producers. Or from Durant's (2010) perspective, it becomes more "demotic" (i.e., democratized).

The transistor radio presents a parallel case. Bliven (1924) made the argument that the "new" medium of the transistor radio would give choice to listeners, enabling them to tune into a variety of stations, rather than being forced to consume the viewpoint of one station. He argued that this would enable listeners to be more democratic in their listening as well as more reflective of content. We can think of Twitter as a new media radio in which the Twitter feed of any user is

Figure 2.1   The Notificator; *Modern Mechanix and Inventions* magazine, 1935

like a station. One can choose to tune into particular tweets or user timelines and tune out of others. Following Bliven's logic, this may be facilitating more democratic and reflective consumption.

Twitter can be traced to a long line of innovations in communication technologies. Besides the telegraph and radio, Twitter resembles early social sharing technologies. For example, Benedictus (2010) compares a 1930s message board, The Notificator, to Twitter. The Notificator, as described by *Modern Mechanix and Inventions* (1935), was a "robot messenger" designed to "aid persons who wish to make or cancel appointments or to inform friends of their whereabouts." It had a "continuous strip of paper" on which passers-by (at railway stations and other public places) could write a brief message after inserting two pennies (see figure 2.1). The passer-by's message stays behind a glass panel for two hours. The parallels to Twitter are numerous. Not only are all the messages on The Notificator readable to any interested passer-by, but any passer-by could also direct a message to anyone they wished. Furthermore, Twitter's timeline is a digital equivalent of The

Notificator's scroll of paper. And, like The Notificator, whether that message gets read is not always guaranteed. Benedictus (2010) also points out that, "[as] with Twitter, the size of [The Notificator's] messages was limited, but what they might say was not."

Of course, Twitter has an exponentially further reach than The Notificator, is public at a global scale, and facilitates interactions between unknown individuals rather than intended recipients. Twitter's ability to broadcast tweets to far-reaching unintended audiences – with the exceptional case being a celebrity seeing one's tweet – marks a major shift from the locality of The Notificator's audience. Twitter's audience can be thought of as networked "global publics" (Delanty 2006), through which divergent groups and individuals from around the world are publicly connected. Nonetheless, it is useful to make the argument that public forms of social media are nothing new and that previous generations had already shifted the public/private boundary through the technological mediation of everyday messages. Furthermore, like The Notificator's messages, the terseness of Twitter does not limit its potential meaningfulness. In other words, Twitter is not as "revolutionary" as one might initially think. Rather, it follows a historical line of communicative shifts in public short-messaging services.

Twitter and the "Global Village"

The global aspect of Twitter's reach is important and can be easily understood through McLuhan and Fiore's (1968) notion of the "global village."[1] McLuhan (1962: 31) argued that the process of "new electronic interdependence recreates the world in the image of a global village." McLuhan was referring to his prediction that globalized electronically mediated communications infrastructure was creating a level of interdependence which would enable all parts of the world to be connected in a sort of "global village." A year after he forwarded this theory,

John F. Kennedy was assassinated and television coverage of the event provided ample evidence of the global reach of this broadcast medium (Bianculli 1992: 86).

Twitter has been similarly associated with an amplification of the global village; Morris (2009) believes that "Twitter is closer to the Global Village than the Internet was envisioned to be." If something happens somewhere in the world – regardless of whether it is banal or profound – someone will tweet about it. Human rights activists can keep tabs on potential human rights violations in distant places, and fashion enthusiasts, regardless of where they live, can interact with fashionistas in London and Paris. Twitter can be viewed as accelerating the reach of McLuhan's global village not just in terms of connectedness, but, importantly, in terms of awareness of others in the village. However, the global village is not without faults and limitations. Ayoo (2009) evaluates the possibility of information communication technology as enabling African universities to gain access to journals and other scholarly materials, thus connecting them to a "global village of higher education." However, Ayoo concludes that not all African universities have equal access, leading to an unequal participation in this global village. Taken within a context of Twitter, students at universities in affluent countries can send tweets to authors of books and follow researchers at non-profit organizations, leveraging the power of the global village to educate them. Their counterparts at less well-off African universities may remain disconnected from this village due to a lack of technical and/or social capital. Ultimately, cases like this demonstrate that the global village – like "local" villages – remains highly stratified, and the idea of being able to be connected with anyone in the world through a 140-character tweet is an ideal rather than a reality. That said, we do seem more "connected," an argument made by Castells (1996) in his conceptualization of the "Network Society." Watts (2003) and Barabási (2003) also argue that computer networks are increasing our connectedness.

However, this perceived connectedness is economically mediated. Facebook, Google, and Twitter are all corporate entities, whose ultimate allegiance is to investors and shareholders. From this perspective, Shah (2008) argues that applying the term "global marketplace" rather than global village is perhaps more apt. In this vein, Twitter is perhaps also a global marketplace for ideas, commodities, and ourselves. This notion of Twitter as a global marketplace is also useful in understanding the power that influential Twitter users have within the medium's global publics. Specifically, a tweet from an African university student has more limited "success" in Twitter's global marketplace than tweets from users who have more Twitter clout. However, at the same time, if that student tweets something profound (e.g., about an imminent labor strike), that tweet could potentially be widely consumed in the marketplace. There is an interesting tension here. Though Twitter as a global marketplace has unequally distributed influence, it has some resemblances to McLuhan's global village in that even far-flung individuals are not only connected to an immense global network, but their voices can potentially be amplified exponentially. Though this is an interesting paradox of the structure of Twitter, it is a paradox that other communications technologies before it have also experienced.

Conclusion

John Dent's play, introduced at the start of this chapter, reveals many of the similarities between the telegraph and Twitter. Sir Peter Curious saw the telegraph as compressing space and time (sending messages quickly across great distances) and bringing the private more into the public (discovering the private actions of Lady Curious and his servants). Twitter follows these historical shifts. But, aided by technological and social change, it has amplified these processes. Just as the telegraph did not determine the erosion of privacy, neither has Twitter. Rather, the private has become more public over time. Indeed,

The Notificator displayed many "private" interactions between people to any railway-station passer-by. Like the telephone, Twitter has not determined social sharing across great distances, but has facilitated already emergent shifts in social behaviors.

This chapter has also explored how Twitter has potentially extended Marshall McLuhan's notion of the "global village," an idea that everyone in the world is connected in the image of a village. However, it is important to emphasize that Twitter follows an already well-trodden path along which the telegraph, telegram, radio, television, telephone, and email have already been before it. Additionally, like these previous technologies, Twitter's access is not universal throughout the "global village" and, as such, there are disjunctures and differences in terms of who is actually connected to the village.

Additionally, this chapter has contextualized the succinctness of tweets. In the past, technology determined the length and duration of the message. In the internet age of today, our ability to communicate is seemingly limitless. However, mediated communication (as opposed to face-to-face communication) has, in many countries, been marked by a new era of brevity (or a perceived era of brevity). In this vein, Twitter is a digital throwback to the analogue succinctness of telegraphs and telegrams – a comparison analogous to Standage's (1998) reference to the telegraph as the "Victorian Internet." Yet what is the significance of this electronically diminished turn to terseness? Does it signal the dumbing down of society, the victory of short attention spans, or the rise of new virtual "me" cultures, in which, as Marshall Berman (1982: 22) puts it, "the individual dares to individuate himself"? Are we saying more with less, or just saying less? These questions are intentionally sweeping. However, they are indicative of questions asked when communication technologies of the past became popular. This chapter has explored some of these questions, and subsequent chapters will build upon these answers.

It is tempting to focus on the relative infancy of Twitter.

However, this is at the expense of gaining a richer under-standing of the historical context of the medium. Ultimately, Twitter, like the telegraph, has gained significant public atten-tion. And, like the telegraph, a new, revolutionary technology in its time, Twitter is experiencing immense growth as well as harsh criticisms. Despite the centuries of separation, the users of both technologies share a common motive: the desire to communicate. James Boaz (1802: 2), in his patent application, talks about one ship vessel approaching another and using an optical telegraph to say: "I wish to speak with you." Though far less cumbersome than the 25 lamps of Boaz's telegraph sign-aling system, perhaps Twitter's hundreds of millions of users are just trying to do the same: "I wish to speak with you." This time around, users do not even have to wait five minutes to hear from the blue mountains. "@SirPeter Pretty well I thank you" would be tweeted back right away. Also, unlike the tel-egraph, anyone in the world could be reading @SirPeter's messages, replying to him, or circulating his thoughts to their friends, family, and colleagues.

Natasha T-R
@NatashaT_R

Lying in bed... Checking twitter and thinking...
Maybe Ill nap and study later.

12:59 PM - 17 Nov 2011

@NatashaT_R[1]

This chapter begins with Kierkegaard's critique of modernity as fantastical in its dreams, but ultimately lazy. The tweet above would be perfect Kierkegaardian fodder. But, rather than view Twitter as redolent of a lazy culture unable to converse in lengths greater than 140 characters, a set of theoretical frames is provided here to better understand the complexities of how Twitter and social media more generally are part of our social lives. Larger questions of whether Twitter exposes us to different worldviews or whether it reinforces existing isomorphic social structures are specifically explored.

CHAPTER THREE

Theorizing Twitter

> [F]or indications are the only thing the present age achieves, and its skill and virtuosity entirely consist in building magical illusions; its momentary enthusiasms which use some projected change in the forms of things as an escape for actually changing the forms of things [and, eventually] this present age tires of its chimerical attempts until it declines back into indolence. Its condition is like one who has just fallen asleep in the morning: first, great dreams, then laziness, and then a witty or clever reason for staying in bed. (Kierkegaard and Dru 1962)

Twitter is not merely a communicative technology. Rather, as Heidegger (1977: 4) warns, regarding technology as "neutral [. . .] makes us utterly blind to the essence of technology." Ultimately, computers and other technology form the medium, but are not divorced from the social. In his essay "The Question Concerning Technology," Heidegger forwards two statements regarding technology: "Technology is a means to an end" and "Technology is a human activity." He argues that the two definitional statements are not mutually exclusive and actually belong together. From this vantage point, technology is "a man-made means to an end established by man" (Heidegger 1977: 5). It is also, from his perspective, a "way of revealing" (Heidegger 1977: 12). This is where Heidegger is particularly useful for understanding the complexities of technology in relation to social media. Specifically, Heidegger conceptualizes this "revealing" through the concept of *Herausfordern*, which can be translated as "to call forth or summon to action, to demand positively, to provoke" (Heidegger 1977: 14). Rather than being neutral, the power of Twitter and other social media is also that they are designed to provoke and call forth regular updates from their users.

This chapter presents the first steps toward a theoretical understanding of Twitter. Rather than rush to breathlessly describe its novel role in contemporary economic, political, and social life, the points put forward in the previous chapter are built on by taking a step back and considering Twitter in broad theoretical terms. This chapter is intended to provide a selected literature review and a set of directions for scholars, students, and practitioners by making connections to scholarship in communication, sociology, and philosophy. A broad array of theoretical perspectives is purposely explored to both explain the nuances of understanding Twitter and provide a framework for understanding later chapters that focus on particular applications of Twitter. In this chapter, particular emphasis is placed on Erving Goffman's interdisciplinary work in order to provide a solid theoretical framework to critically explore Twitter's role in social communication. Other areas explored are democratization, self-identity, community, and the modern "event society." I will start with Lev Manovich's (2001) concept of the digital object as it is useful in understanding how the various components of tweets and Twitter itself come together.

Twitter as a Digital "Object"

Manovich (2001: 13) makes an argument for the theorization of "new media objects" rather than viewing new media as "products" or forms of "interactive media." For him, a new media object "may be a digital still, digital composited film, virtual 3-D environment, computer game, self-contained hypermedia DVD, hypermedia website, or the Web as a whole" (Manovich 2001: 14). Viewing from the perspective of the object in Manovich's invocation allows us to fluidly group together spaces of new media and to explore their cultural significance.

Following Manovich, it is useful to consider the environment of Twitter as a digital object containing further digital objects. Specifically, tweets (individually or actively) can be thought of as digital objects, as can the retweeting of sets of tweets, and so forth. Interactions (e.g., a set of at-mentions) can also be thought of as digital objects. We can then see the emergence in Twitter of discursive objects that have no set configuration. They can be composed of tweets with photographs, hyperlinks to blogs, hyperlinks to articles, and conversations with other Twitter users. A utility of the concept of object in this case is that it lends itself to an exploration of the parts that make the object, leading Manovich (2001: 15) to observe that the object helps us "instead focus on determining the new-media equivalent of a shot, sentence, word, or even letter." In the case of Twitter, we can examine interactions as objects or parts of objects. For example, a set of tweets with photographs of a natural disaster could be thought of as the "new media" equivalent of a photographic essay, all the tweets together forming a visual digital object. Include text from other tweets and a new object emerges. Though this fluidity itself can cause problems, it also highlights the fact that changing these configurations reveals certain social meaning that can be discovered from Twitter (and similar social media). In this case, the object is useful in understanding social representation, refiguration, and reproduction. As Manovich (2001: 15) emphasizes, "new media objects are cultural objects; thus, any new media object [. . .] can be said to represent, as well as help construct, some outside referent: a physically existing object, historical information presented in other documents, a system of categories currently employed by culture as a whole or by particular groups." In other words, the digital objects that emerge from Twitter represent cultural objects that can be meaningful and even potentially evocative in the way physical objects are. Though this sounds quite abstract, computer-mediated communication has been doing this for some time. Just as emoticons and emojis are imbued with meaning as digital objects (Derks et al. 2008; Riordan 2017), Twitter can give birth to similarly meaningful digital objects configured in many different ways (e.g., a highly retweeted tweet can become a digital object in its own right).

I Tweet, Therefore I Am

Self-presentation is an important aspect of Twitter. Though not reductively Cartesian (i.e., "I think therefore I am"), the act of tweeting is born from individual contributions and is about self-production. Indeed, microblogging services depend on regular posting by users. Without this regularity, the utility of social media such as Twitter diminishes significantly. As for status updates on Facebook, users of social media continue to regularly post as the status-updating practice becomes a meaningful part of their identities (Boon and Sinclair 2009; Nosko et al. 2010). Daily tweets that indicate what one had for breakfast or what one is wearing can easily be relegated to the merely banal. Indeed, "good morning twitter" and "goodnight twitter" are not uncommon. But, from Bourdieu's (1984) perspective, the daily, sometimes "banal" is pregnant with meaning. Indeed, Bourdieu (1984) was interested in the banal minutiae, which included what one had for breakfast. Reading the banal historically can also give it new meanings. Dayan (1998: 106–7) gives the example of how everyday, originally personal, discourses of emigrants can then be collectively understood historically to give insights into momentous decisions such as migration. In other words, documentation of the banal can be of direct historical value. Diary entries are another important example. They have traditionally documented everyday events, the "little experiences of everyday life that fill most of our working time and occupy the vast majority of our conscious attention" (Wheeler and Reis, cited in Bolger et al. 2003: 580). Mediated documentation of the banal is also nothing new. Indeed, nineteenth-century cultural critics such as Baudelaire lamented the ubiquity and banality of photography (Baudelaire 1965). Burgess and Green (2009: 25) discuss how the posting of everyday videos on YouTube is a digital version of activities including scrapbooking, family photography, and VHS home movies. The role of the banal and Twitter is best understood within this broader historical context.

In the case of Twitter, "banal" tweets serve as an important vehicle of self-affirmation. We can read tweets such as "had too many espresso shots today" as a means by which individuals affirm their identities in a constantly shifting environment, one that Bauman (2000) terms a "liquid modern" world. The seemingly banal tweet becomes a means for them to say "look at me" or "I exist." This need to affirm their identities keeps regular users invested in the act of tweeting (sometimes daily or hourly). This is part of what Ellerman (2007) extends into the psychological concept of "inventing the self," a cognizant, explicit self-awareness and affirmation of self. Goffman (1981: 21) also notes how our daily communicative rituals have considerations of "ego" and "personal feelings."

It is also useful to draw a comparison between mobile phone text messages and Twitter. Though the former is a private bilateral communicative act, its length and content are often similar to those of Twitter. As Licoppe (2004: 143) found, mobile phone-mediated communication helps people tell each other about their days, which brings the communicating individuals "closer." And this feeling of "closeness" is in no way lessened by its mediated state. Rather, as Putnam (2000: 27) argues, internet-mediated communication presents a counterexample to the "decline of connectedness" we see in many aspects of American community life. Shirky (2010) extends this argument by noting that in recent years the hours of television American youths watch has declined (a first, given its always upward trajectory), a fact he attributes to an increase in hours spent using social media and other internet applications.

Regardless, it is not difficult to make the argument that these forms of self-confirmation are redolent of the nihilism Heidegger associates with aspects of modernity. However, it is critical that we recognize the importance of these posts to the identities of the posters. We can understand this through "Bildung," which Herder (cited in Gadamer et al. 2004: 8) refers to as "cultivating the human." And Gadamer (2004: 8) explains Bildung as the "concept of self-formation." From the perspective of identity, Gadamer (2004: 10) sees Bildung as describing "the result of the process of becoming," which, as such, "constantly remains in a state of continual Bildung." Though it is easy to view tweets merely as a crude mode of communication, doing so misses the impact that tweets have on one's Bildung. For active users of Twitter, posting tweets is part of their identity maintenance, and the constancy of active Twitter users confirms this relationship, or, as a Cartesian aphorism: I tweet, therefore I am.[2] Though tweeting is part of becoming for its users, it departs from Cartesian dualism in that the former is contingent on a community of interactants, whereas the latter makes the argument that the individual mind is thinking and, as such, stands apart from community and, indeed, the body. Examining Twitter alongside Cartesian thought reveals that the former complicates the autonomous individuality of the latter. Specifically, Twitter seems to provide ways for individuals to assert and construct the self which are contingent on a larger community of discourse.[3]

Twitter as Democratizing?

One shortcoming of understanding social media through Bildung is that it does not capture the shift that media have experienced from being exclusively elite forms to more accessible ones. In other words, has the medium of Twitter opened up access to the production of selves by tweeting? Turner (2010: 2) argues that contemporary media forms have experienced a "demotic turn," which refers to "the increasing visibility of the 'ordinary person' as they have turned them-selves into media content through celebrity culture, reality TV, DIY websites, talk radio and the like." Turner (2010: 3) makes the key point that the media have perhaps experienced a shift from "broadcaster of cultural identities" to "a transla-tor or even an author of identities." George Gilder (1994), a dot-com cyber evangelist, extended this idea much further, arguing that new media would be "moving authority from elites and establishments [and that these . . .] new technolo-gies [would] drastically change the cultural balance of power." However, Turner is more cautious, pointing out that the "demotic turn" seen in contemporary media should not be conflated with democratization and the end of the digital divide. Specifically, he argues against Hartley's (1999) notion of "democratainment," arguing that, in neologisms such as this, the democratic is most always secondary (Turner 2010: 16). He argues that no "amount of public participation in game shows, reality TV or DIY celebrity web-sites will alter the fact that, overall, the media industries still remain in con-trol of the symbolic economy" (ibid.).[4] The natural question that arises is whether Twitter is different in any meaningful way. An argument can be made that, within Western society itself, Twitter does represent a significant "demotic turn" (i.e., ordinary people are able to break "news," produce media con-tent, or voice their opinions publicly). Katz et al. (1955: 219–33) argue that "opinion leaders," the "transmitters" of influence, play a key role in the "flow" of influence. They can have rel-ative status in particular settings such as a workplace or interest community. If Twitter helps promote ordinary people into well-known "opinion leaders" (from citizen scientists to citizen fashionistas), the medium may be challenging tradi-tional media hierarchies or, at a minimum, generating new forms of influence and new types of "influencers." However, if most tweeting "opinion leaders" reflect influence already present in traditional broadcast media, Twitter does not repre-sent a significant redress in systems of communicative power.

Twitter may be exposing us to a selection of new viewpoints and voices, but the actual influence of these voices may be relatively limited.

Even if the influence of ordinary people on Twitter is minimal, the medium can potentially be democratizing in that it can be thought of as a megaphone that makes public the voices/conversations of any individual or entity (with the requisite level of technological competence). However, Durant (2010: 5) cautions against "treating media communication as being like an ordinary conversation that has simply been amplified and made public." With Twitter, Durant's advice is particularly applicable in that discourse on Twitter becomes transformed by the medium rather than merely being amplified. Specifically, the ways in which we communicate via social media in general are qualitatively different from traditional face-to-face communication (though not in every respect, of course). Because the medium encourages association, users are already thinking of what hashtags to include in their messages, or who should be @- mentioned. Additionally, each communicative act has an element of self-advertising, so tweets as a mode of communication inherently involve methods to promote the propagator of a tweet to a larger audience. For example, if someone includes a trending hashtag in a tweet, it is many more times likely to be read by others through trending topic searches or through retweets (boyd et al. 2010; Kwak et al. 2010).

Another reason why it is important to think of Twitter as not being simply amplified is that the meanings of messages on Twitter are a product of different circumstances than, for example, a face-to-face muttering to a friend. The same muttering posted on Twitter can take on different meanings, not just in its initial tweeting, but if it gets retweeted. A useful way to think of this is through semiotics, the sociolinguistic practice of understanding signification in communication. Every word we speak or write, argues Saussure (1916), is part of a structure of meaning. Simplified, this meaning can be represented by symbols (or "signs" in his terminology) which signify (i.e., stand for) something. What they stand for is not self-evident or, as Guattari (1995: 52) puts it, "signifying semiotic figures don't simply secrete significations." Similarly, if tweets are read in this way, they do not "secrete significations," but rather need to be interpreted. (Menchik and Tian (2008) do this in their semiotic study of email.) Technological spaces, or, as Guattari refers to them, "mecanospheres," do not merely amplify meaning; rather, the mecanosphere "draws out and actualises configurations" (Guattari 1995: 49). Though pre-dating current interactive Web technologies, Guattari is interested in deterritorialized "ontological universes" (ibid.), spaces where we (re)produce our identities. What is particularly significant is that technological spaces can mediate the connecting together of actors from a seemingly infinite set of combinations.

When one is searching for tweets, whose tweet you may stumble upon and where that will lead you remain unknown variables. This has real impact on the significations individuals intend when they tweet. Ironically, as Enteen (2010: 9) argues, this is a "seductive" aspect of the internet in that it "seduces its users into believing that the entire world can be reached by clicking a mouse [while,] the majority of users traverse only a fraction of available pathways." Though we can think of infinite possible configurations, we still only traverse certain paths on the internet (e.g., Amazon, Wikipedia, eBay, major news sites, and Google). Similarly, Twitter "seduces" its users into thinking tweets will traverse more pathways than they do in practice.

Twitter and the Event-driven Society

Microblogging, more than many web spaces, is event-driven. Indeed, part of Twitter's "seductive" power is the perceived ability of users to be important contributors to an event. Specifically, organizing social life by events presents opportunities for everyday people and traditional media industries to tweet side by side. One way to render this visible is through Twitter's "trending topics" function, a list of the most popular subjects people are tweeting about. Interestingly, there are always "populist" trending topics, such as what people are listening to, celebrities one hates, or the "#ToMyUnbornChild" trending topic which elicited tweets from soon-to-be parents to their unborn children. Simultaneously, a significant number are based around breaking news events (e.g., the death of Prince or the 2016 Kaikoura, New Zealand, earthquake). Though traditional media industries usually determine what events become considered important, some trending topics come into being through a single tweet or a small group of individuals.

The importance of trending topics on Twitter can be understood as part of what Therborn (2000: 42) calls the "event society (*Erlebnisgesellschaft*)." Huyssen (2000: 25) helpfully translates this as a "society of experience," which is event based. Seen as part of the larger cosmology of Twitter, this reflects a particular aspect of modernity in which events, however transient or superficial, are of importance to society. Huyssen's explanation of *Erlebnisgesellschaft* captures these elements well. He writes that the term "refers to a society that privileges intense but superficial experiences oriented toward instant happening in the present and consumption of goods, cultural events, and mass-marketed lifestyles" (2000: 25). Through this reading of *Erlebnisgesellschaft*, the intriguing question of what constitutes an "event" itself emerges (e.g., does it constitute an "event" when Lord Alan Sugar, boss in *The Apprentice* UK television show, is mouthing off to Labour Party politician Ed Balls (Harp 2016)?).

Erlebnisgesellschaft seems to draw from Kierkegaard's (1962) argument that "the present age is an age of advertisement, or an age of publicity: nothing happens, but there is instant publicity about it." Tempting as it is for some, applying Kierkegaard's "nothing happens" argument to Twitter is a potentially dangerous path. Rather, as argued previously, our interpersonal interactions on Twitter, as well as other new media such as Facebook and LinkedIn, are part of our daily happenings. And, following Adorno (1991), our daily interactions with these media are very much a part of our larger socioeconomic life. For Adorno, our interactions with any media are routed through what he calls the "culture industry," institutions which control the production and consumption of culture. What we listen to or what we read are all mediated by the culture industries and, from his perspective, its "commercial character" (Adorno and Bernstein 1991: 61). Ultimately, relegating Twitter to a space where "nothing happens" not only ignores the fact that the interactions we have on Twitter are a product of larger social, political, and economic process, but it also smacks of elitism (a charge which Waldman (1977) argues was, ironically, often leveled at Adorno).

In their work on YouTube, Burgess and Green (2009: 7) observe that there has been an "exponential growth of more mundane and formerly private forms of 'vernacular creativity'." Ultimately, viewing Twitter as mere web chatter ignores this vernacular creativity to which Burgess and Green refer. Instead, there is more analytical purchase in understanding the consumption of perceived "superficial" and "transient" viral videos or tweets, which become constituted as a cultural "event." As people retweet or forward videos to others, and discussions ensue offline and online, the media event is born. Television has been highly successful in constructing media events (especially in the years that people collectively tuned in on a particular day and time for the next installment of a show). For example, the episode "Who shot J.R.?" in *Dallas* and the series finale of *Magnum PI* are considered to be prominent "media events" in television history (Butler 2010: 139). These events were discussed for days and months afterwards and became part of the cultural memory for a generation of American television watchers (Austin 2011: 66). Through viral levels of retweeting and trending topics, Twitter has this ability to construct memorable media events as well.

However, Kierkegaard's argument remains critically important to understanding Twitter. The latter part of his argument is particularly useful. There is definitely an "instant publicity about it" in that everything from one's daily happenings or musings becomes part of a publicity-driven culture. In a sense, Twitter markets us through our tweets and, as such, shifts us more toward "an age of advertisement," where we are not necessarily advertising products, but rather ourselves (and our self-commodification). This can generate a '"lowest common denominator" culture' of exhibitionism (Hogan 2010). And this can also encourage cyberbullying, which has the potential to cause real harm or distress (Whittaker and Kowalski 2015).

Twitter and Homophily

By nature, events are inclusive for certain groups of individuals. For instance, the trending of the soccer World Cup unsurprisingly includes global fans. One important question is whether Twitter is able to bring together dissimilar individuals to events. This is particularly relevant because theorists of "cross-talk," a field of sociolinguistics which studies "intercultural communication" (Connor-Linton 1999), argue that coming into contact with differing or antagonistic perspectives can play a beneficial role in developing an energetic civic culture (Liebmann 1996). What role does Twitter play in cross-talk? Most users do not elect to follow the tweets of people/institutions widely dissimilar to themselves. Rather, as the new media literature has shown, people online, as they do offline, tend to associate with like-minded people (boyd and Ellison 2008; Livingstone 2008). This pattern is known as "homophily" or, more colloquially put, "birds of a feather stick together" (McPherson et al. 2001). In the case of many internet applications, this homophily is combined with an elite bias, making for an even greater digital divide versus email and other more "basic" internet functions (Witte and Mannon 2010). There is no doubt that heterogeneous interactions would increase the diversification of "circles of followers" on Twitter. However, the question is whether Twitter is exposing us to birds of a different feather. This is potentially relevant because heterogeneous interactions within associations/ organizations are directly correlated with increased tolerance and social integration (Coleman 1988). In other words, these groups are positively affected and become more cohesive. The literature on homophily (especially McPherson et al. (2001) and Yuan and Gay (2006)) demonstrates its effect on limiting group heterogeneity offline. McPherson et al. (2001: 415) put this simply: "similarity breeds connection."

Some have argued that Twitter has broken homophily's grip. The usually tempered *Christian Science Monitor* suggests that Twitter should receive the Nobel Peace Prize for exposing us to divergent viewpoints from ordinary people (Pfeifle 2009). However, as McPherson (2001: 415) observes, "people generally only have significant contact with others like themselves." And, unsurprisingly, the "people like us" (McPherson et al. 2001: 416) paradigm of compatibility is self-reinforcing. No significant research has been done to counter homophily on Twitter. Indeed, research has shown that homophily is positively correlated with information diffusion (De Choudhury et al. 2010). However, it is useful to make the hypothesis that it is potentially easier to break homophilic boundaries on Twitter. This, of course, involves willful action by individual users. That being said, some do decide to follow tweets from users very different from them after reading a tweet they posted on a subject of interest. The million-dollar question is whether this has any significant effect on the worldview of Twitter users or whether it disappears in the web of *Erlebnisgesellschaft*. Research demonstrates that "Twitter users are unlikely to be exposed to cross-ideological content from the clusters of users they followed, as these were usually politically homogeneous"

(Himelboim, McCreery, and Smith 2013). In other words, Twitter has a propensity to act as an echo chamber.

Telepresence and Immediacy

The importance of tweeting to homophily and self-production explains some of the reasons people tweet regularly and with conviction. However, this only tells part of the story. That is, tweets, when aggregated in particular combinations, become important digital objects to their interlocutors. One of the ways in which they become particularly important is through their transformation into objects which are no longer perceived as digitally mediated.

In a class I teach on sociological understandings of the internet, the first reading I assign to students is "The Machine Stops" by E. M. Forster ([1909] 1997), a dystopian story which sees an earth devoid of oxygen in which all our interactions with the world take place from our own rooms (mediated by "the machine"). A key section of the story tells of a woman, Vashti, who is engaged in a primitive video chat with her son, Kuno, "who lived on the other side of the earth." Kuno asks her to come visit him in person ("I want you to come and see me"), but Vashti replies, "But I can see you! What more do you want?") (Forster [1909] 1997). The philosopher Hubert Dreyfus (2009: 49) sees Forster's vision as quite prophetic, arguing that we "have almost arrived at this stage of our culture" in that "our bodies seem irrelevant and our minds seem to be present wherever our interest takes us." Dreyfus considers emergent "Web 2.0" technologies as the bringers of a sort of "disembodied telepresence" (2009: 49–71) in which, like Vashti, people do not see computer-mediated communication as mediated communication.

Computer-mediated communication in general often makes us feel as if we're in a non-technological space, which has the immediacy of face-to-face communication. This occurs through the process of "telepresence," which is defined as the "perceptual illusion of nonmediation" (Lombard and Ditton, cited in Bracken and Skalski 2009: 3). The term is often associated with Minsky (1980), the founder of MIT's artificial intelligence laboratory, and has been used to understand immersive technologies such as Skype or virtual reality (VR) in which three-dimensional goggles or other technologies are worn (Bracken and Skalski 2009). Ultimately, telepresence is useful for understanding the perception of users that they are "there" and are not experiencing mediated interactions. However, telepresence is not restricted to immersive graphical technology and this is important for understanding our use of Twitter. Licoppe (2004: 152), for example, argues that the "mostly short and frequent communicative gestures" of mobile phone calls and mobile text messages create a "frequency and continuity" through which "a presence is guaranteed." He adds that it is not so much what is said, but rather the act of calling/texting that facilitates telepresence (ibid.). Twitter resembles texting in that it is not only limited to a maximum of 140 characters, but the social use of the technology is built upon a high frequency of contributions regardless of where the individual is physically located (on a bus, in a club, or with one's children).

One of Ebner and Schiefner's (2008) respondents adds that microblogging can facilitate virtual communities because users feel a "continuous partial presence" of other users. In this vein, Rosen (cited in Crawford 2009) compares aspects of Twitter to a radio. Even if someone does not post on a particular day, they feel an aura of other users through the feed of microblog posts on their PCs. Licoppe (2004) has usefully theorized this as a "connected presence" in which mediated communication (in this case, Twitter) facilitates the construction of social bonds. Specifically, Licoppe (2004: 135) concludes that physically absent parties "[gain] presence through the multiplication of mediated communication gestures on both sides." In other words, a constancy of presence is felt through multiplied interactions – a process Twitter is inherently designed for.

Because of Twitter's ability to inform followers of the daily happenings of another user (e.g., "had espresso and crois- sant," "slept on bus," "laptop stolen," "at police station," etc.), there is a similar perceptual illusion of non-mediation in which a face-to-face interaction has occurred with that person. This not only follows Licoppe's (2004) arguments regard- ing text messages and telepresence, but also Wajcman's (2008: 68) argument that mobile technology has facilitated an "always on," "persistent connection." This is not a coinci- dence. Rather, Twitter adopted elements from the successes of 1980s and 1990s synchronous internet chat technologies, such as Internet Relay Chat (IRC) and the instant messaging client (ICQ), both of which sought to create an "always on" state. What is interesting about Twitter (and other microblog- ging platforms) in juxtaposition to immersive graphically based technologies, such as the virtual worlds Second Life and Twinity, is that simple textual updates throughout the day are what generate telepresence (such as text messages on mobile phones). In the case of individuals following the tweets of people caught in disasters, for instance, there is a sense of "being there" while one hears about the specificity of experi- ences from an "ordinary person" (e.g., "a bomb went off one block away from my office"). Similarly, if one is following the tweets of celebrities and reads about what they are reading, eating, who they are seeing, and so on, telepresence can also occur. One can perceive physical proximity to Justin Bieber or Taylor Swift, for example. Another interesting distinction between textual-based social media and immersive visual technologies is that individuals explicitly choose to enter the latter for their ability to generate telepresence. Social media, on the other hand, are conceived by most users as merely communications media. This illusion of non-mediation is critical to understanding the "unintended" (McAulay 2007) pervasiveness of social media into the lives of everyday users. Gigliotti (1999: 56) emphasizes that this "pervasiveness [is . . .] throughout disparate forms of contemporary human activity." Similarly, if one is tweeting from the bus (or even speaking on a cell phone), that person generally perceives a deterritorialized state where they are no longer on the bus, but rather in a liminal space of telepresence (which is why people can speak so loudly on their phones in a public space and not be aware of the dozens of eyes pointed at them). Bull's (2005) work on iPods and MP3 players reveals similar findings of liminality where the mobile music listener inhabits a distinct space which is there, but not there.

This ultimately speaks to shifts in our rituals of social communication. Part of this change involves less of a boundary between our bodies and our technologies. Clark (2003) argues that "carried devices" have become embedded into our daily lives, making us more "cyborg." More broadly, however, it seems that the embedding of our carried devices (e.g., iPhones, Androids, iPads, and other mobile computing devices) has led to us perceiving interactions mediated by carried devices to be part of our unmediated lives. The perception of non-mediation powerfully shapes our experience of mediated forms. Though communication is ultimately socially embedded, it does not always feel that way. Sometimes this perception of non-mediation becomes highlighted.[5] Anne Power, a grandmother in Ireland who communicates with her emigrant children and grandchildren via social media technologies, puts this succinctly: "you can't hug Skype" (Kenny 2016). As Kenny (2016) argues, Power and other "Skype Grannies" are "feeling the loss" of physical co-presence. Their experiences highlight that technologies such as Skype have become normalized in our social communication, but physical face-to-face contact has particular affordances (e.g. hugs). Power was able to travel to Australia to visit her daughter. This is clearly not possible for many less privileged people across the world, for whom technologies such as Facebook, Periscope, WhatsApp, Skype, and FaceTime are the closest they might get to co-presence.[6] Ultimately, mediated telepresence is extremely meaningful to people in a network society where families, workplaces, and circles of friends span continents. Given the importance of mediated communication in globalized modernity, understanding Twitter is an important task and one in which interactionist theory is particularly valuable.

A Theoretical Framework for Understanding Twitter

Any successful communication technology shapes our social world. However, as Raymond Williams (1990) famously cautioned, technology shaping our social world is different from determining it. Or, as Claude Fischer (1992: 5) puts it, "fundamental" change in communication technology "alters the conditions of daily life, [but they . . .] do not determine the basic character of that life." Fischer's (1992: 5) work on the telephone sees the medium as not "radically alter[ing] American ways of life," but rather the ways in which "Americans used it to more vigorously pursue their characteristic ways of life." In other words, the telephone facilitated the intensification of pre-existing characteristics of social life. In the case of Twitter, it may be intensifying pre-existing characteristics of an erosion of the private in which more quotidian aspects of our lives are publicly shared. These are some of the new messages made possible by the new medium. We learn about other people's daily rituals, habits, happenings, and the places they visit. Not only do we potentially get a certain level of richness that we do not get in other mediated communication, but we are also exposed to a certain candor. We are perhaps getting more truthful portrayals of some sides of people, which were previously kept in the private sphere or what Goffman (1959: 119) calls the "backstage," which refers to "places where the camera is not focused at the moment." Or, most likely, we are getting a posed view of the backstage: we see what people want us to see. Twitter can be thought of as a sanitized backstage pass.

Given that the dramaturgical work of Goffman has been

successfully extended to include mediated communication (e.g., Rettie 2009), it can also be extended to better understanding Twitter. Specifically, work like that of Knorr Cetina (2009) has argued that Goffman's work can be useful for understanding mediated interactions. In the case of Twitter, the work of Goffman and his interactionist followers is helpful in understanding the concepts relating to self-production discussed earlier. For the benefit of those unfamiliar with his work, I will first introduce some basics of Goffman in terms of face-to-face dialogic interaction before delving into Twitter. Goffman's (1981) approach places primacy on interaction and views our face-to-face social situations as critical. From one vantage point, to understand Twitter is to understand how we "talk." Goffman conceptualizes "talk" through three themes – "ritualization," "participation framework," and "embedding." The first refers to his argument that the "movements, looks, and vocal sounds we make as an unintended byproduct of speaking and listening never seem to remain innocent" (Goffman 1981: 2). A key aspect of ritualization is that we acquire gestural conventions over our lifetime and that these gestures cannot be captured by the term "expression" (ibid.: 3). Second, "participation framework" refers to Goffman's theory that "those who happen to be in perceptual range of the event will have some sort of participation status relative to it" and that these positions can be analyzed (ibid.). Lastly, "embedding" refers to the "insufficiently appreciated fact that words we speak are often not our own, at least our current 'own'" and that "who can speak is restricted to the parties present" (ibid.). He adds that "although who speaks is situationally circumscribed, in whose name words are spoken is certainly not." Goffman emphasizes that "[u]ttered words have utterers," but utterances "have subjects (implied or explicit)." He concludes that the subjects may ultimately point to the utterer, but "there is nothing in the syntax of utterances to require this coincidence" (ibid.).

I have intentionally outlined Goffman's three key themes

surrounding "talk," although he is referring to unmediated rather than mediated talk. The literature extending Goffman's ideas of talk to mediated communication is now established (Adkins and Nasarczyk 2009; Bryant and Miron 2004; Riva and Galimberti 1998; Spitzberg 2006; Walther 1996). For example, Rettie (2009) successfully extends Goffman's ideas to mobile phone communication. Knorr Cetina's (2009) work is particularly innovative in extending Goffman's theories to interactive new media. Her work, which studied European stock-market traders, makes the argument that their inter-actions with other traders can be thought of as "synthetic situations," which are "entirely constituted by on-screen pro-jections" (Knorr Cetina 2009: 65). Knorr Cetina begins the process of extending the idea of "synthetic" to Goffman's concept of "situation," but stops at the "synthetic situation." To understand Twitter and other emerging media, we would be well served by extending Knorr Cetina's idea of the synthetic to Goffman's concepts of "embedding" and "encounters." Building from this literature, I will use Goffman's three key themes surrounding "talk" (ritualization, participation frame-work, and embedding) to make some initial extensions of his work to the mediated space of Twitter.

Drawing from "ritualization," tweets seem a-gestural and the term "expression" seems perfectly able to capture what the tweeting individual is trying to "express." However, it is easy to forget that any computer-mediated communication has acquired gestural conventions which also "never seem to remain innocent." Though the gestural conventions may be mediated through graphical avatars, emoticons, emojis, or even unintended typed characters, these can be considered "gestures" and they are laden with meaning. For example, on Twitter, one can decipher a sigh or pause through subtle and not-so-subtle textual cues (e.g., a "..." for an explicit pause). This is a critical point and one supported by the literature that users "compensate textually" in computer-mediated commu-nication (Herring 2001).

In terms of participation framework, computer-mediated communication which is public has a "perceptual range" which cannot actually be fully perceived by the speaker of the word. That being said, there is a "perceptual range" which is at least partially perceived by the sender of the tweet, and those who receive the tweet in their Twitter timelines have a "participation status relative" to the tweets. What I mean by this is that the person sending the tweet knows that there is a potential audience for it and that the readers of the tweet have different participation statuses relative to the tweet. Specifically, a tweet by an individual or group may have triggered the tweet. Or it could be a subtler relationship. Regardless, this participation status is important to understanding social communication on Twitter.

Lastly, and most importantly, is Goffman's idea of embedding. For him, embedding signifies the distinction between the situational circumscription of speaker and the fluidity of who "owns" those utterances. Specifically, he argues that utterances have subjects, but the original utterer need not be preserved in the utterance itself. Additionally, he observes that this "embedding capacity" (1981: 3) is part of our general linguistic ability to embed utterances in "any remove in time," rather than just in "the situated present." Goffman's theoretical perspective is particularly suited to understanding Twitter because of his development of embedding. Specifically, tweets, when they have been broadcasted to the Twitter universe ("Twitterverse"), become removed from the situational circumscription which face-to-face communication provides. Tweet utterances, as the utterances Goffman is referring to, also have subjects. However, the circulation of tweets is largely dependent on whose name the utterance is being attributed to, rather than who is the original utterer. So, if an unknown person sends a profound tweet, it is most likely destined never to be read. Of course, this is true of any medium in that reception depends on audience. But the ability of Twitter to re-embed tweets into the situational space of

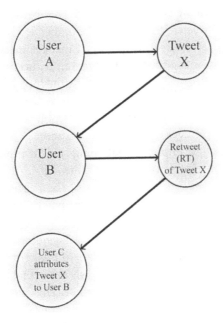

Figure 3.1   Twitter attribution

another Twitter user (through retweets) generates wholly new audiences which feel the utterance to be originating from the retweeter. This is particularly interesting because the retweet most often bears reference to the original Twitterer (through an @-mention (e.g., @whitehouse)). However, this part of the tweet is usually unconsciously or consciously ignored (see figure 3.1). Or, in the case of quoted tweets, where users add comments to tweets by other users, attribution can be particularly challenging as the retweeting user has added some new, original content to their retweet.[7]

Furthermore, embedding is also particularly useful in theorizing Twitter as it also refers to our linguistic ability to fluidly temporalize utterances. Though Twitter, as a medium, can be synchronous in communicative interactions (if Twitterer and tweet recipient are both online at the same time), it most often has some element of asynchronicity. That being said, when tweets are retweeted, they become re-embedded into the situated present of the recipient. And if that recipient retweets, the new recipients also view the tweet utterance in their situated present. Because in virtual spaces "the interacting parties meet in time rather than in a place" (Knorr Cetina 2009: 79), it is useful to think of what I term "synthetic embedding," which places primacy on "response presence" (Goffman 1983) rather than physical place. That being said, synthetic embedding, like physical embedding, reformulates the space in which it is embedded, which happens to be a virtual space.

The difference with Twitter is that the audience range of tweets is not always in congruence with the perceptual range (or indeed intended range) of the original Twitterer. The original tweeter intends the tweet to circulate to their immediate followers. They are not always consciously aware that their tweets have the potential to travel much farther. This is a key distinction between synthetic embedding and embedding. Kwak et al. (2010: 6) note that once a tweet is retweeted (regardless of the number of followers the original Twitterer has), it reaches an average audience size of 1,000. This is quite significant as an "everyday" tweet posted by an ordinary individual has a potentially large readership if it is retweeted. Therefore, as with any utterances with intended audiences, tweets are not only synthetically embedded in some time frame, but also within the context of their audience. And if tweets do become retweeted, they experience synthetic re-embedding in both a different temporal frame and potentially a different social context.

The above does not take into account replies to tweets and the responses to these replies. Rather, it has been restricted to a single tweet utterance and the ways in which we can theorize its production, perception, and reproduction. However, a critical function of Twitter and a reason for its popularity is the ability of users to reply to one another. When replying to a tweet or directing a tweet to a specific user, the site prefixes the reply with an "@" and the intended recipient sees this in their Twitter page when they log on. Like face-to-face communication, utterances on Twitter generate responses. Similarly, these responses are, following Goffman (1981: 5), "realized at different points in 'sequence time'." Conversations on Twitter become marked by the exchange of responses which can be aggregated into a sequence (by time), and this forms a "coherent" conversation.[8] However, having a conversation on Twitter can be more like sitting in a room with a door, not knowing who is going to pop their head round and respond or who is listening behind the door. Additionally, it could be several people coming through that door within seconds of each other. On top of that, there could be any number of other rooms out there with someone retweeting your tweet, and they have respondents. If the user identification of the originating Twitterer is retained (through an at-sign), the originating Twitterer has the ability to see who is retweeting and responding. They can choose to become a respondent to a retweeter, thereby opening the door to one or many of these other rooms. For example, Donald Trump retweeted (RT) this tweet in April 2017 from @DRUDGE_REPORT: "GREAT AGAIN: FEDS ARREST MURDER SUSPECT IN 'FAST AND FURIOUS' SCANDAL ... http://fxn.ws/2o7NY8K."[9] Anyone can retweet this tweet, reply to it, or retweet it with modified text. Each of these configurations entails differences in audience and perceived authorship, with some potentially mistaking that Donald Trump wrote the tweet.

Ultimately, there is a sense of boundedness of the retweet to the new utterer. However, anyone, not just the originating Twitterer, can open any of these doors or they can form a new room and "own" the tweet. This type of computer-mediated communication does have a history in forms of copy-and-paste communication (e.g., if someone copied a discussion idea from one email to another, they become considered the original utterer). However, within the etiquette of emailing lists, the original utterer is preserved and it is customary for an original poster (OP) – even if on another site or mailing list – to be referred to or thanked (Hansen et al. 2010).

Conclusion

> I immediately asked the obvious question: why would some-one want to Twitter? Evan Williams put it this way: "The question 'Why are we interested in this stuff?' – 'Why is this entertainment?' could be flipped on its head when we ask, 'Why is fictionalized, non-real entertainment, normal enter-tainment, interesting?' People are in the world and that's real." (Niedzviecki 2009: 129)

Twitter co-founder Evan Williams believes that the lives of ordinary people are "real," and fictional entertainment which has become the norm is "non-real." The posting of perceived "banal" tweets such as what one had for breakfast or what one is wearing have led some to dismiss Twitter. However, from Williams's point of view, this is what is "real" and the real is interesting. Another aspect that has fueled critics of Twitter is the medium's terseness. Trying to communicate in the restricted format of 140 characters seems unduly limited to some. For some of Twitter's critics (e.g., Keen 2010), it may even be considered a threat to our current modes of com-munication. They argue that new media more generally are leading to the impoverishment of grammar, vocabulary, spell-ing, and so on (Tucker 2009). This is not a "new" argument. Rather, as Baym (2015: 1) argues, every new communications medium sees a cohort of critics who consider the medium as "shallow." Additionally, she highlights that the critics of elec-tronic messages have seen them as "vacuous" and that "new media often stir[s] up fears of moral decline" (Baym 2015: 47).

It is also important to note that many of the things which are concisely tweeted are also expressed tersely not only in other mediated forms, but in face-to-face communication as well. Not all communication needs to be verbose. Goffman refers to these as "truncated verbal forms" (1981: 7). If we are asking someone which direction a subway station is, or how much a newspaper costs, a couple of words will satisfy the questioner. Those such as Keen (2010) who argue that Twitter heralds the death of meaningful communication may be failing to appreciate this. The key to understanding "talk" on Twitter is not to get drawn into a privileging of verbosity in speech acts. This is a slippery slope, ending, more often than not, in stratified communication. Rather, the assumption needs to be made that the actors in Twitter are satisfied by the sub-140-character responses they receive.

Following Goffman (1981: 10), another important conclusion of this chapter is that a "basic normative assumption about talk is that, whatever else, it should be correctly interpretable in the special sense of conveying to the intended recipients what the sender more or less wanted to get across." They need not "agree" with the message; they just need to be in agreement "as to what they have heard" (ibid.). Or, put into linguistic theory, "illocutionary force" (the conventional intention of a statement) is what needs to be in agreement, rather than "perlocutionary effect" (the effect of the statement on the hearer, or in achieving a particular goal). I would add, though, that the recipients of tweets may not be intended and that illocutionary force can be diminished as tweets become increasingly removed from the original tweeting speaker. However, the medium ultimately tends toward the privileging of verbatim tweets rather than insuring the preservation of intended meaning (i.e., what the original speaker "wanted to get across").[10]

Ultimately, this chapter has sought to further our understanding of Twitter by extending interactionist and other social theory. By exploring literature on media democratization, self-production, technological determinism, and interactionism, some basic theoretical frameworks have been introduced by which to understand Twitter's roles in social communication. It has been emphasized that our uses of social media are products of larger social, political, and economic forces and the theoretical frames introduced in this chapter are critical to meaningfully understanding Twitter. The next chapters build on this theoretical base in order to explore the ways in which Twitter has potentially changed self-presentation, the synchronicity of social interaction, and forms of talk (cf. Goffman 1981), as well as power relations between interactants. Later chapters will explore specific topics and empirical case studies in order to investigate these questions.

Cecilia R
@reykai

Replying to @ifahmi

@ifahmi how about this: Twitter is the first realtime flow of worldwide thoughts and consciousness? re: microblogging or chat engine

6:50 AM - 27 Oct 2009

@reykai[1]

If Twitter is a conduit for a global stream of consciousness, it logically follows that the medium is a barometer for revealing everything, from the occurrence of natural disasters to the public perception of political candidates. This chapter explores this potential awareness of "worldwide consciousness" through the examination of Twitter and journalism. Twitter can be understood as a news environment in which news is always present. That includes both professional journalists and "citizen journalists," who cover "news" in their cities, towns, and countries. Likewise, news is highly present through the retweeting of links to news stories. Also considered in this chapter is the question of Twitter as a more democratic space for news production and consumption. Through new forms of Twitter-mediated journalism, the medium may be changing journalistic norms, including the transparency of journalistic practice and a greater role of citizen journalists in overseeing news production.

CHAPTER FOUR

Twitter and Journalism

Twitter has been prominently associated with journalism, both in terms of shifts in journalistic practice and in the facilitation of citizen journalism. An interesting aspect of Twitter is its function as an "ambient" news environment (Hermida 2010b), a media space where news is always present. In Twitter's case, both banal and profound news is present in this ambient environment. This news is produced and consumed by a wide range of individuals, from professional journalists to non-professional citizen journalists. In this way, Twitter presents an opportunity for many types of journalisms rather than strictly traditional modes of journalistic production and consumption. Moreover, the roles of news producer and consumer are often blurred on Twitter. The medium has also influenced some of the ways in which journalists conduct news work. Specifically, as an ambient news space where news is in the air, Twitter-savvy journalists with their fingers on the social media pulse are often on the lookout for newsworthy scoops. They can contact Twitter users who they think are breaking interesting news. As discussed later in this chapter, the reporting journalists need not even be in the physical location of breaking-news events when citizen journalists are on the ground giving them updates via Twitter (which can include embedded photographs and video).

Two key themes are explored in this chapter: Twitter as an ambient news environment and as a space for multiple journalisms. In terms of the latter, two historical case studies of citizen journalists and Twitter are explored in detail. The site's role in the reporting of the Mumbai bomb blasts in 2008 and

the downed US Airways flight in 2009 illustrates the influence of citizen journalism and Twitter. Also explored here
is the question of whether Twitter has transformed ordinary
individuals into citizen journalists whom the newsreading
public follows, or whether their voices are merely subsumed
by traditional media. In other words, has Twitter really produced a new space in which ordinary people meaningfully
interact with other ordinary people around the world who
have rich insider accounts pertaining to diverse forms of socioeconomic life? An argument is made that ordinary people on
Twitter are producing news and consuming news (especially
"breaking news") produced by other ordinary people. And
with the introduction of the Explore (previously Moments)
aggregation features of Twitter, one need not even follow
those who are tweeting out the day's news. However, counter-
arguments are presented which make the case that perhaps
the individual tweets and Twitter users breaking news stories
experience a short-lived fame as the public follows stories of
interest through professional news media outlets. Ultimately,
the rise of citizen journalism on Twitter highlights the complex roles of ordinary people in update cultures and how what
one may tweet merely as a simple update can become transformed into "news," whether traditional media pick up the
tweet or it is retweeted at a large scale (i.e., a Twitter community itself determines "news").

Twitter as a News Environment

There has been some discussion and scholarship on Twitter
and journalism around the idea of "ambient news" (Burns
2010; Hermida 2010b). This idea conceptualizes Twitter
as a space whose ambient environment always contains
news (the analogy here is to oxygen in our physical ambient environment). Hermida (2010b: 301) argues that
"lightweight" and "always on" communication services can
create ontologies where news is part of the "mental model"

of these technologies' users. He adds that Twitter can be thought of as "an awareness system" (ibid.), which facilitates awareness between users even when they are not physically proximate. The awareness is always there, but central attention is activated at moments "when a user feels the need to communicate." The difference between Twitter and visiting the website of a newspaper is that, in the former, news is always present, but potentially at the periphery for a user. Other information or particular individuals may be taking center stage. Hermida offers an interesting model for considering Twitter as an "ambient media system" in that news information is received "in the periphery of their awareness [. . . and] does not require the cognitive attention of, for example, an e-mail" (ibid.). In other words, individual tweets do not inherently represent valuable pieces of information ipso facto. In chapter 3, I conceived of Twitter as consisting of nested "digital objects," which can be composed of anything from a couple of tweets to the combination of tweets, retweets, and hashtags. Hermida's notion of Twitter as an ambient news space is particularly useful in seeing how digital objects may emerge which catch a user's attention and are drawn from periphery to center (whereas an individual tweet may not have the gravity to do this). Collective approvals of, for example, a news story through retweets from certain users can engage tweet consumers in different ways. An important aspect of understanding Twitter as an ambient news space is recognizing that "completeness of awareness is not the goal" (Hermida 2010b: 303). It is useful to think back to the analogy between Twitter and the medium of radio (see chapters 2 and 3). If one had complete awareness of the radio's total band of frequencies, one would be deluged (think of 25 radios all blaring different stations in a room). If all frequencies of one's Twitter feed took center stage simultaneously, this type of incomprehensible cacophony would occur. Rather, for most users, their Twitter feed works more like a single radio station, albeit disjointed, which is always on, though someone can be checking email or working and Twitter can be in the periphery. But if something comes to our attention, the Twitter feed, like the radio station, can come to the center of our cognitive field. The key is that Twitter, unlike a singularly focused radio station, always has news in the ambient environment (excepting news radio, of course). Though not referring to Twitter, Hargreaves and Thomas put it well: "News is, in a word, ambient, like the air we breathe" (cited in Hermida 2010a). This has implications both for news consumption and production. Journalists can "sense" news just as it is unfolding. They could see a digital object constituted of important tweets emerge and decide to contact Twitter users, or research the story on the ground.

New Journalisms

Besides adding to journalists' source mix, Twitter has transformed some journalistic practices and norms. For example, Lasorsa et al. (2011: 19) found that Twitter led to journalists "more freely express[ing] opinions," a behavior which directly challenges "the journalistic norm of objectivity (impartiality and non-partisanship)." They also found a contingent of journalists on Twitter who use the medium for "providing accountability and transparency regarding how they conduct their work" (ibid.). This is an important aspect of how Twitter is shaping some aspects of journalistic practice. Some of the shifts have come about through processes on Twitter that involve users "patrolling" the emergence of news and its authenticity or journalistic rigor. Bruns (2005) describes the process of "gate-watching," wherein users are engaged in "highlighting, sharing, and evaluating the relevant material released by other sources" (Bruns and Burgess 2011: 2). Through sometimes critical evaluations of news, journalists can be held accountable very quickly after an article has been published. In other words, Twitter's ambient news environment has gained an increasingly evaluative role on traditional media, where journalists have "to maintain the trust of audiences" on Twitter (Lasorsa et al. 2011: 23). Journalistic norms have been particularly affected in these ways over the last century (ibid.: 19) as more "democratizing" technologies from the telephone to blogs have emerged.

The medium can also facilitate more collaborative journalistic practices wherein journalists invite Twitter users to "participate in the news production process" (Lasorsa et al. 2011: 26) by eliciting feedback on an article or retweeting unedited messages they think are relevant to a breaking-news event. Another key way in which new media more generally have been shaping journalistic practice is crowdsourcing, where the "wisdom of the crowds" (Surowiecki 2004) is leveraged to analyze large amounts of data or check materials. David Fahrenthold, a reporter at The Washington Post, perhaps exemplifies innovating crowdsourcing on Twitter as part of his journalistic practice. In his 2016 reporting of the Trump Foundation and how it was receiving and spending money, he turned to Twitter to discover and pursue tips and leads. Fahrenthold was tweeting about a $10,000 portrait of Donald Trump purchased via his foundation. Legally, the giant portrait had to be used for charitable purposes and Fahrenthold was trying to track down where it was. Twitter users posted leads of various Trump paintings that might be the painting Fahrenthold was trying to track down. In September, a Washington Post reader found the portrait at Trump's Doral Hotel golf club in Miami through a Tripadvisor.com photo and alerted Fahrenthold via Twitter (Fahrenthold 2016). Enrique Acevedo (@Enrique_Acevedo),[2] a journalist with Univision in Miami, worked close to the Doral and paid a visit to the hotel, eventually finding the painting and tweeting: "Hey @Fahrenthold just checked and the portrait is still hanging at the Champions Lounge. How much did you say it cost the Trump Foundation?" (See figure 4.1).[3] This case not only exemplifies innovative forms of journalistic crowdsourcing, but collaboration between journalists via Twitter who likely would not have been working together.

Enrique Acevedo ✔
@Enrique_Acevedo

👤 Follow

Hey @Fahrenthold just checked and the portrait is still hanging at the Champions Lounge. How much did you say it cost the Trump Foundation?

RETWEETS 545   LIKES 772

11:32 PM - 20 Sep 2016

↩ 62   🔁 545   ♥ 772

Figure 4.1   Tweet from @Enrique_Acevedo discovering the missing Trump portrait; reproduced with permission from Enrique Acevedo

Citizen Journalists Breaking News Through Twitter

Twitter has received significant media attention over the years for the way it disseminates information during breaking-news events, including the 2008 Mumbai bomb blasts (Dolnick 2008), the January 2009 crash of US Airways Flight 1549 (Beaumont 2009),[4] political movements in the 2011 "Arab Spring" (Warf 2011), and the 2016 UK Brexit referendum (Siegel and Tucker 2016). In the case of US Airways Flight 1549, Janis Krums, a passenger on the Midtown Ferry, took a picture of the downed jet floating in the Hudson[5] and uploaded it to Twitter before news crews even arrived on the scene (see figure 4.2). Krums not only uploaded his tweet and photograph with ease, but also continued tweeting as he helped with aid efforts. In an instant, he was transformed from Florida-based businessman to both citizen journalist and emergency aid worker. Though not as striking to us today, we need to remember that this was revolutionary for traditional journalism. During the Mumbai bomb blasts in 2008, Twitter was used to circulate news about the attacks (Beaumont 2008). Seconds after the first blasts, Twitter users were providing eyewitness accounts from Mumbai. For example, on November 26, 2008, the day of the attacks, @ShriNagesh tweeted "a gunman appeared in front of us, carrying machine gun-type weapons & started firing. I just turned & ran in opp direction," and @dupree tweeted "Mumbai terrorists are asking Hotel Reception for room #s of American citizens and holding them hostage on one floor."[6] On November 27, @Ashokjjr tweeted "Oberoi fire under control now,"[7] and @sengupta tweeted "Trident fire seems under control"[8] (all tweets cited in BBC News 2008). Though limited to 140 characters, the information contained in these tweets was invaluable to individuals in Mumbai as well as news media outlets throughout the world. Traffic on Twitter with the #mumbai hashtag grew to such a volume on November 27 that the Indian government asked

Figure 4.2   Miracle on the Hudson; photograph by Janis Krums
(www.janiskrums.com; Twitter @jkrums)

Twitter users to halt their updates: "ALL LIVE UPDATES – PLEASE STOP TWEETING about #Mumbai police and military operations" (BBC News 2008). Some reports indicated that the Indian government was worried that the terrorists were garnering inside information about the situation from internet media sites including Twitter (Courier Mail 2008).

Not only was news in the case of both Flight 1549 and the Mumbai bomb blasts disseminated nearly instantaneously through Twitter, but tweets also included linked photographic documentation. Krums' emotive image was used by traditional news organizations around the world. Though not available in Krums' time, video (even live video via Periscope) can be seamlessly embedded into tweets. And, as with Flight 1549, news organizations continue to face tight budgets and remain hard-pressed to have people on the ground picking up stories this quickly. Twitter, on the other hand, has at its disposal a virtual army of citizen journalists ready to tweet at a moment's notice from their mobile phones or mobile devices. As "smartphones" (e.g., iPhones and Android phones) penetrate markets further, a higher percentage of this army can seamlessly embed high-definition pictures and video into their tweets. At the time of writing, 68 percent of American adults own smartphones (Anderson 2015). Additionally, a majority of American adults use mobile location-based services (Zickuhr 2013) and most American adult mobile users have apps installed (Olmstead and Atkinson 2015). In the American context, a very large segment of the population is capable of sending tweets with linked or embedded high-definition photographs and video. A significant number of these users have location-based services enabled, which would associate location with their tweets. Furthermore, as mentioned previously, it is relatively easy for a user to tweet from their phone. Most smartphone users with a Twitter-based app could take a picture or video and send a tweet in under 45 seconds. This seamless convergence of photographic and textual information from everyday "citizen journalists" made

Twitter a news source during the 2011 "Arab Spring" movements in the Middle East and North Africa (Benn 2011), the 2012 US Republican presidential primary election (Murthy 2015), the 2014 Hong Kong #UmbrellaRevolution (Thandar and Usanavasin 2015), and the 2016 US presidential election (Wells et al. 2016).

The Rise of Twitter-based Citizen Journalists?

Rebillard and Toubol (2010) concluded that the egalitarian promises of the internet as a tool for citizen journalists have not panned out. Rather, professional news media websites are mostly built around content from professional journalistic sources, and most "citizen journalism" online relies on and links back to professional news media websites. Nonetheless, Twitter has made possible some interesting cases of citizen journalism, as discussed in the previous section. Indeed, in the case of US Airways Flight 1549, as already mentioned, it was a citizen journalist, Janis Krums, who took a picture of the downed aircraft and circulated it to the Twitterverse from his iPhone (see figure 4.2) before the traditional media even had any idea of the disaster. Today, journalists often turn to Twitter first, asking those on the ground to live-tweet, or simply embedding relevant tweets directly into their online coverage. Others ask users their permission to reproduce eyewitness photos or video. For example, in the case of United Flight 3411 and the forcible removal of Dr David Dao discussed in chapter 1, journalists asked @JayseDavid for permission to reproduce his video shot on the plane.[9] In such cases it is also not uncommon for other Twitter users to argue such use is exploitative and that the user who took the photo or video should be paid.[10]

Similarly, in the case of the 2015 Paris terror attacks, those "reporting" on the destruction were generally ordinary Parisians. A question of interest in this chapter is whether this signals the rise of citizen journalism or whether it is merely a new means for traditional media to crowdsource stories (and even crowdsource free photographic documentation). Either way, this is a question with significant implications. Jen Leo, a blogger for the *Los Angeles Times*, wrote about Krums' iconic photograph, asking whether it is "becoming more interesting to turn to citizen journalism than traditional broadcast media for coverage?" (Leo 2009). Part of this question, of course, is contingent on the legitimacy of Twitter as a news source itself. Ross McCulloch (2009) of the Third Sector Lab blog emphasizes how Flight 1549 marked a turning point for Twitter's legitimacy.

With the press of a few buttons on his iPhone, Janis Krums changed the way the world looks at Twitter. While the traditional news networks were still searching for the plane in the Hudson, [his] photo was already spreading like wildfire across the Twitterverse.

From McCulloch's perspective, the tipping point whereby Twitter became considered a potentially legitimate source of breaking news was Flight 1549. Not only could interested individuals see Krums' photograph online, but they could also send tweets directly to him, posing questions and requesting clarification. Indeed, Krums' @jkrums Twitter following rocketed from 150 to nearly 6,000. Krums participated in Twitter-led discussions, including one on the Third Sector Lab site. What is unique in this type of citizen journalism is that consumers of Krums' account were able to build (or at least perceive) a rapport with Krums himself. Though this case highlights the use of citizen journalism in breaking news stories, it does not displace the usefulness of traditional news media (or length-unrestricted blogs in the realm of new media) to cover in-depth or longer-running issues and matters. Bianco (2009: 305), for example, argues that Twitter has "notably proved to the world its capacity to transmit real-time information," but is not a medium best designed for reporting "issues and campaigns across a protracted period of time."

Though, from Bianco's perspective, Twitter is not displacing traditional media, news organizations have found the medium useful in their coverage of breaking news. Minutes after Krums posted "The Miracle on the Hudson" photograph on Twitter, media outlets were calling his mobile phone asking for up-to-the-minute information and requesting interviews. As Bianco (2009: 305) notes, within half an hour of taking the picture, Krums was interviewed live by MSNBC. Today, the speed at which citizen journalists are engaged has accelerated and the types of content they can provide has grown both in type and quality. McCulloch (2009) points out that though "The Miracle on the Hudson" may have been a means by which Twitter was legitimatized, this newfound victory was not at the expense of "old media" in that the "newspapers and TV news stations didn't pay a penny to the likes of Reuters and AP when US 1549 hit the Hudson [. . . as they] all got their big photo for free that day" through the internet. Twitter also allows journalists themselves to report from remote or harsh conditions. Swasy (2016: 67) gives the example of a photographer and journalist hiking and biking to a remote mudslide, tweeting before first responders even arrived. In a similar vein, there have been cases where governments have either banned journalists from reporting from their countries or made it extremely dangerous. Iran and Syria are well-known examples. As Palser (2009) notes, major international news organizations such as CNN relied on information from social networking and social media websites, including Twitter. In Syria, Facebook and Twitter were key platforms used by citizen-journalist activists on the ground to get updates to international journalists during the "Arab Spring" (Salama 2012).

During Twitter's infancy, the use of social media by journalists remained exceptional rather than the norm. Lariscy et al. (2009) found that only 7.5 percent of journalists they interviewed described as social media "very important to their work" while 56.5 percent were neutral or considered social media to be "of little or no importance." Today, journalists "are very proud to share how many followers they have and whether they are one of the most followed journalists in their

newsroom" (Swasy 2016: 67). Additionally, sports reporters are taught very specific methods to report via Twitter,
including hashtag use and live-tweeting (Reinardy and Wanta
2015: 33). Twitter is seen by many to be indispensable to
their journalistic practice (Arrabal-Sánchez and De-Guilera-
Moyano 2016). García de Torres and Hermida (2017: 2–3)
highlight that this was not always the case as Twitter was historically seen as a less important news-gathering device once
media correspondents were on the ground. However, news
organizations are now deploying teams for live-tweeting and
are increasingly embracing collaborative practices with citizen
journalists (Clayfield 2012).

But live-tweeting is not without its issues. Writing in the
context of live-tweeting for medical conferences, Weiner (2015:
159) argues that live-tweet feeds "are merely a source of insub-
stantive fragmented news of doubtful significance." Content
aside, ethnographic work with journalists suggests there are
practical and ethical issues with live-tweeting (Barnard 2016:
197). "And although it may pose potential conflicts for journalists affiliated with the Associated Press, BBC, or other
institutions with similarly restrictive social media policies,
live-tweeting is an increasingly common practice among citizens and professionals" (Barnard 2016: 197). Both Weiner's
and Barnard's research results highlight that more conservative groups and organizations (e.g., the medical community,
AP, and BBC) tend to be hesitant of live-tweeting. However, as
Barnard highlights, live-tweeting has become common. Even
in the more conservative scientific community, advice for how
to live-tweet has been published in *Nature* (Sohn 2015). Some
churches have even encouraged live-tweeting to report their
events (Gould 2013).

Twitter as Communal News Space

Some of these changes in journalistic norms involve more
communal journalistic practices, where citizen journal-

ists are helpful to news production (Poell and Rajagopalan 2015). Computer-mediated communication has, as Castells (2000) argues, created a new "social morphology," which is dominated by networks. "Virtual communities" have been noted for their ability to transcend geographical constraints (Rheingold 1993). However, they also represent interesting dialogic spaces where a seemingly individualistic interlocutor is actually being listened to by the larger virtual community. Not only does communication in such spaces become simultaneously individualistic and communal, but so does the negotiation of the culture of news production and consumption. The (re)construction of communication and culture on Twitter represents a particularly interesting case. Specifically, Twitter is a "public space" with anyone able to see, respond, or forward ("retweet") messages. On Twitter, users can break news, comment on larger political issues, local concerns, and fads – all publicly.

Hashtag categories illustrate the ability of Twitter to be both an individual and communal news space simultaneously. For example, #breakingnews, a hashtag used to tweet breaking news, has been a regular hashtag topic. Any tweets with #breakingnews are aggregated into a communal meta-thread which represents what Twitter users consider breaking news at the moment. In December 2016, the hashtag #JoeMcKnight trended on Twitter as the man thought to have shot and killed American football star Joe McKnight was released without charge. Twitter users actively contributed their thoughts, forming a communal thread on the topic which was simultaneously individualistic. Users quickly tied the case to #BlackLivesMatter and contributed to discourse on American race relations. Furthermore, a claim (albeit easily refutable) can be made that Twitter has made opinion the result of a "democratic" confluence of voices, rather than the privileging of elite individual or institutional voices. This may be particularly poignant where marginalized groups (in this case, African Americans) feel they are not being heard in mainstream media. The act of tweeting breaking news or one's opinions regarding #JoeMcKnight can also serve as a means to affirm individuals' identities (e.g. as marginalized African Americans) rather than as an intended form of journalism. DiMicco and Millen (2007), in their work researching the use of Facebook at a large software development company, found that employees used status updates to, for example, affirm their identity as business professionals[11] or, on the other hand, as fresh out of college.[12] In other words, #break ingnews or #JoeMcKnight tweets are being used by some as a means to assert their individual and group identities (see chapter 3 for a theoretically grounded discussion of identities and Twitter). And even if these individuals tweet without journalism in mind, it may be that a "journalistic community" surrounding a hashtag topic nonetheless emerges. Gibbs et al. (2015: 260) have similarly argued that bereavement communities have emerged on the photo-sharing platform Instagram around #Funeral.

Digital Divides and Twitterized Journalism

As this chapter has discussed, Twitter has fostered an active ambient news environment with many forms of journalism emerging (from professional to citizen journalism). However, it should be noted that news production and consumption on Twitter remain a socially stratified practice. As Hargittai and Jennrich (2016) argue, "Women, members of under-represented racial and ethnic groups, and those of lower socioeconomic status tend to contribute to online conversations at lower levels." Even amongst children – a demographic which is painted as a homogeneously net-savvy generation – digital divides (including smartphones) based upon lines of class and other socioeconomic factors continue to exist (Mascheroni and Ólafsson 2015).[13] Hobson (2008) has persuasively argued that the internet continues to be "raced" and racial digital divides remain pervasive (Kolko et al. 2000,

2008; Cisneros and Nakayama 2015); Twitter is no exception to this. Another important distinction that needs to be made in terms of digital divides is that between access to the internet and being "internet savvy" – an understanding that sees internet use as different for different kinds of users (DiMaggio et al. 2001). For instance, Piwek and Joinson (2016: 361) found that 89 percent of Snapchat users in their studies were white and 88 percent were heterosexual. In terms of access, studies have shown that smartphone ownership and internet usage continue to grow worldwide (Poushter 2016), but access does not inherently translate into equal usage. Specifically, people with disabilities (Ellcessor 2010) and populations which are socioeconomically marginalized are more likely to use the internet for the simplest of tasks (often email) and remain ignorant of or ill versed in the use of newer social media tools (Witte and Mannon 2010). At a more basic level, Hargittai (2006) found that respondents with lower educational levels had a higher frequency of spelling and typographical errors when using internet search engines, resulting in an internet experience which is limited from the start.

Digital divides also continue to be age-related (Friemel 2016). Physical disabilities too have been found to affect online usage of such services as online banking, social networking sites, and e-commerce (Dobransky and Hargittai 2016: 23). However, the internet-enabled middle classes were already using online bill payment systems, for example, at the start of the millennium (Hayashi and Klee 2003). The amplification of digital divides in the face of more advanced internet applications should not be read as fodder for a Luddite argument. Rather, technology can be harnessed to more equitably disseminate news. For example, the reach of text messages is less socially stratified than tweets, given the levels of mobile penetration in many countries. Text message-based information services have successfully been deployed in less developed countries. For example, FrontlineSMS[14] was used during the 2004 Indian Ocean tsunami to keep disaster-affected individuals informed.[15] Additionally, text messages continue to be frequently used to disseminate health messages in less developed countries (Chib, van Velthoven, and Car 2015). The point here is to be aware of how digital divides affect news production and consumption on Twitter.

Another limitation of Twitter is the issue of information integrity. Tweets regarding breaking news, disasters, and public health epidemics can be misleading, incorrect, or even fraudulent (Goolsby 2009). In the case of the 2014 Ebola epidemic, significant levels of tweets tagged with #ebola contained false or misleading information (Kalyanam, Velupillai, Doan, Conway, and Lanckriet 2015). Similarly, during the 2011 UK riots, misinformation on Twitter potentially created further tension and unrest (Geere 2011). For instance, Geere (2011) observes that a widely circulated tweet which linked to an image of tanks and soldiers was claiming to be proof of the British army assembling in central London. In fact, the image turned out to be of an army presence in Egypt. Geere (2011) also gives the example of how a set of tweets "even claimed that rioters had attacked the London Zoo and set free a selection of animals, including a tiger."[16] Again, this was a hoax. Marginalized and vulnerable populations are disproportionately affected by such information. It is impossible to monitor the integrity of information flowing on Twitter. Though individuals can follow trusted news outlets on Twitter, some users can and do pose as traditional news organizations by employing a username which sounds or looks like a newspaper or television station. Indeed, someone who posed as the Dalai Lama on Twitter attracted 20,000 followers in 48 hours (Moore 2009). Though Twitter eventually shut down this impersonating account, the openness of the medium enables significant fraudulence, and the implications of this should not be underestimated.

Post-Fact Journalism, "Fake News," and Twitter

Another interesting aspect of how journalism has been changed by Twitter is the emergence of viral fake news. Fake news has been a part of Twitter for many years now. For example, during Hurricane Sandy, news stories and images circulated that reported that subways were completely flooded (Murthy and Gross 2017). However, what has changed since early instances of fake news on Twitter is not only the volume of fake news, but its noticeable influence. Fake news occurrence during the 2016 US presidential election is particularly stark. One particular case exemplifies this well. In the days running up to the election, Eric Tucker, a 35-year-old cofounder of a marketing company from Austin, Texas, tweeted a photo of buses alongside text that asserted that paid protesters were being bussed in to demonstrate against Donald Trump, hashtagging #fakeprotests #trump2016 and #Austin (Maheshwari 2016). Though the story was later proved as false and it was established that the Clinton campaign did not bus in paid protesters to Trump rallies, the damage had been done. The tweet went viral, quickly retweeted by 16,000 and liked by 14,000. The story crossed to Facebook, where it was shared over 350,000 times, with rapid comments on Reddit (Maheshwari 2016). In many ways, this case suggests the victory of the speed of information dissemination over fact-checking and verification. However, this is not solely a Twitter problem. Others have argued that we have entered a "post-fact" society (Manjoo 2008). Automated bots, non-human Twitter accounts, also play a part in the circulation of fake news, and this is likely to play an increasing role in shaping what news appears on our Twitter feeds (Larsson Anders and Hallvard 2015).

The dissemination of fake news on Twitter is also not always intentional. Take the example of Hugo Rifkind (@hugorifkind), a Scottish journalist, who on Thanksgiving morning, November 24, 2016, tweeted: "Searching old cuts. Odd thing. Why does the world recall Trump saying 'If she wasn't my daughter, I'd be dating her' but not Ivanka's reply," adding a screenshot from the August 24, 2006, "Quotables" section of the *Chicago Tribune* of Ivanka Trump replying, "If he wasn't my father, I would spray him with Mace."[17] Shortly after Rifkind posted his tweet, another journalist, Sarah Kendzior (@sarahkendzior), tweeted the screenshot with a comment saying she had not seen much reporting about Ivanka's comment.[18] Several interesting things happened. First, Kendzior's tweet was retweeted over 3,500 times and liked by more than 4,000 users, making it go viral and get picked up by a range of news organizations. Second, Rifkind tweeted to Kendzior: "you are stealing from me," as he was not attributed as the source. Third, and most importantly, the news was actually fake; Ivanka never said this and it likely originates from US comedian Conan O'Brien (Seipel 2016). On a BBC radio program (Hewlett 2016), Rifkind stated that he did not know what he had done wrong as he posted on his personal Twitter and did not ever state the quote was "news" or fact-checked. And Kendzior not only took credit for the fake news story but also did not fact-check it, leading major publications to subsequently apologize for publishing the story (Gauthier 2016). This case not only highlights how easily this one tweet became a "fake" news sensation, but also that journalists did not uphold the same fact-checking standards they would place on themselves in a traditional journalistic venue. In addition, the initial discussion between Rifkind, Kendzior, and others about whether the story was stolen from Rifkind or not took place publicly on Twitter. All the while, the story was actually fake.

Ultimately, Twitter is not shaping a turn toward fake news or the rise of non-fact-checked information, but is echoing our current relationship with the need for speed in terms of information flow and the acceptability (or perhaps expectation) of erroneous information. This is the case with both citizen and professional journalists. Part of this argument connects back to arguments made in chapter 3 about Twitter being part of "always on" event-driven culture, whose prioritization of immediacy can have significant implications. There, I argued that we should not be technologically deterministic about Twitter (i.e., Twitter is making us this or that). Rather, the ways in which Twitter has evolved and is being used are a manifestation of our social, political, and economic beliefs and realities.

Twitter and Journalism: A Blessing or a Curse?

Journalists have had an important relationship with Twitter since its infancy. Since the birth of the microblogging platform, newsroom budgets have been in steady decline. Initially, many journalists were wary of using the platform as a fount of local information and potential sources. The situation today has dramatically changed, and journalists who are not familiar with Twitter are very much in the minority, leading BBC Global News Director Peter Horrocks to tell his staff: "Tweet or be sacked [fired]" (Barnard 2016: 191). Social media courses are not only an integral part of journalism education now, but also are being integrated into the professional curriculum for practicing journalists. In addition, data journalism, where large amounts of data are studied using a variety of computational data research methods, uses Twitter as a data source quite heavily. This has helped journalists decipher a signal amongst the vast quantities of noisy tweets.

Twitter has over a relatively short time gone from a source of information for a select few technologically literate journalists to a resource leveraged by newsrooms across the world, whether they are large or small. In addition, coverage by newsrooms of issues or events that are far away often draw heavily from Twitter. For example, immediately after Donald Trump was announced as the US president-elect in 2016, the BBC World Service's radio coverage of the surprising election result had a reporter canvassing people around the USA via

Twitter to elicit their feedback. One country that was thought to have been deeply affected by the election result was Iran, given the thawing of relations between the USA and Iran that former US president Barack Obama initiated. Significant coverage on November 9, 2016, by the BBC World Service on opinions from Iran came from tweets that were being interpreted by a BBC Persian Service correspondent. Indeed, when the reporter who was running the segment asked if there was anything else to add, the Iran-based reporter said that she had many more tweets she could continue to share.

In this context, tweets are often seen as replacing the age-old word-on-the-street *vox populi* interview that has been a mainstay of reporting. On the one hand, time and space are being compressed in order to provide real-time updates from people who are actually on the ground (though there are many issues in terms of validating the authenticity of whether potential sources are actually on the ground in a location). On the other hand, Twitter remains a biased sample, not representative of country populations at large (Blank 2016). So, if newsrooms need to turn to Twitter for on-the-ground information, they are immediately going to be biased towards Twitter demographics, which vary heavily depending on national, cultural, and other contexts. Some countries are more representative than others. Combining on-the-ground reporting with Twitter and other social media is perhaps the gold standard, but it is a more expensive form of journalism than social media alone.

The importance of Twitter to journalism perhaps cannot be overstated. First, reporters have their Twitter IDs accessible via stories they publish online or Twitter IDs displayed next to their names in broadcast media. Second, reporters may be more frank and unguarded on Twitter, as was the case of many journalists responding negatively to Donald Trump during the 2016 US presidential elections (Farhi 2016). Twitter users are also not shy about interacting with reporters to ask questions or to share information. In the case of the November 6, 2016, earthquake in Cushing, Oklahoma, for example, local journalists were being @-mentioned by earthquake victims with eyewitness photos of the damage they had encountered. Some of these images, such as one taken by @sgrfree51, became incorporated in broadcast, online, or other reporting by journalists nationwide (KHOU.com 2016). Whereas, in the past, journalists had to trawl through Twitter to discover potential sources, users involved in a particular event/situation/issue are proactively reaching out to journalists because they want to be part of the process of making the story.

Part of this motivation for everyday people to be engaged in collaborative newsmaking comes from a paradigm shift in terms of sharing itself. In its early days, Twitter's critics argued that the medium was encouraging over-sharing (i.e., TMI – "Too Much Information"). However, our social norms around the world are changing in terms of what people feel comfortable sharing online and the level of detail of their sharing. As privacy norms have shifted, we see images such as in the 2016 Cushing, Oklahoma, earthquake that report actual earthquake damage with visible street signs that provided a precise location of where the photo was taken and where the user likely lives. This is a major change from prior Twitter use. In addition, the photographic quality has increased substantially since Krums' "Miracle on the Hudson" photo. The richness of photos does not replace the need for professional photographers, but does decrease some of the disparity between them and citizen journalists snapping photos on their smartphones. In other words, the gap between production quality is narrowing between the two forms of photojournalism, and this is part of the broader trend of the "prosumer" (Ritzer and Jurgenson 2010). This is not only attributable to the technology, in terms of the smartphones we carry that have extremely high-megapixel cameras, but also the ability of those experiencing an issue to be right in the heart of the situation, while journalists may be quite far away. By the time the press are able to mobilize resources, the story might have moved on and the types of pictures they are able to take might have also changed.

Conclusion

This chapter has sought to explore the manner in which journalism has been influenced by Twitter. Because of Twitter's ubiquity in developed countries (and increasingly in developing countries), it has become an important "ambient" news environment (Hermida 2010b). Specifically, news is always present: it is in the environment of Twitter. This chapter has discussed how news need not always be at the center of a Twitter user's cognitive field. Rather, like a radio, a user's Twitter timeline could be playing in the background, and if the user becomes interested in a particular story, Twitter moves from the ambient periphery to the active center. Some of this is facilitated by digital objects on Twitter, the confluence of tweets, hashtags, retweets, pictures, and hyperlinks. The update culture on Twitter lends itself particularly well to new forms of journalism. In this chapter, shifts towards collaborative journalistic practices (e.g., crowdsourcing) and citizen journalism have been explored.

Research has shown that print media readership is declining (Gulati and Just 2006; Wahl 2006) and that, as Vivian Schiller (cited in Emmett 2008) of NYTimes.com nearly a decade ago observed, "social media [. . .] is one of several essential strategies for disseminating news online – and for surviving [as a news organization]." Though news organizations tend to send tweets with the headlines of their breaking-news stories, many smaller, local news organizations do not have multi-dimensional engagement with Twitter (Meyer and Tang 2015). In the field of journalism, it is easy to see how social media are redefining centuries-old journalistic practices. "Citizen journalists," non-professional journalists, are taking photos and videos from their smartphones and embedding them in tweets, and this material has now become part of some journalists' source mix. As newspapers cut back on staff, citizen journalists fill the void, always ready to "report" via Twitter what they consider to be an important scoop.

Another issue which is pertinent to journalism and Twitter is the persistence of digital divides. As this chapter has argued, there remain persisting digital divides in many Western countries, which keep marginalized and vulnerable populations away from Twitter. Though new social networks and communities of knowledge are supported by Twitter, they are strongly socioeconomically stratified. This keeps Twitter inaccessible to much of the newsreading public, relegating the medium to the more technologically literate "Twittering classes" (this is especially true in developing countries). Furthermore, the issues of information integrity on Twitter (e.g., misleading information/updates, news hoaxes, and state propaganda) also, generally, disproportionately affect marginalized populations. Hoaxes and patent misinformation can have potentially disastrous ramifications for vulnerable populations if issues of health, for example, are concerned. And state-sponsored propaganda, often employing automated bots, could influence the efficacy of a social movement or election domestically or internationally, given Twitter's worldwide reach. Ultimately, news production and consumption on Twitter are highly stratified.

Though we must be cognizant of digital divides and differing levels of information literacy, this is not to say that Twitter has not altered news production and consumption. Indeed, journalistic norms surrounding transparency and accountability have been affected by Twitter's ambient news environment (Hermida 2010b). Just as journalists use crowdsourcing to help with stories, the crowds are watching journalists on Twitter. Journalists on Twitter have had to open the gates to their craft, bringing news production further into the public eye, at least in terms of higher levels of accountability (Hayes et al. 2007). This chapter has also illustrated how professional news media have become more open to using tweets for picking up breaking news such as the downing of Flight 1549 and the Paris terror attacks. When tweets have been picked up by major media outlets in cases such as these, this coverage has brought attention to Twitter itself. However, the public ultimately takes interest in the stories themselves and not so much in the original source tweets or the individual Twitterer responsible for breaking the story. If this is the case (and chapter 3 specifically discusses issues of tweet attribution), Twittering citizen journalists are ephemeral, vanishing after their 15 minutes in the limelight (affirming the continuing importance of Andy Warhol's prophecy). In most instances, they are left unpaid and unknown. Those citizen journalists who do become "known" represent elites in the medium. This is an interesting tension in that Twitter is viewed as an alternative news media. Yet, as Poell and Borra (2011: 14) found in the case of the 2010 Toronto G20 protests, the "resulting account was based on the observations and experiences of a small group of insiders." In other words, Twitter's citizen journalism is not exempt from the hierarchies endemic in traditional media industries. Rather, new forms of elitism are emerging.

Ultimately, Twitter has gained prominence as a powerful media outlet. Shirky (cited in Last 2009) argues that the 2009 anti-government Iranian protests were "transformed by social media" and, through Twitter, "people throughout the world are not only listening but responding." In 2011, many in the media asserted a similar conclusion in reference to the "Arab Spring" social movements (see chapter 6 for a full discussion claims of "Twitter revolutions"). Though Shirky's conclusion is itself debatable,[19] it is important to respond to his assertion that global citizens are not only consuming breaking news but producing news in a globalized Twitter-mediated public sphere, which emphasizes an instantaneous "stream of news [which] combines news, opinion, and emotion" (Papacharissi and de Fatima Oliveira 2012: 1). Even Mark Pfeifle of the usually cautious Christian Science Monitor argued that Twitter should be given the Nobel Peace Prize (Last 2009). Regardless of one's opinion on that, the power of the medium lies in the fact that profound tweets appear side by side with banal ones – second by second, minute by minute, and hour by hour. It is from this perspective that Twitter affords citizen journalists the possibility to break profound news stories to a global public and to interact with journalists in new ways. Even if professional news media dominates coverage of the story and the original Twitterer is left with only 15 minutes of fame, the power of Twitter to citizen journalism should not be underestimated. Additionally, Twitter has facilitated new, particularly collaborative journalistic practices and is shaping journalistic norms such as transparency.

Vicky Soni
@vickkysoni

Follow

First experience with #earthquake in Gurgaon at 4.30 AM today, not able to sleep now.

LIKE
1

3:40 PM - 16 Nov 2016

@vickkysoni[1]

As the tweet above illustrates, some users tweet during a natural disaster. This tweet was sent by a user in India on November 16, 2016, almost immediately after an earthquake registering 4.2 on the Richter scale was reported in Haryana, India. Another user, @ZeherAkash, tweeted around the same time: "#Earthquake in delhi, and what people do??? . . . yes, they tweet."[2] As these tweets suggest, the information conveyed by the messages may not be rich in each individual instance. However, collectively, as seen in cases such as the Haryana earthquake in India, the information disseminated and gleaned can be of great value to disaster victims and relief workers alike. Indeed, early news coverage of the earthquake highlighted relevant tweets (Chatterji 2016) as the quake occurred at 4.30 a.m. local time and news crews had not been assembled. This chapter explores the significance of Twitter during and after natural disasters.

CHAPTER FIVE

Twitter and Disasters

Throughout this book, Twitter has been explained as a communications technology which is best understood as part of a larger trend towards "update cultures." As discussed in previous chapters, there is a pervasive culture in quite a few countries where individuals take a picture and want to share it online, or have had an exceptional meal and want to update their friends about the amazing restaurant they found. However, there are gradients of the type of updating that occurs on Twitter (i.e., updating ranges on the spectrum between banal and profound). Previous chapters have discussed the platform's role in updating about the banal, including both the significance and perception of such updating (chapters 2 and 3).

However, the previous chapter began the discussion of more extraordinary forms of updates through citizen journalism. In this chapter, update culture is discussed in the context of diverse people being in extreme situations that they feel the world needs to be updated about: disasters. On Twitter, citizen journalists have updated the world during earthquakes, plane crashes, tsunamis, wildfires, and other disasters. In all of these situations, people felt the need to update via tweets.

The focus of the previous chapter was to discuss Twitter's role in terms of changes to journalistic practice. This chapter seeks to understand the nuances of update cultures by examining one extreme end of the continuum from the banal to the profound: tweets about extreme disasters. Disasters are specifically useful for understanding Twitter in that those who are affected are completely broken from normal routines, potentially at risk of injury or death, anxious about the short term, and usually in some form of shock or another trauma. Additionally, internet access can be severely limited or potentially dangerous if traveling is needed for access. Yet individuals in disaster epicenters tweet. And they use Twitter in new and innovative ways in these situations. Here, the unique case of Twitter and disasters is explored, to understand both Twitter's specific role and some of the complexities surrounding update cultures.

Gathering news information about disasters is an act of following a fast-moving target. In the minutes between news broadcasts, things on the ground can change so rapidly in particularly acute disasters. Traditional news media often cannot catch up in a timely manner. Before the internet became pervasive, television (and, before that, radio) served as the first line for individuals to access fast-breaking news regarding disasters. Now social media have become important sources of disaster information. In particular, Twitter is commonly used by individuals to follow breaking news regarding disasters, and to keep abreast of the updates that may be coming in frequently throughout the day. Twitter and similar social media sites are inherently built for individual users to subscribe to flows of information, a structure that works efficiently for information dissemination during disasters. In the case of Twitter, users who are interested in breaking news often "follow" the Twitter feeds of traditional news media. What is also particularly unique to Twitter is that users can then elect to follow the updates of users who they feel are close to a disaster. Twitter users can choose to follow the tweets of those "reporting" on the disaster (e.g., traditional and citizen journalists as discussed in the previous chapter), or they can simply read the feeds of these users. In other words, disasters offer a particularly unique case to see the ways in which journalistic practice has been changed by Twitter, a key theme discussed in the previous chapter. This chapter begins by introducing the study of disasters. It discusses the social embeddedness of disasters and then provides a historical context through an exploration of relevant information technology and disasters literature. Twitter has been used during disasters for nearly a decade. This chapter reflects this history by exploring the 2010 Pakistan floods and the 2016 Kaikoura, New Zealand, earthquake as cases. These examples serve to present an examination of Twitter's differential usage in developed and developing countries, and to highlight extreme forms of update culture (e.g., a user tweeting as they feel the earth shake under them).

Disaster as Socially Mediated

Disasters, as Clarke (2004: 137) observes, may be destructive, but are ultimately "prosaic" and, as such, help us glean "important things about how and why society works as it does." (The same holds true for understanding how Twitter "works" during disasters.) Sorokin (1943: 244), in his seminal *Man and Society in Calamity*, noted that disasters "offer an opportunity to examine many aspects of social life which in normal times are hidden." Forms of kindness between members of a community or existent social hierarchies are made highly visible in disaster situations, despite less altruistic behavior at other times. For example, in the aftermath of the 2004 Indian Ocean tsunami, the Sri Lankan government tried to appropriate land from devastated coastal villages for hotel development.[3] Steinberg (2000: 178) notes that, during the 1971 San Fernando earthquake in California, middle-class individuals were quickly approved for federally funded loans, while the poor, elderly, and ethnic minorities were largely ignored.[4] Despite these inequalities, disaster situations have the ability to activate "disaster communities," usually ad hoc communities of people affected by or involved with a disaster. Using the case of a munitions ship explosion in Halifax, Canada, in 1917, Samuel Prince (1920: 19) argued that the violence of disaster situations creates a state of "flux" from "which it [life] must reset upon a principle, a creed, or purpose" and, from this, "a new sense of unity in dealing with common problems" (Prince 1920: 139) can emerge.

Like in Halifax, contemporary natural disasters cause a flux and various virtual communities can emerge in a common creed of reconstruction. The cyber-presences of disaster communities have blurred a disaster's physical spatial borders as individuals and aid agencies in disaster-struck areas form online coalitions (Murthy 2013). Fischer's (1998: 18) observation that "[g]roups of survivors tend to emerge to begin automatically responding to the needs of one another" is affirmed virtually in some disaster cases (though not in others). Whether these were activist oriented or scientific (e.g., geological change affecting water supply issues), individuals and groups in some twenty-first-century disasters have worked together virtually. Online communities can be important to the social fabric of certain groups of disaster victims. For example, from the day the 2004 Indian Ocean tsunami hit subcontinental shores, the web forum and chat sections of India's and Sri Lanka's most popular websites filled with posts. On the popular Indian site rediff.com, a bevy of sympathetic posts appeared on December 26, 2004, the day the tsunami hit the Indian subcontinent. One year after the tsunami, the forum section of the popular Sri Lankan website spot.lk hosted several discussion threads in which users posted images and text (including in the Tamil language) in remembrance of victims of the disaster (Murthy 2013).

Scholarship on disasters illustrates that new media spaces such as these functioned as collective spaces which brought together disparate people and communities who experienced similar traumas (Palen 2008; Yan 2009). Though they are relatively recent phenomena, these digital communities of disaster victims are reminiscent of what Barton (1969: 226–7) termed communities with "segmental integration." What he meant by this was that the community had "close ties" within particular social "segments," but had "few ties" between the segments (ibid.). Applied to virtual communities, groups could have "close ties" online, but not necessarily to other groups of online posters. However, Barton (p. 227) argues that despite this diversity between segmental groups, "intense discussion and awareness within all groups" can occur as "each has some of its members affected" by the disaster.

Loft (2005) suggests that blogs (the longer-length cousin of Twitter) can encourage community-building.[5] Specialized roles emerge on media including blogs, and solidarity can develop from the specialized roles that people have in this virtual community. In my research on new media and disasters (Murthy 2013), I found that tsunami-related blogs can be understood as communities through the complex mesh of online interactions between those with missing relatives, individuals affected locally by the aftermath, aid workers, volunteers (specialist and non-specialist), and the general public (some encouraging donations and others expressing support online). Just the fact of empathetic expressions of support by anonymous virtual participants in a community is powerful. In the 2007 Virginia Tech shooting, anonymous individuals contributed their condolences to an online virtual Memorial in Second Life, and this was found to be meaningful by those affected by the disaster (Hughes et al. 2008).

Information Technology and Disasters

The diffusion of innovative technologies within a state of extreme disaster seems at some level counterintuitive. Rather than conjuring up *ad hoc* networks of Twitter users, which update others of road closures and fatalities, one would think a disaster would sweep away any proclivity for technological invention. However, as Pitirim Sorokin (1943: 243) prophetically noted in the 1940s, disaster can "stimulate and foster" society's "scientific and technological work." Twitter becomes, in some disasters, one of the tools for this innovative work to which Sorokin is alluding. That being said, the introduction of new technologies in disaster situations, as Bates and

Peacock (1987: 305) note, is not a zero-sum game. They give the example of a society where water was traditionally obtained from public fountains or watering places. Besides serving the purpose of providing water, they also functioned as key community spaces where women met and socialized. In reconstruction efforts, these villages could be given piped water to their houses or village centers (perhaps due to well contamination), an action which Bates and Peacock (1987: 305–6) argue constitutes a change in social life (e.g., for women who regularly socialize at fountains). Additionally, if victims turn to Twitter because of a disaster, tweeting may persist as part of their life after the disaster. However, in this situation, Twitter most likely "augments" (Jurgenson 2012) their social communication rather than eliminating or severely reducing face-to-face interactions.

Cutting-edge communications networks have historically been associated with developed countries. Recent scholarship shows that this trend is changing (Nadiri and Nandi 2015; Wei 2016). The ability to tweet and post YouTube videos of your "disaster experience" has the potential for normally marginalized individuals and groups to update the world about their situation. This is hardly unproblematic. Although it fosters a perceived sense of empowerment amongst disaster victims,[6] there is also a globally induced pressure to update the world by "representing"[7] one's village/town/city/country, as international media scramble to arrive in remote disaster-stricken areas.

Whether the people have become more empowered or not, online dispatches from developing countries (despite usually coming from social and economic elites) not only shape international views of disaster victims, but can also affect aid campaigns.[8] For example, Instagram photographs and their accompanying text regarding the 2015 earthquake in Nuwakot, Nepal, flowed out of the country while traditional forms of news dissemination were severely limited (Traveler24 2015). One YouTube user, Anil Mahato, shot nearly five minutes of video as the quake hit on May 12, 2015, and managed to upload it the next day, garnering tens of thousands of views.[9] In addition, comments were later added, below his video. A Facebook group called nepalphotoproject[10] encouraged Instagram users to hashtag #nepalphotoproject and share eyewitness accounts of the earthquake. Images shared by users document both physical damage as well as Nepalis trying to get back to daily life (Traveler24 2015). Though on a small scale and usually dependent on local digital knowledge, these representations of disaster experiences via social media can provide a counterbalance to sometimes exploitative and ethnocentric accounts.[11] Tweets coming out of disaster areas can have similar effects, particularly if they are used to disseminate content from another platform to Twitter, a medium known for its use by journalists. Moreover, tweets can be cross-posted either automatically or with the click of a button, enabling content on Twitter to circulate to a variety of other social media platforms used by the tweeter. This can potentially increase visibility of the original tweet, sometimes dramatically.

Before specifically exploring Twitter and disasters, it is useful to further examine the history of information-sharing technology in disasters. As in other chapters, this historical context is critically important to viewing Twitter alongside other sociotechnical innovations in disaster communication. Stephenson and Anderson's (1997) forward-looking essay "Disasters and the Information Technology Revolution," though well over a decade old now, remains a useful review of the subject. Beginning with "time-sharing" mainframes (where clusters of users shared room-sized computers) in the 1970s, followed by the advent of personal computers in the 1980s, they argue that disaster relief operations have been heavily shaped by technological change. They observe that online modem-networked bulletin boards (very early precursors to Twitter), such as ADMIN in Australia and the Emergency Preparedness Information Exchange (EPIX) in Canada, had been adopted by a small minority of emergency professionals by the late 1980s (Stephenson and Anderson 1997: 311). They single out the 1990s as having perhaps the most profound effect on disaster relief operations, with innovations in digital radio, Geographic Information Systems (GIS), email (and email list servers), Gopher (software used to create information portals), remote sensing, and the internet (ibid.: 311–15). Fischer (1998) also notes that disaster victims in the USA during the 1990s could complete online applications for disaster relief from the Federal Emergency Management Agency (FEMA) website directly, and that the information on various websites (governmental and otherwise) announced disaster mitigation and response. It is important to reflect on the evolution of information technology with regard to disasters, not only to contextualize the importance of these changes, but also to remember that these technologies have not always been ubiquitous. The same goes for tweets during disasters – something that has become ubiquitous in developed countries.

During contemporary disasters, the world not only expects and assumes a barrage of tweets, but also digital videos and photographs that chronicle the events surrounding a disaster. But, in 1995, the use of the internet as "a self-help network" for relaying information about the Kobe earthquake in Japan (through digital maps, digital photographs, and online forums) was noteworthy (Stephenson and Anderson 1997: 315). Similarly, the use of web pages during flooding in North Dakota and Manitoba in April and May 1997 "played a crucial role [. . .] in maintaining a sense of community among evacuated people dispersed throughout the region" (Stephenson and Anderson 1997: 317). This latter point that the internet can (and has over a decade) influenced social cohesion during natural disasters is one compellingly made by Shklovski et al. (2008). That said, there are downsides to increasing internet and telephony usage during disasters. Specifically, a greater reliance on the internet also translates to a greater demand on electricity. Additionally, using mobile devices to upload videos and photos can easily overload cellular phone systems and cause outages. (Twitter is an interesting exception in that tweets are low bandwidth consumers; individuals can tweet more regularly and from more locations in the disaster area, whereas video uploading is often a much more difficult action to accomplish.) In the case of the 2004 Indian Ocean tsunami, the disaster created large-scale interruptions to the electricity and telephone grids. In developed countries this is much less of a problem, though even affluent New York City faced power outages during Hurricane Sandy (Murthy and Gross 2017).

Twitter Research and Disasters

As already noted, Twitter has been prominently associated with contemporary disasters. Research on the usage of social media and disaster events has been growing, covering a range of sites, including social networking, photo repository, and microblogging sites (Kireyev et al. 2009). The discussion of natural disasters on Twitter has been part of a general trend that has brought Twitter significant mainstream attention. As McCulloch (2009) argues, the downing of US Airways Flight 1549 in the Hudson River in New York in 2009 and Twitter's use in covering the story legitimized the site as a journalistic space (a case discussed in detail in the previous chapter). Specifically, the media used by Janis Krums to circulate a picture taken on his iPhone of the downed aircraft was Twitter's photo-sharing portal, TwitPic. This happened well before any news crews arrived and many major news media used his iPhone picture in print media, with the Associated Press eventually purchasing distribution rights. And MSNBC had him on the phone within 30 minutes of him tweeting.

The October 2007 wildfires in Southern California were perhaps the first natural disaster that put Twitter on the map. As Hughes and Palen (2009: 1) note, Twitter was used "to inform citizens of the time-critical information about road closures, community evacuations, shifts in fire lines, and shelter information." A man-made disaster in which Twitter became important and, indeed, controversial was that of the Mumbai bomb blasts of 2008, where everyday Indians were tweeting about which hotels had been taken over by armed gunmen, where fires were still burning, and where shots had been fired (see chapter 4). Because tweets are so short, researchers have found them to be a medium especially well suited to communicating real-time information during disasters (Hughes and Palen 2009). As Palen et al. note (2010), "the implications of social media are significant for mass emergency events." Additionally, social media are being used by government officials to assist in organizing volunteer efforts during disasters (Tucker 2011). Indeed, a formal framework that identifies 15 distinct disaster-related social media uses has been developed to enable effective engagement of social media at all stages, from disaster preparedness to disaster recovery (Houston et al. 2015).

The 2010 Pakistan Floods

Though I introduce a more recent disaster, the 2016 Kaikoura, New Zealand, earthquake, next, it is useful to provide some historical context to Twitter's use in disasters. I do this through the 2010 Pakistan floods, which were the third most popular trending topic in 2010 in Twitter's News Events category (Twitter.com 2010).[12] The floods caused enormous loss of life, significant environmental destruction, and a large-scale humanitarian crisis. The United Nations quickly labeled the situation in Pakistan as a "catastrophe." There were 1,802 people reported dead and 2,994 injured (Associated Press of Pakistan 2010). The United Nations World Food Programme estimated that 1.8 million people "were in dire need of water, food and shelter" (*The Irish Times* 2010). In the case of the floods, the vast majority of the affected population consisted of digital have-nots prior to the flooding. National broadband penetration was a mere 0.31 percent (International

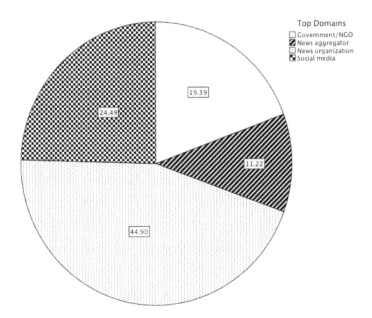

Top Domains
☐ Government/NGO
▨ News aggregator
☐ News organization
▨ Social media

19.39

24.49

11.22

44.90

Figure 5.1   Top 100 domain categories to which #Pakistan tweets linked (by percent)

Telecommunication Union 2010) at the time of the disaster. (Since then, broadband and cellular penetration has grown significantly (Imtiaz, Khan, and Shakir 2015). Additionally, the areas that were affected are predominantly home to Urdu-language speakers, rather than English-language speakers. Language and Twitter use are linked, with English being the dominant language for tweets (Mocanu et al. 2013).

I investigated the 2010 Pakistan floods on Twitter by studying 113,862 tweets with the trending hashtag "Pakistan" (collected during August 2010).[13] Which websites people were linking to in their tweets were also examined. What is immediately noteworthy is that traditional media were the most frequently linked media types during the 2010 Pakistan floods (see figure 5.1). This finding highlights several aspects of Twitter's use in this case. Twitter users place primacy on circulating information from traditional news media rather than information/news from social media (which includes blogs). In many ways, this affirms an argument that Twitter as a whole does not give much voice to alternative news sources (including alternative disaster accounts from citizen journalists). Rather, CNN, the BBC, and other traditional media dominate the list of sites to which individual tweeters linked during the floods. Although this indicates the continuing strength of traditional media, it does not highlight the eclipse of social media. Rather, it affirms the place of traditional news media alongside social media in disasters. Indeed, Dailey and Starbird (2016) argue that both legacy and social media play an important role in disasters, as they found in their study of Hurricane Irene in upstate New York.

In terms of content, most Pakistan-related tweets refer to the floods in passing and often recommend a news article. Many users retweet headline stories tweeted by traditional news organizations. One of the questions explored in this book is how transformative Twitter – as a medium – is in terms of forming communities, whether around health (see chapter 7) or social movements (see chapter 6). In the case of disasters, the scholarship has argued that Twitter can facilitate the formation of effective disaster communities (Houston et al. 2015; Ling et al. 2015). However, if most are tweeting in passing, does a disaster "community" emerge?

Although these communities can and do exist – for instance, individuals in a disaster zone tweet the location of victims or report road closures (Palen et al. 2010) – the majority are tweeting news stories from traditional media. Additionally, the vast majority of users are only tweeting once about the floods (see figure 5.2). Such infrequent involvement points to the fact that these users are not part of a cohesive disaster community. Rather, Twitter users passively retweet about humanitarian crises, political movements, and other "causes" from the comfort of their chair (akin to the "slacktivism" discussed in chapter 6). This low-stakes involvement in the disaster creates a public identity for themselves as global individuals who

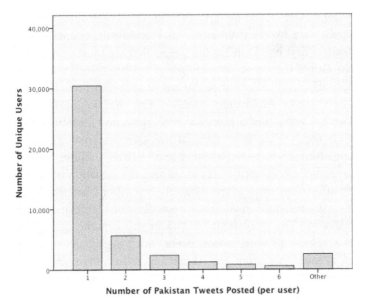

Figure 5.2   Frequency of tweets per user with Pakistan trending topic tag

are immersed in humanitarian causes. It takes just a second to tweet about a disaster and one's followers potentially see a user as an empathetic cosmopolitan. Rather than deep engagement, these masses of users are only superficially engaged with a disaster or other humanitarian event.

This behavior should not be viewed as normatively inferior to tweets contributed from on-the-ground aid workers and citizen journalists. Rather, these types of users themselves are qualitatively different and not comparable. What the involvement of these casual tweets reveals is a relatively high level of focused interest toward the floods. Interestingly, many Twitter users (with the majority in Western countries) at least had the floods on their mind, even if it was only in passing (see figure 5.2). This is further substantiated by the fact that Pakistan was one of the top trending topics of 2010 (Twitter.com 2010).[14]

The Pakistan floods also shed light on whose tweets are

being picked up and being circulated. Besides traditional news media, are tweets from users in Pakistan experiencing the disaster first hand among the tweets that are most retweeted? No. Out of the top 20 @-mentions, a celebrity (Jemima Khan) outranks UNICEF. Four of the top 10 are celebrities (Jemima Khan, Lance Armstrong, Stephen Fry, and Justin Bieber). Two are news media (the *New York Times* and the *Huffington Post*) and two are governmental/non-governmental organizations (the US State Department and UNICEF). Either Twitter users believe celebrities could impact the situation of disaster-affected victims or the data reflect Twitter's propensity to involve celebrities in all topics, regardless of their expertise or relevance. The scholarship on Twitter supports the latter (Cha et al. 2010). In other words, users with a significant number of at-mentions were the exception rather than the rule. Specifically, the directedness of the conversations regarding the Pakistan floods had a significant weight toward mentioning celebrities rather than individuals or organizations on the ground in Pakistan. Additionally, only 10 of the top 100 users who were @-mentioned and one of the top 20 @-mentioned users were located in Pakistan, which supports the theory that Twitter functioned more as a clearing house of "news" passing through the hands of mainstream media or celebrities during the disaster, rather than Pakistani individuals and institutions. Research in celebrity studies highlights the emergence of "development celebrities," celebrities who have cultivated influence in development politics through a variety of modes, including Twitter (Goodman and Barnes 2011). Prominent celebrities have had their "development celebrity" status emphasized via Twitter by tweeting about disasters such as the Haitian earthquake. Celebrities including Paris Hilton, Dannii Minogue, Chris Martin, and Ben Stiller took to their Twitter accounts to alert their followers after the Haitian earthquake; Wyclef Jean tweeted ". . . on my way to the DR to get to Haiti. Please urge your councilmen, governors, etc; we need a state of emergency for Haiti"[15] and that "Haiti today faces a natural

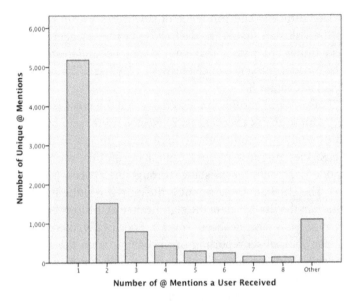

Figure 5.3   Frequency of @-mentions per user with Pakistan trending topic hashtag

disaster of unprecedented proportion, an earthquake unlike anything the country has ever experienced" (Goodman and Barnes 2011). Two years after the earthquake, Ashton Kutcher, a celebrity whom users often ask to retweet development-related content, tweeted "On this 2 year anniversary of the #Haiti Earthquake - #HelpHaitiHome: http://bit.ly/yPgons."[16]

Twitter provides a highly efficient medium for "development celebrities" to make known their development credentials. In the case of Stiller, only a vague tweet about Haiti is tweeted, but it makes clear Stiller's interest in the Haitian disaster. Even in developed countries, celebrities take to Twitter during disasters, though for different reasons. In the case of the Kaikoura, New Zealand, earthquake discussed next, Daniel Gillies, a New Zealand actor known for his role in *The Vampire Diaries*, asked his followers to donate to the Red Cross.[17]

The authority and influence of celebrities within the case of the Pakistan floods (as well as in Twitter in general) are also important points that should not be underestimated. The broader influence of celebrities in Twitter is discussed in detail in chapter 8.

Tweets by celebrities are also retweeted the most (see table 5.1). Out of the 15 tweets most retweeted, nine were by celebrities. Only two non-celebrity individuals appear in this list. Celebrities are most interested in raising awareness about the floods and money for assistance through their tweets (see table 5.1). The US State Department is the only governmental institution in the list. Much of the significance of this retweet list is derived from what is absent from it. Specifically, there are no citizen journalists reporting on the floods from the ground. Indeed, there are no individuals from Pakistan who appear in the list. From the vantage point of retweets, Twitter seems to be disproportionately focused as a medium for celebrities to promote fundraising efforts rather than disseminating first-hand information about the floods. That said, tweets by social-media savvy Pakistanis did help raise money during the disaster (Toosi 2011). However, the majority of retweeted messages are linked to celebrities or other influential Twitter users. Celebrities ultimately had a powerful voice within the context of the Pakistan floods, a voice that is seemingly louder than individual journalists and individuals in Pakistan.

This highlights the larger power of celebrities within Twitter and within update cultures. Many individuals follow celebrities because they are interested in their updates on celebrity culture (Hargittai and Litt 2011), whether these are banal or profound. Individuals are tuning into celebrity Twitter feeds whether to read their breakfast selection, romantic interest, or about development causes. Another way to think about celebrities tweeting on disasters is as "brokers," who introduce large sections of the public to a disaster the celebrity thinks matters (e.g., Wyclef Jean's tweet about the Haitian earthquake). The retweeting of a celebrity tweet can potentially have

Table 5.1 Top 15 retweets with identifiable users

(numbers 5 and 13 had no identifiable users and were categorized as spam)

Ranking	Retweet text
1	RT @Yunaaaa: Flood-affected children in north-western Pakistan urgently need aid – Help @UNICEF help these children – Please visit http: ...
2	RT @JemKhan: My article re Pakistan floods. Please read, RT, donate if poss. Thanks http://www.thesundaytimes.co.uk/sto/public/article37 ...
3	RT @DalaiLama: His Holiness the Dalai Lama prays for the loss of life caused by floods in Pakistan, India, and landslides in Drugchu htt ...
4	RT @rainnwilson: We give a billion a year to Pakistan which aids the Taliban. Why not give it to the poor or to the debt?
6	RT @Sascha1976: Wat #carglasszuigt kan, kan ook voor een goed doel... Hashtag #giro555open om Pakistan te helpen. 14 miljoen mensen hebb ...
7	RT @oncefelin: Moscow mortuaries full. Floods in India. Floods in China. Floods in Pakistan. Millions affected. Climate change is real. ...
8	RT @stephenfry: Amazing article by @JemKhan on Pakistan, its floods, its future and what we can do. http://bit.ly/95Knjq
9	RT @UncleRUSH: 20 million left homeless by Pakistan flooding...plz raise awareness
10	RT @StateDept: Text \SWAT\" to 50555 from your phone to contribute $10 to help flood victims in #Pakistan. http://go.usa.gov/cxS #UNHCR #UN"
11	RT @TheEconomist: How the heatwave in Russia is connected to floods in Pakistan http://econ.st/cvZWWX #economist #heatwave #russia #pakistan
12	RT @stephenfry: To donate to Red Cross http://bit.ly/aW9DAs or to give £5 text DONATE to 70700. Those stricken by the Pakistan floods ne ..
14	RT @TheVijayMallya: My website-mallyainparliament.in hacked by d Pakistan Cyber Army Shocked when I opened site to update it Saw the Pak ...
15	RT @QueenRania: Dire needs in Pakistan for flood-affected children – Help @UNICEF Please help these children by visiting http://www.unic ...

real impacts on the prominence of disasters from the eyes of Twitter users in developed countries. The knock-on effect could be increased media attention. Ultimately – if one sees Twitter as a powerful political force – these public elevations of a disaster to prominence could potentially influence governmental humanitarian aid decisions (that is, if politicians see Twitter as a barometer of constituent sentiment).

Twitter and the 2016 Kaikoura, New Zealand, Earthquake

On November 14, 2016, an earthquake with a 7.8 magnitude hit the South Island of New Zealand (with the earthquake's epicenter close to Culverden). Many coastal and other cities were affected and aftershocks were felt in the following days. This earthquake triggered a tsunami with waves 8 feet above normal tidal levels, the highest seen in 38 years (Dewan, Grinberg, and O'Sullivan 2016). Power and telephone lines were knocked out in some areas (Australian Broadcasting Corporation News 2016), but social media enabled affected individuals to communicate by Twitter, Instagram, and Facebook. Though there was a mobile outage initially, this was quickly fixed (Wheatstone et al. 2016). During previous earthquakes in New Zealand, celebrities tweeted their support to disaster victims (the edge 2010). More substantially, Twitter has been used as a support community, especially when quakes hit in the middle of the night (Cropp 2016).

Twitter was even carrying reliable earthquake reports of Kaikoura before major news media began reporting on the disaster. In addition, Twitter provided narratives of the earthquake that might not have been covered by international news media in the past. But, as tweets went viral, these stories were covered. For example, three cows were stranded on an earthquake-induced "island." A local New Zealand news service, Newshub, posted a tweet with video footage of the cows,[18] which went viral on Twitter[19] and caught the attention of

Newshub Breaking
@NewshubBreaking   ☼   ⚋ Follow

The cows left stranded on a quake-created island near Kaikoura have been brought to safety bit.ly/2fOwrPu #SaveTheCows

RETWEETS   LIKES
540   732

5:02 PM - 14 Nov 2016

↰ 29   ⇄ 540   ♥ 732   •••

Figure 5.4   "Stranded Cows" tweet; reproduced with permission from Newshub (www.newshub.co.nz)

news media worldwide, spawning the hashtag #SaveTheCows (Bloom 2016); see figure 5.4. The cows were eventually rescued and the video garnered over 2 million views on YouTube.[20] The tweets during the earthquake and in the aftermath were found to be related to the earthquake/tsunami, the collapse of the cliff that blocked New Zealand's major highway, the stranded cows, and earthquake safety. Tweets covered a wide range of topics, ranging from power outages to worrying about relatives in New Zealand. A word cloud depicting the top terms gathered from 33,800 tweets posted on November 17–18, 2016 is illustrated in figure 5.5 What this pattern reveals is that tweets were flowing rapidly from the moment the Kaikoura earthquake was felt, and useful information was succinctly conveyed in a timely fashion. Reporting on the 2016 Haryana earthquake supports people's immediate turn to tweeting no matter when a disaster hits: "Many people

Figure 5.5   Word cloud of 33,800 Kaikoura earthquake tweets, produced using netlytic (Gruzd 2016)

tweeted about the earthquake despite the tremor hitting early in the morning" (Zee Media Bureau 2016).

New Zealand is in the top 20 "Twitter Countries" (Sysomos 2014: 14) in terms of Twitter usage per capita. Because of its large user-base and high frequency of earthquakes, researchers had already begun investigating Twitter and earthquake notification in New Zealand, including during the 2011 Christchurch earthquake (Yin et al. 2015). However, in its infancy, Twitter's ability to filter important information from experts during disasters is questionable. Rather, Twitter's infrastructure is based around prioritizing the circulation of tweets from more "popular" Twitter users. Indeed, Twitter's search results default to "top" tweets rather than all "live" tweets. No analysis is made concerning whether or not a user has expertise in an area. For example, in the aftermath of Kaikoura, the New Zealand Earthquake Commission (@EQCNZ) and New Zealand Civil Defence (@NZCivilDefence) tweeted advice about "drop, cover, and hold"[21] as well as avoiding beaches and coastal areas.[22] These tweets were retweeted 58 and 155 times respectively but paled into insignificance in comparison to the 3,300 retweets Sky News' (@SkyNews) stranded cows tweet[23] received. Figure 5.6, a network graph of 33,800 tweets from 11,672 unique Twitter users, puts this into perspective by

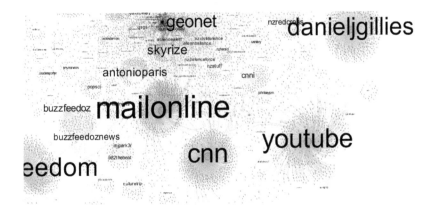

Figure 5.6   Close-up of network of 33,800 earthquake tweets from 11,672 unique Twitter users (November 17–18, 2016)

illustrating the impact of particular Twitter users during the earthquake, including the smaller reach of @NZCivilDefence. As figure 5.6 illustrates, CNN, YouTube, and the *Daily Mail* feature prominently. The previous case explored, the 2010 Pakistan floods, was different, both in the type of disaster and locale, and tweets from popular Twitter users – especially celebrities – were disproportionately influential.

Like the Pakistan floods, one of the top users within the network is a celebrity, Daniel Gillies (@danieljgillies), known for his role in *The Vampire Diaries*. As figure 5.6 illustrates, @danieljgillies received a substantial share of retweets and mentions. Indeed, the network has the most focused activity around particular users, which are referred to as "star"/"wheel" formations. Other important accounts were news outlets such as CNN, BuzzFeed, and, interestingly, the UK's *Daily Mail* (@mailonline), which covered the stranded cows extensively. Indeed, "cows" was one of the top words in the word cloud (see figure 5.5). Relief agencies do appear within the network. In figure 5.6, around @geonet, New Zealand Civil Defence (@nzcivildefence) and the US Geological Survey (@USGS) are present, but are not highly prominent. News organizations

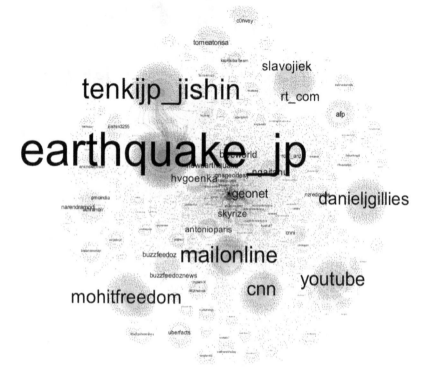

Figure 5.7   Whole network of 33,800 earthquake tweets from
11,672 unique Twitter users (November 17–18, 2016)

and celebrities are clearly more visible in the overall network.
Interestingly, several Japanese earthquake bot accounts actually had the highest number of retweet/mentions (as figure
5.7 reveals). They are not central to the conversation related to
New Zealand, but they numerically predominate the data set.
Additionally, figure 5.7 visualizes discernible influencers and
their position within the network as a whole.

What is interesting about the earthquake data is not only
that news organizations continue to be important during disasters on Twitter, but also that the tweets of everyday people
do not seem to be directly picked up on Twitter. That is not
to say that their voice is not crossing over to being heard, as
many news stories use images taken by local New Zealand
users on Instagram, Twitter, Facebook, and other social media
platforms. However, they are not distinctly identified within

the graph network. Rather, the news organization publishing the story generally is.

In terms of relief organizations, New Zealand Red Cross (@nzredcross) is the seventh most mentioned user within the data collected. This is similar to my work done on Hurricane Sandy, which found that the US Red Cross was noticeable on Twitter (Murthy and Gross 2017). Historically speaking, in the case of the Pakistan floods, the Red Cross was significant, as this chapter previously discussed. The continued visibility of Red Cross accounts on Twitter demonstrates that during disasters, Twitter provides specific affordances for fundraising efforts. Tweets are easy to send and users are clearly motivated to retweet content aimed at garnering donations to aid agencies. Chapter 6 discusses the motivation for some Twitter users to want to support fundraising efforts within their social networks.

Conclusion

This chapter has explored, the unique ways in which Twitter is used in disasters, extreme events which render visible many aspects of social life which are otherwise obscured or invisible. When a disaster strikes, otherwise disparate groups become joined together across the common experience of being disaster victims. In this way, Twitter may be helping form far-reaching communities that transcend traditional socioeconomic barriers. Or it may be reinforcing these hierarchies. A key reason this chapter explored disasters rather than another area is that disasters are highly unique in their extreme nature and their ability to instantaneously affect everyone regardless of social position. Most disaster victims feel anxious and, at a minimum, disoriented. Some may have even witnessed death (and tweeted about it). This extreme situation can lead to an update culture whose content can be highly profound. Additionally, the stakes of getting tweets out from a disaster zone can be much higher. Lives could potentially be saved through tweets warning people of flash-flood areas or other dangerous situations. Therefore, even if internet access is difficult to come by, some individuals may feel a direct need to update the world of what they know about a disaster situation.

Even if their tweets do not save a life, one thing is certain. The world turns to Twitter to learn of minute-to-minute detail during disasters. This chapter has discussed how Twitter has shaped journalistic practice, using disaster reporting as a case study. Disaster victims who are tweeting to help other victims also simultaneously become citizen journalists. This practice has not infringed upon the role of traditional media and disaster reporting. Rather, it has augmented the information available to journalists in their reporting (i.e., being much more timely and far-reaching in their reports). Examining Twitter's use during natural disasters reveals both the forest and the trees. We see individual citizen journalists, aid workers, and victims going to great lengths to interact with each other on Twitter. However, the macro view suggests that those who have a powerful voice regarding any topic on Twitter (i.e., celebrities and other "popular" Twitter users) have the most powerful voice during natural disasters. For example, James Corden (@JKCorden) tweeted on the day of the 2016 Kaikoura, New Zealand, earthquake: "Stay safe New Zealand. We're all pulling for you right now x,"[24] which was retweeted nearly 2,000 times. Similarly, Richard Armitage (@RCArmitage) tweeted, "Hope everyone is ok in NZ. thinking about you this morning. Stay safe," gaining nearly 1000 retweets.[25] This is a trend not restricted to disasters, but includes many topics on Twitter (Cha et al. 2010). The fact that celebrities including Stephen Fry, Jemima Khan, Rainn Wilson, Yuna Kim, and Russell Simmons commanded the most retweets during the 2010 Pakistan floods (see table 5.1) reveals how much of a celebrity-oriented culture many of Twitter's trending topics have developed. Indeed, celebrities appear to be at the forefront of Twitter-based fundraising efforts for flood victims, and a more extended discussion of celebrities can be found in chapter 8.

In this chapter, the twofold significance of this has been explored. First, celebrity cultures are powerful and involve the ability to set the agenda regarding important events far beyond celebrity gossip. Second, as "development celebrities," their voice within disaster discourses is indicative of update cultures themselves. Specifically, Twitter users see celebrities as a key source of "important" updates, whether about Hollywood gossip, fashion trends, or important world events. Celebrities command our attention on a range of topics regardless of their superficial engagement, and they can steer discourse on Twitter in terms of raising disasters to prominence, which potentially has real impacts on fundraising efforts.

This chapter also highlights the varying locales and types of disasters that are tweeted. Twitter's more extensive use in the 2016 Kaikoura, New Zealand, earthquake reveals that, in a country with exceptionally high rates of internet use per capita (International Telecommunications Union, 2015), the medium was perceived as having significant effects on communication during the disaster. Though the two disasters are different (floods versus an earthquake/tsunami), they were similar in becoming trending topics on Twitter. However, in Pakistan's case, Western Twitter users (especially celebrities) were most responsible for the propagation of tweets and the catapulting of #pakistan to one of the most popular trending topics of 2010. In the case of Kaikoura, many tweets were geolocated as originating from users in New Zealand. Though there are differing uses of Twitter by users in developed versus developing countries, the use of Twitter by Indians during the Haryana earthquake illustrates how things have changed on Twitter in the six years since the Pakistan floods.

New Zealand and other developed (or emergent affluent economies, such as Brazil) have large Twitter user-bases and are able to have agency, control, and voice regarding disasters which occur on their home soil. In developing countries, updates usually had to travel through celebrities or other highly followed Twitter users, but now are coming from everyday users. It is important to note this change. As discussed in the following chapter, it was mostly Twitter users outside of Egypt who were tweeting about Egypt during the "Arab Spring," and it is these users who received attention in traditional media coverage, rather than Egyptians. Though in the past Twitter may not have been changing the power of both Western individuals and traditional news media, and Twitter is hardly devoid of this power relationship, it seems that those in developing countries have much more of a voice on Twitter than was the case six years ago. This is partially attributable to an increased user-base of Twitter in countries such as India, but also to huge surges in smartphone ownership (Poushter 2016).

Overall, Twitter presents a valuable mode of dissemination of information when disasters hit. Though a Twittering elite remains in many developing countries, user-bases have also grown substantially and tweeting has become more democratic (though still quite stratified) in countries like India, for example. Nevertheless, the effect of one tweet during a disaster can be profound or, as Serino puts it, "In 140 characters, [. . . a] person on a cell phone on a beach can tell hundreds of people around them that a tsunami is coming" (cited in Tucker 2011). Disasters present us with unique glimpses of the complexity of update cultures. On the one hand, updating the world can seem banal and evidence of a moral decay (if one agrees with the arguments of Twitter pessimists). On the other hand, a tweet from that person on the beach is still a terse update, but one that is extremely profound.

Tim Pool
@Timcast
Follow
Looks like there is some action in the air nycga.net/events/event/g … 2pm March from Washington Square to Liberty Plaza. #OWS #Occupy #Theother99
RETWEETS
4
9:36 AM - 27 Nov 2011

@TimCast[1]

The tweet above is part of the stream of tweets from the Occupy Wall Street-related hashtags of #OWS and #Occupy. Occupy Wall Street was a series of activist movements started in New York City in 2011 to protest against perceived financial inequalities symbolized by Wall Street. The movement spread to many global cities. #TheOther99 refers to the hashtag used by the Occupy and related movements which seek to redress the wealth disparity gap in the USA (in which wealth is ultra-concentrated amongst the richest 1 percent of the American population at the expense of the remaining 99 percent). Both #TheOther99 and #Occupy saw a resurgence with the 2016 US presidential election of Donald Trump. The tweet above is attempting to solicit participants for an Occupy Wall Street-related march at 2 p.m. in New York City on the day the tweet was posted. The march is part of a campaign within Occupy Wall Street for environmental justice. This chapter explores the role of Twitter in activism and whether tweets like the one above can bring feet to the street during social movements. The 2011 "Arab Spring" movements in the Middle East and North Africa and #BlackLivesMatter are used as case studies to evaluate what role Twitter may have played in the movements. The former remains important today, as many attribute the "Arab Spring" uprisings as key to Twitter's association with social movements (Gerbaudo 2012).

CHAPTER SIX

Twitter and Activism

Facebook and Twitter turned out to be far more effective agents of change than any "martyrdom" attacks on apostates, crusaders and Zionists – the most familiar objects of hatred in the jihadi lexicon. (Black 2011)

In the decade since Twitter's inception, the medium has been prominently associated with wide-ranging forms of sociopolitical activism. In addition to Occupy and the Indignados Movement in Spain, one of the more prominent associations is with the so-called "Arab Spring," a rough grouping of diverse anti-government movements in the Middle East and North Africa (MENA) in late 2010 and early 2011. The movements, which included Tunisia, Egypt, Libya, Bahrain, Syria, and Yemen (with substantial protests occurring in many other countries in the region), received particular media attention for the ways in which Twitter was used in them. Whether or not Twitter "turned out to be [a] far more effective [agent] of change," as Black (2011) argues above, Twitter became recurrently associated with MENA movements since 2009 and #iranelection was the top Twitter news story in 2009. Like the case of the downing of US Airways Flight 1549, discussed in chapter 4, the unrest in Tunisia in 2011 hit Twitter before mainstream international media (Moore et al. 2011), making it a valuable news source for international journalists and news-consuming individuals around the world. Though it is tempting to label many of the movements as Twitter revolutions, this does not accurately capture the medium's role. Marcell Shewaro, a prominent Syrian blogger, observes that "[t]he street led the bloggers" in the case of the Syrian unrest (cited in Moore et al. 2011). Or, paraphrasing Shewaro, the street led the tweeters. This is in distinction to some scholarship which has found that the "efficacy of the streets has changed" and that new media have become critical centers of progressive political resistance and protest (Raley 2009). Gerbaudo (2012) usefully adds that there is an intersection between "tweets and the streets" rather than one necessarily leading the other. This chapter explores activist movements and Twitter by critically examining the case of the Egyptian unrest in January 2011 ("25 January Revolution"), though it refers to other countries grouped into the collective "Arab Spring" uprisings. This chapter asserts that it is important to critically approach Twitter's use in these movements. Specifically, the idea of technological determinism is explored and the case is made that Twitter has great potential in organizing activists' movements (as seen in Egypt), but we should be careful about concluding Twitter's value ipso facto, nor should we regard Twitter as "causing" these very diverse movements. Additionally, Twitter's impact on complex, large-scale sociopolitical activism is examined through Mark Granovetter's sociological work in which he argues that there is "strength" in having a multitude of "weak" connections (the type of connections Twitter most often facilitates). Though the chapter does not present original empirical data, it synthesizes empirical data from an array of sources in order to present comprehensive conclusions on Twitter's role in the "Arab Spring." The chapter provides a more nuanced conclusion to Twitter's role in recent social movements without falling victim to a strict binary distinction of whether Twitter caused/didn't cause the 25 January and other revolutions associated with the "Arab Spring."

Cairo Tweeting

Egypt has experienced varying levels of control of media content in recent years (Cottle 2011). During the 25 January

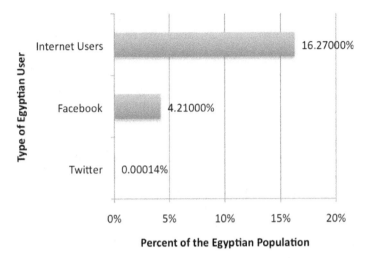

Figure 6.1   Internet, Facebook, and Twitter users in Egypt

Revolution, the Egyptian government began by targeting online social platforms, including Facebook and Twitter, and then moved to the communication infrastructure itself (Dunn 2011: 16). In Egypt, at the time of the unrest, there were approximately 3.5 million registered Facebook users (4.21 percent of the population), 12,000 registered Twitter users (0.00014 percent of the population), and 13.5 million internet users (16.27 percent of the population) (Dunn 2011: 18; United Nations Department of Economic and Social Affairs 2010: 63). Figure 6.1 provides a visual representation (with Twitter users almost invisible on the figure above).

Given these data, it is clear that the percentage of the Egyptian population who were tweeting or consuming tweets was minuscule. That is not to say that .00014 percent of the Egyptian population could not start the movement. Rather, the actual direct reach of Twitter within Egypt was extremely minimal. That said, the perception of the Egyptian government concerning online social networking and social media was that they were a threat. This can be partially explained by media representation of Twitter's and Facebook's influence, but also Twitter's reach outside of Egypt. International mainstream news media were regularly using scoops garnered from Twitter as an integral part of their source mix (Lotan et al. 2011). Whether it was over-egging the pudding by Western journalists, or for other reasons, the Egyptian authorities shut down the internet for five days in January 2011. Because this internet shutdown had major impacts on what Dunn (2011: 20) terms "apolitical" groups of Egyptian society, including the business community, these previously apathetic groups began to exhibit anti-government sentiment. Ultimately, what we can conclude is that the tiny base of Twitter users in Egypt did not matter in terms of the real effects Twitter had on Egypt. If anything, global news media hype potentially had more of a causal effect on Egypt. Specifically, Twitter's perception as a threat by the authorities mattered more than any concerted statistical quantification of the pervasiveness of the medium in the country. We can extrapolate this to mean that user uptake of Twitter is not the sole variable in activism.

The Egyptian authorities ultimately stoked massive interest by everyday Egyptians in Twitter through the internet shutdown. The notoriety of/interest in Twitter reached the level where Google worked with Twitter to quickly develop a "speak2tweet" system enabling Egyptians to dial an international number and leave a message which would be recorded and tweeted with a #Egypt hashtag. Tweets could also be listened to by dialing the number. The situation reached a point where P. J. Crowley, the US Assistant Secretary of State at the time, felt compelled to tweet:

> We are concerned that communication services, including the Internet, social media and even this #tweet, are being blocked in #Egypt. (Farber 2011)

Though his view is the opposite of the Egyptian government's, Crowley's normative position on the utility of Twitter and other social media to Egypt is quite similar to that of the Egyptian government in that both ultimately legitimize Twitter and its role in the social movements in Egypt in 2011. The fact that Crowley emphasized that his tweet might even be blocked additionally legitimates the power of individual tweets (i.e., his). What is particularly interesting is that it is not individual tweets per se which most fueled activism, but, as Hassanpour (2011: 2) argues, Egypt's internet shutdown (which involved blocking Twitter a day before Facebook), which he describes as acting more as a "catalyst of the revolutionary process and hastens the disintegration of the status quo." In other words, his conclusion is highly counterintuitive in that we would expect the disruption of tweets and Facebook updates to have fragmented revolutionary unrest, rather than strengthen it. Additionally, because government loyalists were using Twitter to launch "smear campaigns against opposition forces" (Tomlinson 2011), the blocking of Twitter – simultaneously and serendipitously – diminished the medium's use as a tool of repression.

Hassanpour (2011: 4) observes that "[i]n the absence of the mass media, information is communicated locally" and local face-to-face communication with friends, family, colleagues, and one's local community is a powerful contributor to on-the-ground revolutionary movements. Specifically, "it forced more face-to-face communication, i.e. more physical presence in streets" (ibid.: 28). Looking at the "schedule" of when the Egyptian government shut down different services also reveals an interesting pattern. Twitter was blocked on January 25, 2011, Facebook on January 26, 2011, and – a whole six days after Twitter was blocked – Cairo's Al-Jazeera bureau was shut down on January 30, 2011 (ibid.: 32). Should we take this to mean that tweets were perceived as more threatening than traditional satellite news reporting done by Al-Jazeera? Ultimately, by March 2011, the number of active Twitter users in Egypt was estimated at over 131,000 (Salem and Mourtada 2011: 16), more than a tenfold increase from January 2011.

Twitter Revolution?

On a more macro level, over 122,000 tweets with keywords pertaining to the Egyptian movements were circulated during January 16–23, 2011, jumping to over 1.3 million during January 24–30, 2011 (O'Dell 2011). Though tweets containing Egypt-related keywords and hashtags jumped over tenfold in January 2011, this should not be conflated with the medium's influence in the movements or even whether it "started" the movements, even though various contemporary movements in the Middle East and North Africa have been labeled as "Twitter revolutions" (Christensen 2011; Warf 2011). As discussed earlier in chapter 3, it is critical that we evaluate the actual uses of Twitter rather than falling into the trap of being technologically deterministic in terms of the medium. Claiming that the movements in Iran, Egypt, Tunisia, Bahrain, and other MENA states were the result of social networking sites and social media is, according to Warf (2011), an untenable point. Warf (2011: 166) not only observes that a mere 0.3 percent of Iranians were Twitter users at the time of the uprisings, but also adds that it is highly unrealistic to think that it was the case that "dictatorships staffed with passive bumbling incompetents [were] patiently wait[ing] to be toppled by savvy young Arab bloggers and cyber-dissidents." Or, as Moore et al. (2011) put it, "Could a simple text message, sent by enough people, depose dictators everywhere?" A key observation by Warf is that Twitter, Facebook, and mobile phones may have "enabled" mass movements in the "Arab Spring," but they did not "cause" them. Rather, he argues that it was high unemployment, persistent poverty, and frequent police brutality that were key factors in civil unrest in the region (Warf 2011: 167). El-Din Haseeb (2011: 118) argues that an over-emphasis on the role of social media in the "Arab Spring" uprisings is at the expense of understanding these events as the result of over 40 years of accumulated political consciousness. This slip in logic in terms of causality and new media is one which Morozov (2009; 2011) frequently highlights in his work. In other words, Twitter played an important role in the "Arab Spring," but did not cause it. As Gerbaudo (2012) highlights, Twitter can act like "Lenin's classic description of the Party newspaper as 'propagandist', 'agitator', and 'organiser' of collective action." Just as we should be careful about accusing newspapers of causing the Bolshevik revolutions, we should be cautious with Twitter and contemporary revolutions.

Ultimately, in the case of Iran, as only 0.3 percent of the Iranian population had a Twitter account in 2011, it seems premature to label it a "Twitter Revolution." At the time of the uprisings, 5.5 percent of the Libyan population were internet users, and in Yemen it was a mere 1.8 percent (World Bank 2010). Nonetheless, the "Arab Spring" uprisings, collectively including anti-government movements in Egypt, Tunisia, Yemen, Syria, Libya, and Bahrain in 2011, have been treated by some media commentators as "Twitter Revolutions" (Beaumont 2011). Though social media and social networking technologies played a part in organizing activist movements and, especially, disseminating information out of MENA countries to the West, Twitter ultimately is a communications medium. Like any communications medium, it is merely a tool, and imbuing it with more meaning diverts attention from the fact that Twitter's use and its perception of utility is socially constructed. Rosen (2011) captures this well:

> Internet schminternet. Revolutions happen when they happen. Whatever means are lying around will get used.

The logic here is that modes of communication have historically been integral to revolutions (whether it be the telegraph, rotary phone, cell phone, email, or Twitter). McLuhan (1952: 192) remarks that "[there] have been so many domestic and social revolutions associated with the consequences of the mechanization of writing." Historicizing Twitter's role within social movements in the broader context of technology and political change becomes crucial because, as Motadel (2011) argues, that "communication has played a role in spreading revolutionary ideas throughout history." Mowlana (1979: 111) observes that in the Iranian revolution of 1978–9, "new" media technology was important to the movement:

> the Iranian revolution was also aided by *these modern mass media.* "Small media" – cassette tapes, Xerox, tape recorders, and telephone – could be used to communicate and still escape the control of the regime. From Paris, Ayatollah Khomeini sent his messages through telephone and tapes to Iran, where they were copied by the thousands and made their way through the informal and traditional communication networks to the nation. This method of communication provided both the credibility and excitement of oral messages and the permanence and accessibility of written messages. (Mowlana 1979: 111, my emphasis)

During the late 1970s, these "small media" were the Twitter of the time. Many countries leveraged these "democratic" technologies to record and disseminate written and oral revolutionary messages (Fandy 1999), or to create impromptu "radio stations" with a cassette deck attached to a speaker (Sheldon 1991).

   One of the differences emblematic of Twitter (and similar social media) in comparison to previous modes of communication – stretching back to a letter carried by ship and more recently email – is that it is near instantaneous, multiplex, globalized, socially networked, and public. This, as opposed to earlier forms of communication, has not just speeded up information dissemination, but the ways in which activists can organize. In this way, Twitter as a medium is "revolutionary," but so was the telegraph, as Motadel (2011) argues (though the telegraph's messages were slightly longer than tweets[2] as senders had to include words containing the sender's information (Green 1889: 37)). Motadel (2011) observes that even trains and steamers speeded up communication delivery significantly. In other words, time has incrementally become less and less of a barrier. Along with space, time has become "compressed" (Robertson 1992). As a medium, Twitter extends this type of time/space compression that the telegraph revolutionized.

"Twitter Can't Topple Dictators"

Rosen (2011) wrote the "Twitter Can't Topple Dictators" article, a now notorious online piece, in which he argues that a genre of journalism has emerged which took the title of his article as their premise. Perhaps the most controversial piece of journalism in the genre is Malcolm Gladwell's (2010) article in *The New Yorker*. Contra Lotan et al. (2011), Gladwell argues that revolutions are not tweeted. Rather, he agrees with Morozov (2009) that social activism, for example in Iran and Moldova, was inappropriately associated with Twitter. His argument is particularly compelling in that it draws from the empirical facts that very few Twitter accounts existed in Iran during the movement (Morozov 2009) and almost all #iranelection tweets were in English (Gladwell 2010). Indeed, he cites Esfandiari (2010) who comments that "no one seemed to wonder why people trying to coordinate protests in Iran would be writing in any language other than Farsi." This is a fundamental question. Prima facie, it appears that the association of these movements with Twitter and Facebook was more of a journalistic and diplomatic invention, rather than a reality on the ground. However, though it may not have been a frontline tool on the ground, it was highly effective in quickly getting messages out of the MENA region and into the hands of Western journalists, as Lotan et al. (2011) argue.

Gladwell broadens his argument beyond revolutions in the MENA region and argues that Twitter is, generally speaking, not ideal for carrying out revolutions, movements that inherently need a tightly organized hierarchy. He asserts that Twitter is about loose networks of "followers" rather than a structured organization with leadership. Gladwell gives the example of events during the American civil rights movement, which he terms "high-risk": actions which involved the real possibility of injury or even death, but which had an immense potential for social change. He labels their organization "militaristic." This leads him to the succinct conclusion that "Activism [. . .] is not for the faint of heart." This also leads Gladwell to conclude that these types of activism need "strong ties" rather than "weak ties." Following the sociologist Granovetter's (1973) seminal work on the subject, Nelson (1989: 380) sums up the former as ties which are "frequent contacts that almost invariably have affective, often friendly, overtones and may include reciprocal favors," while the latter are "infrequent contacts that because they are episodic, do not necessarily have affective content." In terms of the strength of ties, Granovetter (1973: 1361) conceptualizes tie strength as based around the "combination of the amount of time, the emotional intensity, the intimacy (mutual confiding), and the reciprocal services which characterize the tie." While Granovetter makes a case for the strength of weak ties, Nelson (1989: 381) asserts that the strength of strong ties lies in the fact that they are likely to foster a less conflictual situation.

Indeed, in Gladwell's example of the civil rights movement, participants became involved through strong ties (a friend, roommate, or family member who was part of the movement) and, as such, developed a stronger commitment to the cause, which helped breed a cohesive network. Ultimately, Gladwell decides Twitter is of minimal use to high-risk activism which requires substantial commitment and dedication to a cause, and concludes that it is best used for "buffing the edges" of existing social orders. In other words, Twitter, from Gladwell's perspective, is better for boycotting a company over a specific product, or lobbying for the release of a particular political prisoner, than for bringing down a government.

In a way, the elephant in the room is not whether strong ties can foster successful activist movements, but whether the strength of weak ties Granovetter hypothesizes can be sufficiently coalesced on Twitter and similar social media to foster successful activist movements. In an age of Twitter and Facebook status updates, where some think talk online is mere "web chatter," could social media spur the sort of action that strong ties can engender? Put another way: can a tweet convince people to take to high-risk streets? Of course, this is a straw man. Even Martin Luther King generally needed more than 140 characters to capture people's hearts. But he ultimately persuaded followers to make significant personal sacrifices for the movement, including participating in high-risk marches and sit-ins.

The key question that needs to be asked is whether a tweet or a group of tweets can bring feet to the street. In some cases, this is possible and in others it is not. Always, this is something that needs to be evaluated on a case-by-case basis. In cases of low risk, there seems a greater likelihood of people being mobilized by tweets. However, even in low-risk cases, often there seems to be an online/offline disconnect. For example, Moore et al. (2011) give the example of the #walk 2work hashtag used in Uganda in February 2011 to coordinate street-level protests against rising fuel and food costs. They conclude that though "the movement seemed strong on Twitter, it failed to catch on in the streets" (Moore et al. 2011). Or, put in terms of leadership, "[the] online arena proves ideal at coordinating protests but not so much at forging leaders" (Tomlinson 2011). However, in high-risk situations, it is even harder to discern whether activism brewed on Twitter can alone muster the strong ties needed for people to hit the streets. This is an important distinction.

Ultimately, Gladwell's argument, though compelling on many levels, creates a strict binary between weak and strong ties. This position forces a choice between the two, when such a choice need not be made. Bennett and Toft (2009: 258) argue that a combination of weak and strong ties (which they refer to as thin and thick network ties) is a desirable configuration for many modern activist movements. Their work on the 2003 anti-Iraq War protests, and the ongoing Fair Trade movements in the UK and the USA, highlights not only the efficiency of combining online weak-tie networks with more centralized strong-tie networks, but also emphasizes that not all movements need strong ties. They observe that political mobilization to drive an election campaign may work best with centrally organized authority, but the Fair Trade movement they studied thrived with "bottom-up," "decentralized" actors participating when an issue they were interested in came up, such as lobbying McDonald's or Monsanto (Bennett and Toft 2009: 250). Additionally, another issue with Gladwell's argument is that it seems to imply that large-scale online networks on Twitter effortlessly appear without involving strong tie-based coalition-building. However, these networks regularly involve a confluence of complex, often transnational, networks, which include both offline and online interactions and weak/strong ties. As the global 2011 Occupy Wall Street campaigns highlight, modern social movements can use Twitter's efficiently distributed weak-tie networks to disseminate real-time information about an activist movement, or to recruit participants. Additionally, movements that actively involve Twitter may be reaching out to new audiences who historically have not been involved in social or political organizations. This is a critical point. Put another way, as formal memberships in collective organizations have declined (Putnam 2000), loose-tie networks are left to fill the void. So, ultimately, pitting strong-tie against weak-tie networks is at the expense of including these latent informal networks of potentially interested activists. It should also be noted that the privileging of strong-tie networks in some cases may be elitist. Many mobilization efforts are cash-strapped, and if movements are organized via digital technologies the cost is greatly reduced (Bennett and Toft 2009: 247). So, even if the effective strength of weak ties is not equal to that of strong ties (and this is not inherently the case), there are issues of access and reach that Gladwell does not fully take into account.

Tweeting Information from #Syria and #Egypt to the World?

In the case of the "Arab Spring," weak ties played an important role both because of cost and a need to disseminate information from the MENA region to the West. Many of these movements were not looking for Twitter to bring feet to, for example, Tahrir Square, but rather to transmit up-to-the-minute updates to Western media in the face of telephone and other communication outages. Many MENA governments have banned or severely restricted social media in recent years. Interestingly, in February 2011, Syria decided to remove a ban on social media sites, including Facebook and YouTube, which had been instituted in 2007 (Mroue 2011). However, as Tomlinson (2011) notes, shortly afterwards the government was reported to have kidnapped and tortured civilian activists to obtain their Facebook passwords, in order to target other suspected activists or scupper their planned actions. Twitter was used in MENA revolutions both by anti-government activists to transmit updates and by governments to find and detain activists. Also, several MENA states created "phantom" Twitter accounts (i.e., automated spam-generating accounts), using these to post banal information with a trending hashtag to dilute activist messages (e.g., this was done in Syria, with tweets about falafels and the weather, to dilute the #syria hashtag). These types of state-sponsored hashtag spam continue today on Twitter and other social media platforms. Twitter and Facebook, Comninos (2011) believes, lend themselves to being used by authorities to "spy" on activists and to uncover their identities to make arrests. Christensen

(2011: 156) observes that the Iranian government uses new media to monitor internet users and argues that "it [new media] served to simplify surveillance, disinformation, and repression." Another issue with Twitter is that of information integrity. The platform has been used to successfully spread rumors and misinformation (via both image and text) to wide audiences (see chapter 4 for a fuller discussion). Fearn-Banks (2010: 58) argues that "Citizen journalists have nothing and no one preventing them from disseminating misinformation to a global audience in seconds." Esfandiari (2010) gives the example of rumors being spread on Twitter during the Iran unrest of "police helicopters pouring acid and boiling water on protesters [, but . . . a] year later it remains just that: a rumor." As a medium, Twitter's skill in propagating information can just as easily be turned to campaigns of misinformation. Additionally, as Lotan et al. (2011: 1380) argue, rumors on Twitter are often difficult to detect as misinformation. As was the case in Iran in 2009, social media can be highly effective as a mode of facilitating "impromptu social networks" (Morán et al. 2010) for activism, but the corporeal violence deployed by some dictators is being used to counter digital dissent. In addition, state-sponsored propaganda on Twitter is becoming more noticeable in many global contexts.

But, even if the efficacy of digital dissent is being curbed by repression, the fact of the matter is that tweets got out of MENA countries even when mobile networks were shut down (Idle and Nunns 2011: 65). These tweets provided a constantly updating stream of information to the world from Egypt (Idle and Nunns 2011). Interestingly, social media also served as a powerful tool of news dissemination to other MENA countries with restricted national news media. Idle and Nunns (2011) observe that Egyptians "were avid recipients of [Twitter] reports coming out of Tunisia," and they argue that Egyptian tweets had a knock-on effect, that "inspire[d] uprisings across the region." Egyptians saw Tunisian tweets not only as a "first-hand" source of information during the events, but also as a vital source of information, given incomplete media coverage by the Egyptian press. Importantly, the tweets served as a catalyst to already fomented revolutionary feelings. With a revolution brewing in their backyard, the tweets flowing from Tunisia – even if they did not directly contribute to the movements – helped draw international attention to the region. Though many Tahrir activists were not involved online, the tiny minority of English-speaking activists tweeting from Tahrir did have tweets picked up by the international news media, and those on Twitter in Egypt felt that they "were not only talking to their fellow Egyptians but to the international media and the world" (Idle and Nunns 2011: 20).

Twitter Didn't Topple Dictators, But It Rattled Them

Even in Tahrir, there was no single leadership. Shehata et al. (cited in Hassanpour 2011) state that "Nobody was in charge of Tahrir," and "a lot of those who joined the protests on January 25 in Tahrir were not aware of the Facebook campaign, they had heard about it from the protesters in the square and surrounding streets." Morozov (2011: 16), speaking about the "Green Movement" in Iran, agrees, observing that people in Tehran "didn't need to go online to notice that there was a big public protest going on in the middle of Tehran [as the . . .] raging horns of cars stuck in traffic were a pretty good indicator."

In looking at the number of active Twitter users in the MENA region between January 1 and March 30, 2011, countries with the highest Twitter user-bases (over 100,000) are Israel, Kuwait, Saudi Arabia, Egypt, Qatar, the UAE, and Turkey (Salem and Mourtada 2011). Only Egypt is an "Arab Spring" country.[3] However, Egypt has a large population and its Twitter user-base, estimated at just over 131,000 by March 30, 2011, translates to a mere 0.00158 percent of the population (see figure 6.2), which puts it as having extremely low

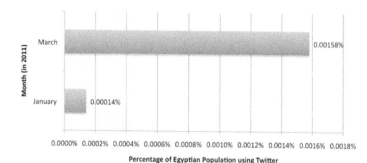

Figure 6.2   Egyptian population using Twitter (January and March 2011)

Twitter user penetration in comparison with other MENA countries (Salem and Mourtada 2011: 16–17, 24). That said, the number of Twitter users in Egypt from January to the end of March, 2011, is estimated to have increased over tenfold from about 12,000 (Dunn 2011) users to 131,000 (Salem and Mourtada 2011). This is indeed significant in and of itself, as it provides empirical data that suggest a rapid growth in Twitter usage during the 25 January Revolution.

Interestingly, tweet volume in MENA states roughly doubled during a day of protests or particular civil unrest. For instance, Tunisia's tweet volume on January 14, the day of protests there, doubled from roughly 4,000 to 8,000 (Salem and Mourtada 2011: 21) and, interestingly, tweet volume in Egypt more than doubled on January 14 as Egyptians tweeted about the events in Tunisia (Salem and Mourtada 2011: 20). As discussed previously, some have dismissed these data given the extremely low penetration of Twitter in many MENA states. Others have argued that coverage of Twitter has been micro-focused around individual Twitter users, making it difficult to discern Twitter's impact. For example, Esfandiari (2010) discusses the case of @oxfordgirl – an Iranian-born writer, former journalist in Tehran, and Twitter user from Oxford, England – who was profiled by the mainstream British press as a "prominent and much-followed source during the

[Iranian] protests" and as "Ahmadinejad's nemesis" (Weaver 2010a, 2010b). And @oxfordgirl states that she coordinated individual movements on the street and warned people to stay away from particular streets where the Iranian militia was waiting (Weaver 2010b). In the case of Iran, @oxfordgirl believes that "Twitter has saved lots of lives by warning people not to go down certain roads" (Weaver 2010b). Esfandiari (2010) sees @oxfordgirl as emblematic of the "myopic" focus of Twitter and its role in Iran. Specifically, she argues that the focus on individual "prominent" Western-based Twitter users brings increased exposure to individual Twitter users, but did little for activists on the ground in Tehran. Though Esfandiari (2010) disputes the legitimacy of @oxfordgirl's claim of being a quasi-air traffic controller of street-level movements, Morozov (2011: 5) states that from her Oxfordshire village she "did an excellent job – but only as an information hub." The difference in opinion between Esfandiari and Morozov clearly reveals the divergent views regarding what role tweets play in social movements, with the former arguing the streets were more important than distant tweets, and the latter not disagreeing but highlighting the utility of tweets as sources of information during activist movements.

Another example concerns a prominent Twitter user during the Egyptian movements, Wael Ghonim, the Head of Marketing for Google Middle East and North Africa. Ghonim started a Facebook page in June 2010, titled "We are all Khaled Said" (Kirkpatrick and Preston 2011). The page was initially launched to raise awareness of a young Egyptian business-man who was tortured to death by Alexandria police. Ghonim ultimately used this Facebook page and his highly followed Twitter profile (@ghonim) to help recruit online followers to the 25 January protests. *Time Magazine* listed him in its 2011 TIME100 list of most influential people of the year for his con-tribution to the 25 January Revolution (*Time Magazine* 2011). Ghonim himself was jailed and tortured for 11 days in early 2011 for his role in the "We are all Khaled Said" Facebook page.

Ghonim was prolific on Twitter, and he has become known for labeling the 25 January Revolution as "Revolution 2.0" and comparing it to Wikipedia, in that 25 January, like Wikipedia, was a grassroots user-contributed revolution without individual contributors receiving credit (CBS 2011). Papacharissi and Oliveira (2011) label him as one of the digitally prominent "opinion leaders" of 25 January.

Take these two cases together (and many more cases abound of prominent "game-changing" tweeters during the "Arab Spring" and earlier movements) and what emerges is that Twitter helped focus the international spotlight on these events and disseminate timely, personal, and relevant breaking news to international news media and the global public. As a medium, what is impressive is the dissemination power of Twitter to circulate this information from Tahrir and other activist hotspots to networks and subnetworks of Twitter users around the world. Tweets from activists in Tahrir ended up being covered by international news media and were picked up quickly. This dissemination was not only important in terms of circulation of information, but also critical to building "unprecedented moral solidarity" (Esfandiari 2010). It was also an important tool for maintaining links between activist movements in various MENA countries and even farther afield. That said, empirical research reveals that perhaps Twitter was of more value to the revolution outside of Egypt than within. As previously discussed, Twitter had even caught the attention of high-ranking State Department officials. However, only 1 percent of (relatively well-off) Egyptians reported using Twitter for 25 January-related information, with the bulk using television and word of mouth (see figure 6.3).

The data illustrated in figure 6.3 are unsurprising in that, as Hounshell (2011a: 22) observes, "many Egyptian Twitterati are upper-crust graduates of the American University in Cairo," and Gitlin (2011) observes that they are "tech-savvy, cosmopolitan, often from elite origins, well educated and tend to speak excellent English." In other words, the Twitterati was

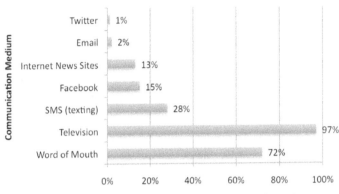

Figure 6.3   Use of communication media during the 25 January
Revolution; data cited in Zhuo et al. (2011)

not representative of the general Egyptian population. But
that is not inherently relevant to the medium's impact within
social movements. Zhuo et al. (2011) argue that social media
sites brought together young, urban Egyptian men (and I
would add "elite") into a "networked individualism" (Rainie
and Wellman 2012), where disparate individuals became
formed into loosely structured networks. This argument provides a more nuanced conclusion to Twitter's role in social
movements without falling victim to a strict binary distinction
of whether Twitter caused/didn't cause the revolution.

Marginalized Groups Having a Voice? The Case of #BlackLivesMatter

Traditionally marginalized groups in the USA, such as young
urban African Americans, may be turning to Twitter as they
perceive the medium is able to individually or collectively
provide some level of voice. Given the response by African
Americans on Twitter to the shooting of Michael Brown, an
unarmed 18-year-old black man in Ferguson, Missouri, in

2014, studying social media use within this context is particularly relevant. Twitter has been seen as an important venue to the black community when expressing their outrage at the time of Michael Brown's shooting, as well as after the acquittal of the white police officer, Darren Wilson, who fatally shot him. The #BlackLivesMatter hashtag has been used over the years to highlight how black lives have been marginalized institutionally in the USA and that contemporary social media-based movements draw from the fact that African Americans have historically had little voice in mainstream media. The hashtag was initially used as a call to action after Trayvon Martin, an unarmed black 17-year-old, was shot by neighborhood watch coordinator George Zimmerman. Focused outrage on Twitter not only helped bring the case of Ferguson to national attention, but has the potential to do so in other black social movements. Indeed, in the case of #BlackLivesMatter, the hashtag was formed around Trayvon, but was redeployed during Ferguson and subsequent shootings, including #JoeMcKnight, which was discussed earlier in the book.

#BlackLivesMatter

Black Lives Matter was started by Alicia Garza with Patrisse Cullors and Opal Tometi in the aftermath of the shooting of 17-year-old Trayvon Martin by George Zimmerman, who shot him 12 times on February 26, 2012. The #BlackLivesMatter hashtag became known internationally when 18-year-old Mike Brown was shot by Darren Wilson in Ferguson on August 9, 2014. It became re-mobilized with 25-year-old Freddy Gray in Baltimore when he died in April, 2015, after severe injuries in a police van which stopped many times. Initial forensic work suggests he had a "rough ride," a practice when someone is not strapped in with a seatbelt and left to bounce around a police van. Gray died seven days after he was assaulted. The hashtag also saw an upsurge with the 2016 US presidential election of Donald Trump.

Figure 6.4   Word Cloud of #BlackLivesMatter, produced using netlytic (Gruzd 2016)

In the case of Ferguson, this tweet was posted about an hour after Brown was shot on August 9, 2014, at 12.03 p.m.: "I just saw someone die," and an image of his uncovered body was posted (Bonilla and Rosa 2015). The circulation of this and other images on Twitter, Facebook, and other social media of his body, visible blood, and Brown making hands up/don't shoot gestures were critical to national news coverage of the shooting (Edwards and Harris 2016: 9–10). In the first week after Brown was shot, over 3.6 million tweets were posted (Bonilla and Rosa 2015: 4).

In order to better understand #BlackLivesMatter content on Twitter, I collected 99,126 #BlackLivesMatter tweets from November 17–26, 2016. Figure 6.4 uses a word cloud to illustrate the most commonly used words within the hashtag. As the data were collected after the 2016 US presidential election, #notmypresident features prominently, with over 2,000 tweets posted in opposition to Trump. One of the more frequently mentioned terms was #jamesmeans, which trended after William Pulliam, a white man from Charleston, West Virginia, shot an unarmed black 15-year-old, James Means. The incident occurred when Means accidentally bumped into Pulliam outside a dollar store on November

21, 2016. Two shots were fired by Pulliam. After the murder, he ate dinner and went to a friend's house. When arrested, Pulliam stated, "The way I look at it, that's another piece of trash off the street" (Abbey-Lambertz 2016), causing a backlash on Twitter, particularly within #BlackLivesMatter. Figure 6.5 illustrates key influencers derived from the 99,126 tweets. Unlike other social movements, individual Twitter users, rather than news organizations, are prominently featured in the network. Examples of this are @blkgrlnae, @gloed_up, @trayneshacole, @carlosnotweird, and @crystal1johnson, who are clearly visible in Figure 6.5, and provide a juxtaposition to the disaster hashtags discussed in chapter 5. One of most frequently mentioned users in the data set, @trayneshacole, acts as an important #BlackLivesMatter information dissemination hub, posting relevant news. For example, on December 6, 2016, she aggregated four tweets about a teacher in California, who wore a #BlackLivesMatter button to class and was banned, into a single tweet that was retweeted over 500 times.[4] She has also played an important hub role by retweeting relevant news from users in the movement, including influential ones such as @gloed_up and @BleepThePolice, as well as from Twitter users more generally.

Though Black Lives Matter activists are right to highlight how much more inequality, discrimination, and abuse they continue to face, it is important to note that these activists are effecting change, albeit not as quickly as they would like. For example, in public health, an area where African Americans have faced long-standing health inequalities, public health professionals have seen #BlackLivesMatter as a "challenge" to spur them to do better, both in terms of diversifying the physician workforce in the USA and improving care to racial minorities (Bassett 2015). Rickford (2016) argues that since its birth from a Twitter hashtag in 2014, "the young movement has reinvigorated confrontation politics." However, as #BlackLivesMatter has gained prominence, a counter hashtag #AllLivesMatter was launched and has high volumes

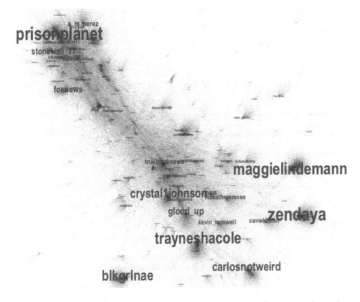

Figure 6.5   Visualization of #BlackLivesMatter influencers based
on 99,126 tweets collected November 17–26, 2016

of Twitter activity. This hashtag has vocally supported white
police officers (including mentioning #PoliceLivesMatter)
and conservative viewpoints (Gallagher et al. 2016).

Ultimately, we can see that through the case study of Black
Lives Matter, the ways in which Twitter is being deployed,
especially by those who were previously marginalized or
underrepresented in mainstream media discourses, has
from many people's perspective changed substantially. As
figure 6.5 illustrates, particular individuals, through videos
or through viral tweets, were able to have an influence on the
articulation of the Black Lives Matter narrative. Also, we have
seen the growth of hashtags that have been kept alive over
time by the movement, meaning that hashtags involved with
movements can potentially have a very long shelf life and be
used instrumentally to keep the movement known within the
public mind, as well as providing an accessible way to obtain

information and updates regarding the movement. This shows a certain maturity of Twitter within social movement organizations (SMOs).[5]

From #BlackLivesMatter to #NoDAPL

Twitter has become associated with prominent social activism movements, including Occupy Wall Street, Black Lives Matter, and the Indignados Movement. The medium has been viewed by some movements such as Black Lives Matter as integral to promoting grassroots-organizing and giving voice to populations who have historically been marginalized. The argument many of these groups are making is that not only is Twitter easy to use, but this ease of use combined with the ubiquity of smartphones has made the platform ideal for organizing as well as interacting with stakeholders. In the case of Black Lives Matter, individuals involved in the movement have been asked to tweet when they have experienced inequalities, including violence by police. Marginalized minorities are increasingly turning on their smartphones and recording video if they are pulled over by a police officer so that they can tweet the video if they encounter police misconduct. Apps such as *Stop and Frisk Watch, Mobile Justice, Cop Watch Video Recorder,* and *Hands Up 4 Justice* have been designed specifically for this purpose (Puente and Tan 2015). For some black people, Twitter may provide a perceived feeling of empowerment both by giving voice and acting as an avenue for accountability. This perception cannot be overstated as this is an important feature of the platform for many users involved in activist movements. The medium also makes it easy for stakeholders to be involved in activist movements even if they are not physically co-present. In the case of the Standing Rock Lakota Sioux Indian water dispute, for example, those who were unable to go to the Dakotas in person were able to raise awareness on Twitter through active use of #NoDAPL (No Dakota Access Pipleline) as well as interacting with those on the ground, supporting them virtually. Twitter has been important for those who support the NoDAPL movement (Petronzio 2016). Specifically, a change.org petition was launched in April 2016 and circulated on Twitter, Facebook, Instagram, and YouTube through #NoDAPL, #ReZpectOurWater, and #StandWithStandingRock. Indeed, when the NoDAPL movement began to target banks which had invested in the pipeline, they used Twitter to keep pressure on these public corporations. For example, a Native American activist, Ruth Hopkins, tweeted pictures of a letter from Wells Fargo,[6] which is an investor in the DAPL project. This pressure ultimately led to Wells Fargo being tweeted at by activists and, in February 2017, some major contracts cited DAPL as a reason for disinvesting from Wells Fargo (Egan 2017).

Indeed, when the Obama administration reacted to the DAPL protests and ordered a halt, key Republican politicians turned to Twitter to voice their discontent, including the speaker of the house, Paul Ryan (see figure 6.6).[7]

Movements such as NoDAPL, which are much smaller than movements like Black Lives Matter, have made the point that they have benefited tremendously from Twitter. Twitter's association with social movements has motivated governments such as China, North Korea, and Iran to install country-level filters to block out traffic to Twitter. The "Great Firewall of China" (GFC) was one of the first to do so, encouraging home-grown microblogging variants such as Sina

 **Paul Ryan**
@SpeakerRyan

This is big-government decision-making at its worst. I look forward to putting this anti-energy presidency behind us.
twitter.com/WSJ/status/805...

4:02 PM - 4 Dec 2016

785   1,445

Figure 6.6   Paul Ryan DAPL tweet (<https://twitter.com/SpeakerRyan/status/805562892921831424>)

Weibo for Chinese consumers to use in lieu of Twitter. The use of Twitter in social movements has perhaps changed since the medium's infancy, where there was a clear Twitter elite. The platform has become ubiquitous. Of course, social capital is important for us to consider in terms of Twitter use. However, as recent work indicates, uptake of Twitter in the British context, for example, has changed substantially (Longley et al. 2015; Sloan et al. 2015) since the publication of the first edition of this book.

Social movements such as the 2011 "Arab Spring" were seen as some of the first "Twitter Revolutions." Now, every major social movement involves Twitter in some way. This is partially attributable to the fact that journalists use the medium as a way to put their finger on the pulse of what is happening around a particular issue. That being said, the medium has played an important role in voicing concerns during movements such as the Euromaidan protests in Ukraine, where #Euromaidan trended. Young Ukrainians were able to use the hashtag and related hashtags in order to vocalize their views on the Russian annexation of Crimea as well as Ukrainian distancing from the European Union.

Conclusion

> [W]e believe we're going to put our experience on a CD-Rom and give an iPad to these would-be democrats in Tunisia and Egypt, and they're going to replicate what's taken us eight centuries to produce. I think that's probably not going to happen and it speaks to the kind of ahistorical viewpoint that we bring to the world. (Scheuer, in Moore 2011)

This chapter has sought to understand Twitter's role in activist movements by exploring the cases of the 2011 "Arab Spring" uprisings and the Black Lives Matter (#BlackLivesMatter) movement. Diverse positions (favorable and unfavorable to Twitter) were presented in order to critically evaluate the effect of social media on a set of highly prominent activist movements. The factors that contributed to these movements in various Middle East and North African (MENA) countries were also diverse. The economic situation played a central role in demonstrations in Egypt and Tunisia, religious tensions were important to unrest in Syria and Bahrain, and tribal differences played a part in movements in Libya and Yemen (Hadar 2011b). The use of Twitter reveals the fact that information about the revolutions from ordinary people had a potentially global reach. However, though the message may have gotten across, was the medium (Twitter), paraphrasing McLuhan, the "message," which ultimately "massaged" us into a feeling of cybertopia? There are scores of voices in the camps of the cybertopians and cyberdystopians who, in the case of the former, argue for Twitter to be given a Nobel Peace Prize (Pfeifle 2009) and, in the case of the latter, argue that Twitter is emblematic of ineffectual "pseudo-laptop/iPad revolutionaries" (Hadar 2011a), where Twitter's role in the movements is a canard. An important point to understand from this tension is to pay heed to McLuhan's distinction between medium and message, and to understand that the medium itself can easily become the message. In other words, did Twitter itself become the message heard or did the medium actually play a crucial role in helping form, articulate, and ultimately disseminate the message? Specifically, what was the causal relationship – if any – between the multitude of tweets sent and activist movements? Or, as Morozov (2011: 16) puts it, "If a tree falls in the forest and everyone tweets about it, it may not be the tweets that moved it." Mehdi Yahyanejad, who runs one of the most popular Farsi-language websites, Balatarin, believes that Twitter's impact inside Iran was non-existent, and adds that the Iranian "Twitter Revolution" consisted of "Americans tweeting among themselves" (cited in Esfandiari 2010). Hounshell (2011b: 20) concludes that Twitter's role in the "Arab Spring" has been as a "real-time information stream for international-news junkies." Hounshell's conclusion, despite holding water, ends up being excessively reductive.

Specifically, during the "Arab Spring," Twitter was a more multifunctional medium across not only the MENA region, but globally. Twitter served three purposes for Egyptian activists: (1) a real-time information stream maintained by Egyptian citizen journalists (for Egyptian consumption); (2) a means for local information and updates to reach an international audience (including international journalists); and (3) a means to organize disparate activist groups on the ground. Perhaps its greatest impact was in the second purpose and its least in the third purpose.

Another important conclusion we can draw is that though we think Twitter's mode of internationalizing otherwise "national" revolutions is unique, revolutions, along with other types of rises and falls of state power, have historically been "germane international events" whose domestic and international causal forces cannot be neatly untangled into a "hermetic" separation (Philpott 2001). However, what is different is that citizen journalists in Egypt, Tunisia, Libya, and other countries were part of that international revolutionary process in an almost real-time interactive experience.

In fact, much of Twitter's prominence in relation to the "Arab Spring" arose from individuals in the West tweeting and retweeting. Lotan et al. (2011) studied tweets during the 25 January Revolution and found that @exiledsurfer, a Vienna-based "activist," was an integral part of information flow to journalists during the 25 January Revolution. Cases like this raise the important question of what actually constitutes activism in social media (as @exiledsurfer is based in Austria and not Egypt). Gladwell's (2010) answer is that becoming an "activist" on Twitter is a low-risk proposition in most cases;[8] @exiledsurfer, for example, was not putting himself at personal risk.[9] Terms to describe the perceived low-stakes effort of online activism have emerged, labeling these activists as "latte activists," "armchair warriors," and "slacktivists" (Siegle 2005; Vitak et al. 2011). Needless to say, it is "low effort" to sip one's latte in a Starbucks and retweet an #egypt tweet to your followers. However, it is, in many ways, a wholly different qualitative proposition to be tweeting from inside MENA countries, where government officials were recruited to carefully monitor Twitter to track down and detain these activists. The argument that emerges is not new, but remains just as important. The social, political, and economic context of any mediated social communication needs to be carefully interpreted to pass normative judgments on that social communication itself.

In other words, judging an #egypt tweet requires a lot of context. Though retweeting an #egypt tweet can be reductively judged as "slacktivism," would the same verdict be applied if those retweets from Western Twitter users not only led to greater global awareness about #egypt, but also led to increased fundraising for humanitarian relief? Therefore, even if the tweets from Egypt did not "help" the movements in Egypt themselves, they did raise global awareness, which directly led to increased diplomatic pressure and humanitarian aid. Depending on one's vantage point, this may not have been revolutionary per se, but it did have some discernible impact. Gladwell's answer, as discussed in this chapter, concerns the privileging of strong-tie networks. However, weak ties have a lot to offer modern transnational mobilizations. Bennett and Toft's (2009: 252) work on transnational activism and social networks highlights the fact that weak ties can "empower individuals to mobilize their own diverse political networks." Twitter may have also democratized participation in the movement. Ultimately, even if tweets did not bring feet to the Egyptian streets, they helped facilitate a diverse global network of individuals who participated in a wide-ranging set of mobilization efforts (from the retweeters in Starbucks to those sending letters to their congresspeople/ ministers, or participating in activist movements both online and offline). However, there is also real potential for historically marginalized groups, such as young black people, as #BlackLivesMatter tweets illustrate. Because of major biases in terms of access and representation in traditional media outlets, social media have become much more important. The influencers in #BlackLivesMatter, who are not professional journalists, caught the attention of broadcast and traditional media and their previously silent voices were finally heard. That being said, their voices are not being heard enough and Twitter continues to be an important mechanism for activists to point out cases of police brutality, everyday racism, and inequalities faced by black people.

The #BlackLivesMatter and #NoDAPL cases discussed in this chapter differ from the "Arab Spring" in several ways. First, African Americans and Native Americans have greater literacy and access to Twitter than most Iranians and Egyptians. Second, the content on Twitter is not dominated by retweets of celebrities and news organizations. Rather, individual activists tend to be driving what is being "heard" within the hashtag. Third, the stakes of tweeting are very different, with people's lives potentially on the line if they are identified via social media, as in the case of the "Arab Spring." In other words, the level of repression is different. However, both cases highlight the potential for Twitter to get information about a social movement to stakeholders within the movement as well as others interested in the movement, including news organizations.

June Louise
@_Tattycoram_

Replying to @Madmattyg

@Madmattyg @LesleyBryning got told at clinic today my cancer has come back. Need urgent surgery and then chemo before Christmas x

12:40 PM - 28 Nov 2011

@_Tattycoram[1]

As the tweet above illustrates, individuals are tweeting about their health. In this particular case, the user tweeting has been told her cancer has returned and she needs surgery and chemo. The posting of such intimate health information has become a familiar sight on Twitter. This chapter explores some of the ways Twitter is being used by patients, medical researchers, and doctors. The medium is critically examined to highlight both the pros and cons of Twitter's health-related uses. It also illustrates ways in which our bodies have become a subject of Twitter's update culture. The medium's update cultures have been discussed in previous chapters as being highly pervasive in our lives. However, tweeting about one's body marks an even greater shift in this direction. This chapter investigates some of the ways in which Twitter and its role of updating may become particularly routinized in the lives of some users.

CHAPTER SEVEN

Twitter and Health

In chapter 5, the profundity of disasters was used to highlight some of the complexities of update cultures and how every-thing from the banal to the profound is tweeted. Another spectrum that tweets cover is that of the public and the pri-vate. Previous chapters (especially chapter 3) have discussed the historical trend towards more disclosure of "private" information in the public sphere. Twitter's ease, location independence, and its ubiquitous role in the routines of many users have led to very intimate tweets. An important exam-ple of this is Twitter's use in health. An individual's body has traditionally been a very private domain. Tweeting about the state of our bodies in detail sheds light on several important areas of the medium. Not only does it reveal many interest-ing aspects of Twitter's pervasiveness in traditionally private spheres, but the posting of tweets about health also potentially affects the relationships between doctors and patients as well as giving authority and expertise to non-medical professionals (especially fellow patients and their families).

Traditionally, patients have received health-related infor-mation by meeting personally with health professionals, and would normally only share details of their condition in this environment or with someone close to them. As the popularity of online social networking and social media sites has increased, individual patients, their families, and their caregivers have bypassed the traditional controls of the healthcare and life-science industries by volunteering private information about themselves on publicly accessible internet sites. Additionally, they have become more trusting of health messages on these sites; 78.8 percent of US citizens sampled reported using the internet to obtain health information, and "social media have recently become an important alternative for seeking health information" (Jiang and Beaudoin 2016: 240, 242). One reason for this is that these individuals form support networks with strangers who have the same chronic illness.

This is not a phenomenon restricted to Twitter, but rather, as Orsini (2010: 3) observes, people are able to use new media to create support communities on virtual social networks such as patientslikeme.com. The argument that an activity may be "good for your health" has raised important questions for the healthcare community. One study found that moderate Facebook use increases longevity (Hobbs et al. 2016). Rajani et al. (2011: 819) argue that, because of online health networks, illness has "virtually been removed as [a factor] contributing to social isolation and it is now not uncommon for individuals to have networks that number in the hundreds." They add that these virtual networks can function as support groups that motivate others to follow weight loss and other treatment regimes. In the context of Twitter, the platform might provide a more accurate picture of what patients are experiencing every day and what their daily activities actually are, rather than what they may selectively report to doctors. With this in mind, researchers have developed a tool to identify health issues and unhealthy behaviors from people's Twitter activity and deliver custom-made feedback to physicians who could then advise their patients (Fatima et al. 2015). The rise of these health-related communities on Twitter is a unique case in that tweets about one's health may be very regular and involve both a stable and a shifting audience. Not only are these fellow Twitter users a trusted audience (despite the public nature of Twitter), but the Twitterverse is imbued as a space which has some level of authority and expertise in health-related matters. This is not to say that Twitter is replacing doctors. However, health professionals have also started tweeting, as some of them have seen the importance of Twitter to patients (Widmer et al. 2016).

This chapter also explores the manner in which Twitter is used by individuals who have/had a significant health event (as well as by their families). Twitter is used by them to find out about new treatment options, referrals to specialists, and as a support network (to monitor and support each other in terms of medications, treatments, and clinical trials). These networks also serve a role in political activism and patient advocacy. This chapter presents two brief case studies – Lou Gehrig's Disease and cancer – to illustrate how Twitter has become involved in our health. Besides tweets updating others about one's health, the posting of treatment or health status as a tweet can also generate immediate responses from known individuals and strangers. The immediacy of tweet responses can also foster a feeling of "telepresence," the notion that one's communicators are an unmediated "present" rather than relating through mediated communication (see chapter 3 for a fuller discussion). In other words, we can feel a "physical" community within Twitter, which has an audience who shares our highs and lows and can potentially "be there" for us when we receive a shocking diagnosis. One can even make the argument that society has become more and more atomistic and individualistic, with certain community structures becoming weak or inaccessible (Putnam 2000), and, in this context, Twitter becomes an important venue for people to share with others their concerns, joys, and downright fears about their health. For example, instead of going to a local community center to participate in a weekly cancer support group, these individuals may opt to turn to their keyboards and smartphones, gaining strength and support one tweet at a time.

Twitter-mediated Healthcare

Public and private boundaries regarding health have shifted. For some, telling the world about one's health has become part of the larger trend of an "update culture" (see chapters 1–3). For them, updating others about their health via Twitter is on a continuum that includes anything from updating others about what they had for breakfast to the break-up of a relationship. Though the boundaries of public and private have been shifting historically regarding health (e.g., call-in radio shows with doctors), Twitter represents an acceleration of this trend. Not only does Twitter provide a medium for individuals to write about their health at the time (e.g., "i just got diagnosed with cancer. the depression is crippling. one panic attack after another, over and over...",[2] "Might be coming down with the flu... ?"[3], or "My teeth hurt"[4]), but it connects these messages to other health messages on Twitter through hashtags such as #lymphoma and #diabetes. Additionally, this act of sharing one's health situation (sometimes even from a doctor's office) further highlights shifts toward a powerful update culture which includes the "status" of our bodies. For example, individuals tweeting about diagnoses may be updating the world about having cancer, but, usually, their intended target audience is their family and friends. With the increased adoption of fitness trackers and other wearable devices, our bodies are also auto-tweeting heart rate, number of steps, and weight, for example. As discussed previously, these instances potentially highlight a dissonance between perceived and actual audiences on Twitter.

Ultimately, Twitter has become more ubiquitous in health contexts.[5] Take the example of a heart transplant for a woman in Dallas, Texas, in 2015, which was tweeted real-time by Dr Gonzo Gonzalez (@HRTTRNSPLNTMD), chief of cardiac surgery and heart transplant at Baylor University Medical Center, under the hashtags #HeartTXLive and #heartTX (Firger 2015). This is believed to be the first time a heart transplant was live-tweeted. Tweets chronicled the arrival of the donor heart[6] and video from the operation,[7] as well as images of removed and donor hearts.[8] The patient, a woman in her thirties with children, gave consent for the surgery to be tweeted, though all names were anonymized. A 2011 episode of *Grey's Anatomy* fictionalizes such occurrences through a portrayal of doctors tweeting during a surgery. But reality has caught up with fiction as the public is keen for a glimpse into procedures rarely seen, such as heart transplants, and Twitter has become a preferred medium to do so.

Live-tweeting surgeries is, of course, not the norm. The preparation for the Baylor University heart transplant live-tweet event was hardly insignificant. A more representative example of Twitter's use by healthcare institutions is the Boston Public Health Commission (@healthyBoston), which tweets every couple of days regarding public health. A November 30, 2016, tweet states: "#WednesdayWisdom #Smokers ask your MD if you're at risk for lung cancer #LungCancerAwareness."[9] Such everyday tweets, it should be noted, also tend to have low interaction rates. This tweet, for example, was not retweeted and liked only two times. During the 2015–16 Zika virus epidemic, many health organizations worldwide used Twitter to inform local communities of measures to take to minimize risks associated with travel to Brazil, given the 2016 Olympics in Rio.

As the heart transplant case highlights, a key difference with Twitter is that responses are often almost synchronous and can occur regularly throughout the day as individuals check their timelines at work, home, and on their smartphones. One does not even have to be waiting in the hospital to keep tabs on a family member's surgery. Indeed, the Twitter stream in this example contained detailed information that those in the waiting room were not synchronously receiving. Additionally, as Licoppe (2004) has shown, repeated mediated interactions foster "telepresence," the perception of mediated communication as face-to-face communication. For example, a video call using Skype, FaceTime, or WhatsApp is perceived by the conversation participants as being face to face rather than being mediated by Skype (see chapter 3 for a fuller discussion of this). In the heart transplant case, anyone could – via Twitter – feel as if they were "there" in the hospital. As McNab (2009: 566) puts it: "Instant and borderless, it [Twitter] elevates electronic communication to near face-to-face." Grandparents can follow births, and far-flung relatives can relieve their anxieties during a loved one's operation via tweets. Twitter also potentially provides a unique historical opportunity for more accurate health information to be disseminated to broader audiences. McNab (2009: 566) observes that, "one fact sheet or an emergency message about an outbreak can be spread through Twitter faster than any influenza virus." Lastly, Twitter changes the relationship between health institutions (including individual doctors) and the public in that previously monologic health dicta and warnings can now be interrogated, individually situated, or affirmed through an interaction with the institution or person tweeting that information.

Similarly, Twitter presents new opportunities for patient support networks. Hawn (2009: 364) describes the case of Rachel Baumgartel, 33, a diabetic who lives in Boulder, Colorado, and sends tweets almost daily on "what she had for breakfast, what her hemoglobin Alc level is, or how much exercise she got on the elliptical equipment at the gym." As Hawn notes, Baumgartel often receives reply tweets from followers, which encourage her to stick to her "arduous health regimen." Hawn finds that those who are chronically ill are successfully using social media, including Twitter, in this way. Baumgartel herself observes:

> Because I have people who follow me on Twitter . . . it means I have some kind of audience that is caring for me in the background. It's helpful if I'm having a rough day, if things are not going so well with my blood sugar. I find support there, and it keeps me in line, too. (cited in Hawn 2009: 365)

The example of Baumgartel reveals the complex interplay in which tweets can reveal private health information (like hemoglobin Alc levels), while the regular disclosure of this information via tweets to an amorphous audience led to the formation of a more coherent audience – a support community – which had real impacts on Baumgartel's life. Continuing with the example of diabetes, hashtags such as #bgnow are used by Twitter users to share their real-time blood-sugar levels (Liu et al. 2016), while #ShowMeYourPump encourages users to tweet selfies and group photos of their insulin pumps. The hashtag went viral after a Miss America contestant, Sierra Sandison, wore hers visibly in 2015 (Tucker 2015).

Attai et al. (2015: np) argue that social media like Twitter are more "patient-driven in contrast with older models of health care education [. . .] that are unidirectional and paternalistic." Their study investigates the hashtag #BCSM (the Breast Cancer Social Media Tweet Chat). The importance of hashtag-based communities like this is that they repurpose Twitter in innovative ways to create new health communities. In this case, the focus is not on individual tweets, but a single hashtag is used much like a Facebook group, and doctors volunteered as co-moderators to "provide credible, evidence-based information and support for anyone affected by breast cancer" (Attai et al. 2015: np). Heaivilin et al.'s (2011: 1047) work on tweets referring to dental pain found that users' tweets describe levels of pain, treatments taken, and the effect of this pain on their lives. They believe that Twitter may be a useful medium for dental professionals to disseminate relevant health information, including recommendations to visit the dentist if they experience certain symptoms. As a support group, Heaivilin et al. (2011: 1050) argue that individuals "may find comfort in the fact others are simultaneously facing the challenge" of the same medical condition. This illustrates one way in which individuals are using Twitter to ask fellow users for medical advice (e.g., dental pain management). The last example highlights some of the ways in which not only doctor/patient relationships may be changing due to the medium, but also that the authority and legitimacy of fellow Twitter users as sources of medical advice are reasonably high. The importance of this should not be underestimated.

Figure 7.1   @ALSUntangled Twitter Stream; reproduced with permission from Dr Richard Bedlack of ALSUntangled

Within the healthcare community, Twitter is being used by medical researchers and doctors to interact with each other to enhance drug discovery. Interestingly, it is also being used by medical researchers to directly interact with patients. One example is the Amyotrophic Lateral Sclerosis Untangled (ALSU) Twitter research project.[10] Begun in 2009 at Johns Hopkins University, ALSU uses Twitter to connect with people with ALS (commonly known as Lou Gehrig's Disease) by asking people with ALS to tweet about alternative and off-label treatments (AOTs) with the hashtag "ALSUntangled" (Bedlack and Hardiman 2009). This information is then used by researchers at the ALSU project, which has completed nearly 40 reviews of alternative and off-label treatments (ALSUntangled 2016) through a network of 94 researchers in 10 countries (ALSUntangled 2015). At the time of writing, the ALSU project has over 2,700 followers and responds publicly to individual questions from Twitter users. For example, one Twitter user asked whether fecal transplants have been found effective in ALS, a question posed after a Vice Staff (2016) report on the subject. The ALSU team tweeted back that there are micro-biome studies under way to determine fecal transplant utility. This type of interaction potentially represents a turn in scientific dissemination where patients can have direct contact with the research process and formulation of research questions by interacting directly with prominent researchers. Individuals with ALS and their caregivers are able to interact directly with ALSU via Twitter (see figure 7.1). Additionally, their tweets can be seen by members of the public, thereby creating a publicly accessible record of these discussions for those not actively participating. When designing the ALSU project, Bedlack and Hardiman (2009) chose Twitter as they believe that the medium is "simple" to join and to use. However, the ALS network on Twitter is far from simple. Specifically, in addition to discussing AOTs, individuals with ALS and their caregivers become part of a broader ALS support and knowledge network. The ease of communication likely fosters more regular interactions. And the time and effort it takes to tweet @ALSUntangled are minimal for Twitter users with ALS. This potentially breaks down traditional barriers and signals fundamental shifts in doctor/researcher/patient boundaries. Additionally, this type of Twitter use legitimizes the medium's role in health. Lastly, it illustrates how tweets, considered by some as banal updates, can be of direct use in profound medical research.

ALSUntangled is an interesting case as it is attached to a prominent ALS-research center. The trust in and reputation of ALSUntangled has facilitated high levels of sharing about a patient's or a family member's ALS situation and treatment experiences via tweets. Similarly, the individual doctors who are regularly tweeting command a high level of trust both within the ALS patient community and the medical community itself (e.g., one ALSUntangled tweet asks a doctor who has been tweeting within the ALSUntangled hashtag to send his CV to the ALSU research team). Not only does this trust lead to cases of people asking them about potential tests, treatment options, and referrals, but it also reveals the presence of a far-reaching network of followers (who receive this doctor's tweets). As Twitter offers dialogic interaction, any of these followers at any time can choose to respond to one of these doctors' tweets or ask an unrelated question regarding their personal ALS or other medical situation. In the case of ALS, Twitter may be breaking down boundaries between doctors, researchers, and patients, which could ultimately have a positive impact on the psychological and physical well-being of ALS patients. However, this example also highlights the fact that the divulging of private health information most likely needs a trusted mediator (in this case, a university affiliated ALS center).

The Shift of Health Information from Monologic to Dialogic

Traditionally, health organizations, non-profit organizations, and other health-related institutions have followed a monologic dissemination model, where the consumers of this information do not interact with its creator. For example, a health organization issues a swine flu warning, but receivers of this warning do not have the opportunity to ask questions or interact with the health organization. McNab (2009: 566) argues that social media have shifted this relationship in the context of health information in that it "has changed the monologue to a dialogue, where anyone with internet access can be a content creator and communicator." This is part of a larger trend in media more generally which has seen a shift from unidirectional mass media to interactivity. Chapter 4, for example, highlighted shifts toward interactive journalistic practices. Media have become more interactive, with readers able to comment on content and have discussions with other readers or even the author (Chung 2008). Electronic books have also marked significant shifts in interactivity (Larson 2010). In other words, media are generally becoming more dialogical. In the case of health, medical information itself becomes a product of a dialogic community mediated by information technology. Joshua Schwimmer, a nephrologist at Lenox Hill Hospital, believes that part of Twitter's popularity amongst doctors is that it creates "instant online communities of people with similar interests" (cited in Victorian 2010: 16). The instantaneity helps build the community. Individuals tweeting perceive an active audience rather than tweeting into a black hole. This expanded audience also potentially translates to an extended reach of tweets and the dissemination of relevant health information. In the case of ALSUntangled, Twitter was found to extend the reach of ALS clinical trials. Physicians increasingly believe that Twitter could be an effective tool to communicate with patients about clinical trials. Sedrak et al. (2016), for example, found this to be the case with cancer clinical trials.

Examples such as ALSUntangled highlight how the interactivity of Twitter has provided new ways for the healthcare community to interact with patients. Rather than posters on hospital walls or even posts on internet forums, Twitter-mediated platforms such as @ALSUntangled facilitate a highly interactive experience with researchers. This represents a potential shift in the norms of medical research itself. However, regardless of the promise of these Twitter-mediated research spaces, it is most likely that many patients will feel uncomfortable publicly tweeting their age, health information, and location. The boundaries between public and private have shifted significantly, but just how much are patients willing to reveal? Indeed, this cuts to a larger issue of Twitter and health: privacy.

Potential Downsides: From Privacy Issues to Medical Misinformation

Twitter is underused by public health professionals (Panahi et al. 2014). In 2011, only 16 percent of US hospitals surveyed used Twitter officially (Thaker et al. 2011: 707) and this jumped to over 50 percent by 2014 (Griffis et al. 2014). Privacy is a major issue which can affect physician uptake. Leaking of patients' personal information onto Twitter would create a Health Insurance Portability and Accountability Act (HIPAA) violation in the case of American patients (Loeb et al. 2015). Patients may inadvertently offer "too much information" in their tweets (Herron 2015). Or they may tweet to a doctor and expect a response (which the doctor most likely cannot provide due to privacy legislation in most countries). Twitter has also been attributed to spreading medical misinformation, as Oyeyemi et al. (2014) found in the case of Ebola. Chou et al. (2009: 3) add that though "the participatory nature of social media entails an open forum for information exchange," this also leads to a greater possibility of disseminating "noncredible, and potentially erroneous, health information." This is part of a larger issue of information integrity on Twitter (Murthy 2011). Rajani et al. (2011) state that if virtual support groups replace support that would have been provided by healthcare professionals, they may receive medical misinformation as opposed to validated information from the healthcare community. This is an important point. Indeed, some believe that medical professionals need to be present online to ensure the integrity of health information that the public receives, given that patients increasingly consume health information online, as a lack of participation by physicians may ultimately lead to their declining influence in individuals' medical decision-making (Kubetin 2011; Herron 2015).

Twitter can also be used to correct prevalent medical misinformation. For example, H. Michael Dreher, a professor and registered nurse of 25 years, tweets under @RNmakingsense to provide "quick, concise health information" to his followers and, given his experience, feels comfortable "being a filter for health information" through Twitter (Dreher 2009: 220). In another example, the American Cancer Society (ACS) credits Twitter with rectifying "a long-standing communication problem" in which blogs and other internet sites were stating that the ACS was recommending routine screening for prostate cancer (Butcher 2009: 36–8). After tweeting that the ACS recommends men consult with their doctor on the necessity of screening, they have found that blogs and the mainstream media have picked this up.

However, others argue that health professionals using social media run the risk of sharing personal information if they respond to the questions of patients on a site like Twitter (Twaddell, cited in Krowchuk 2010: 7). Additionally, Otto (2011) observes that doctors believe that "offhand remarks" on social media "could show up later in legal proceedings." In highly litigious countries such as the USA, this is particularly relevant. Privacy is also an issue in terms of clinical interactions. For example, Michael Lara, a board-certified psychiatrist and neurologist, had a patient track him down on Twitter and ask him questions specific to his treatment options (Terry 2009: 508). Lara had his staff contact the patient by telephone to resolve the issue and also to make clear that Twitter was not an appropriate medium to contact Lara (Terry 2009: 508). Certainly, the prospect of patients publicly tweeting at any time about sensitive medical questions and remaining in an expectant state is not "just what the doctor ordered." The relationship between doctors and patients can be very personal. However, its intimacy does have various formal constraints, and Lara's case highlights this.

Other potential downsides have to do with medical professionals and institutions "following" people on Twitter. Specifically, some in the healthcare industry are worried that the act of following may be conflated with an endorsement of that particular Twitter user. Terry (2009: 508) gives the example of the Anne Arundel Medical Center, an American hospital which maintains a Twitter profile, but with a disclaimer on their page which makes clear no such endorsement exists. That said, the act of following may be perceived by other Twitter users as an endorsement regardless of any disclaimer. The act of following users on Twitter usually indicates (though not always) some level of – even minuscule – interest in that user. Equating this to the validation of that user is a slippery slope, but a slope that continues to be well greased.

Another issue is differential access to Twitter given persisting digital divides. Blank (2016) observes that British Twitter users, for example, are "younger, wealthier, and better educated than other internet users." As discussed in previous chapters,[11] Twitter is socially stratified along class, race, gender, age, and other lines. Patients from lower socioeconomic backgrounds may be unable to use social media due to limitations of access, skills, interests, and costs (Helsper and Reisdorf 2016). Liang and Mackey (2011: 824) observe that pharmaceutical companies use Twitter accounts for direct-to-consumer advertising where tweets advertising specific treatment options are sent to users. Some marginalized groups may lack the social capital[12] to responsibly consume this hyper-targeted advertising. Chou et al. (2009: 3) also note the presence of a "double divide" where those without internet access are doubly impacted in that they are unable to obtain health information freely available on the internet. That said, the International Telecommunications Union (2016) reports that over 40 percent of people globally use the internet, and smartphones have become an increasingly popular platform for e-health in developing countries (Xu et al. 2015). Additionally, developing countries have increased smartphone usage, aided by the introduction of ultra-low-cost smartphones (Ghosh et al. 2016). Though many of the phones being purchased in developing countries have only basic internet services, Kahn et al. (2010) argue there are opportunities for mobile health (m-health), which involve basic mobile phones. Twitter may be an ideal medium for pushing vital health information to these individuals with basic mobile phones via text messages.

Cancer Networks and Twitter

The illnesses which tend to have the most active Twitter networks are either chronic or life-changing. Cancer patients, their friends/family, and a diverse set of oncology-related professionals are prominent examples of active health networks on Twitter. Cancer survivors are very active on Twitter.[13] Some users insert the phrase "cancer survivor" into their Twitter biographies, affirming this part of their Twitter persona. The case of cancer networks on Twitter provides a glimpse not only of how doctors and health institutions are dialogically interacting with individuals, but also how these networks have an international reach and, most of the time, involve strangers, rather than strengthening existing offline relationships. Though some patients do follow their doctor's Twitter timeline (if they are Twitter users), most often doctors and health institutions are interacting with "far-flung" colleagues or members of the public (Victorian 2010). In the case of cancer, Twitter can be "used to design new health-related interventions" such as pap smear and mammogram screening (Lyles et al. 2013). The clinical trial literature frequently discusses under-representation of certain groups (Rochon et al. 2004), and Twitter may also be an ideal medium to engage marginalized populations who most need health messaging (Murthy and Eldredge 2016).

As discussed earlier in this chapter, these recruitment efforts are premised on the far reach of cancer networks on Twitter. For example, Breast Cancer Social Media (#BCSM), mentioned earlier in this chapter, gained national prominence in the USA and has been labeled as a "social movement" (Szabo 2012). For example, Butcher (2010b) gives the example of Naoto T. Ueno (@TeamOncology), a doctor at the M.D. Anderson Cancer Center in the USA and a cancer survivor, who tweets in English and Japanese and has about 5,500 followers. In the past, he has tweeted about emergent oncology research such as proceedings from the Asian Clinical Oncology Society conference in Japan. This aspect of the public being able to follow medical conferences through Twitter is highlighted by McNab (2009). Ueno also uses Twitter to correct misinformation regarding cancer. For example, one of his tweets, which criticized a breast cancer screening program in Japan, led to the program undergoing a "rethink" (Butcher 2010b: 38). Ueno is an interesting case in that he tweets in the evening in Japanese and during the day in English, so that Twitter users in Japan are online when he is tweeting in Japanese. His Twitter timeline straddles two distinct sociolinguistic spaces within Twitter itself. Second, he makes a point of tweeting about aspects of his daily life, especially food and music, alongside tweets about cancer. At the time of writing, his timeline included tweets about Japanese pop music and a link to an article in *Oncology Times*, which discusses his work on inflammatory breast cancer. He believes that by tweeting about non-cancer topics, he draws an audience "that has nothing to do with cancer," but when he tweets about cancer (which he does about 40 percent of the time), these followers still pay attention to his cancer-related tweets (Butcher 2010b: 38). From his perspective, Twitter "is fantastic in the way that you can disseminate information to people who don't care about cancer." This aspect of drawing individuals who may be interested in one part of your life into another part of your life is a unique aspect of the medium, and it shows how social networks can be intentionally or unintentionally bridged. Of course, this characteristic of Twitter is not limited to health. As discussed in chapter 5, some celebrities regularly tweet about humanitarian crises in addition to other topics (e.g., Hollywood gossip). Though not a bait and switch, this ability of Twitter to expose followers to "unexpected" topical information is important. Indeed, it shapes the ways in which Twitter is able to disseminate information to non-homophilous groups (see chapter 3 for a discussion of homophily).

Another active oncologist using Twitter is Dr Anas Younes, also of the M.D. Anderson Cancer Center. Butcher (2010a) interviewed Younes and describes how he has configured his computer to search for every mention of "lymphoma" posted on Twitter. He uses these incoming tweets as a basis from which to reach a large number of people, whether he knows them personally or not. For instance, a stranger (@Dozyhead) directed the following tweet to him:

> @DrAnasYounes Hi i need your advice pls, both parents had non hodgkins lymphoma, my dad died, do my genes increase my chance of getting it?[14]

Dr Younes quickly responded that there is currently no genetic test to predict familial lymphoma.[15] This sort of interaction between a member of the public (of an unknown location) and a prominent oncologist is a product of Twitter's ability to connect health practitioners with new audiences. It also highlights how Twitter is changing some doctor/patient relationships by not only breaking down traditional barriers between doctors and patients, but also connecting patients with doctors who are experts in the field (regardless of where they live). These interactions can also potentially eclipse racial (Manfredi et al. 2010), gender (Celik et al. 2009), and other barriers between doctors and patients. Older patients are also keen to use electronic communication with their doctors (Singh et al. 2009). Teens report that they find it difficult to discuss drug use and sexual health topics and feel less anxiety using computer-mediated communication (Lenhart et al. 2010: 4). Twitter may be shaping medical practice by providing an avenue for these groups to interact with interested medical professionals.

Twitter also enables doctors to keep a finger on the pulse of what patients are interested in or worried about. As for the case of journalism discussed in chapter 4, doctors can use Twitter as an awareness system in which health is in the ambient environment of the medium. Steven Tucker, an American oncologist based in Singapore, notes that Twitter is an excellent platform from which to listen to patients as well as interested members of the public (Butcher 2010a: 8). Ueno, a cancer survivor himself, stresses the importance of Twitter to patient empowerment. Indeed, he feels this is the "most important thing" regarding his use of Twitter (Butcher 2010b: 38). Specifically, individuals diagnosed with cancer, carers, and family members can use Twitter to gather information on particular cancer treatment options and clinical trials, but can also put questions about their specific cases to leading oncologists in the field. Patients, carers, and family perceive this level of agency as a critically important utility of Twitter. Chou et al. (2009: 3) argue that online social networks "may increase perceived social support." Importantly, they add that social media have facilitated an increase in patient-generated content, which is "seen as more democratic and patient controlled, enabling users to exchange health-related information that they need and therefore making information more patient/consumer-centered" (Chou et al. 2009: 3). As Turner (2010) argues, this is part of a perceived "turn" in which new media breaks down traditional power relations between content creators and public consumers. In other words, patients become both authors and content consumers, giving them more of a locus of control.

I explored some of these questions empirically through a five-month study of cancer-related tweets.[16] The study will be briefly introduced as it gives another example of how Twitter is used in update cultures focused on health. A total of 90,986 cancer-related tweets was collected during the five-month period of 2010–11 (with the breakdown listed in figure 7.2). Most individuals tweeting were from the USA and, out of the top 15 cities being tweeted from, only three were non-US (London, Toronto, and Sydney). The majority of tweets referred to chemotherapy or melanoma (see figure 7.2). Throughout

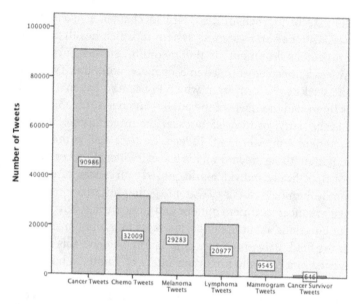

Figure 7.2   Frequency of tweets by cancer-related keywords; left-hand bar indicates total number of cancer tweets. Some tweets mention more than one keyword, leading to a total larger than the left-hand bar.

this book, it has been argued that Twitter is part of a larger societal trend toward "update cultures." In the case of cancer, the succinctness of the medium, combined with users' desire to update their friends, family, and the larger Twitterverse of their everyday and exceptional health circumstances, contributes to an update culture. For example, some tweets collected in this study aim to inform their audience of the commencement of chemotherapy treatment and to update about ongoing treatment. Individuals were found tweeting that they have a chemotherapy appointment today, that they are anxiously waiting at their appointment, or that they have just had treatment and feel physically and emotionally exhausted.

A significant pattern which emerges is that individuals see Twitter as a means to share aspects about their (or a loved one's) chemotherapy regime, which includes tweets proclaiming final chemotherapy sessions as well as some in which chemotherapy is attributed to their cancer's remission. In other words, users often tweet about chemotherapy multiple times and in diverse contexts. For some, updating about their chemotherapy is similar to diary writing. Others who, for example, are having difficulty with side effects may be actively soliciting responses of support from fellow Twitter users.[17]

In the case of melanoma, an interesting trend emerges which often includes users tweeting about their own experiences of melanoma, the loss of a family member, and organizations fundraising or providing melanoma-related information. For instance, at the time of writing, tweets ranged from a user who discussed losing her father to melanoma a decade earlier, to another user tweeting about how she had melanoma two years ago and has to be vigilant about moles. Another user tweeted about wanting to get a tan, but refusing to use a tanning bed for fear of melanoma. Clearly, there is a diversity of melanoma-related tweets across the spectrum, from current patients to skeptical tanners. In the case of chemotherapy-related tweets, individuals either had or were having chemotherapy, or knew of people in that situation. The melanoma tweets varied more widely. However, what they share in common with chemotherapy tweets is that the succinctness of the tweet, combined with its efficient and wide-ranging distribution, encourages users to tweet as a form of diary writing and as a means to solicit support.

These insights into Twitter intuitively make sense. In the collected data, there regularly appear tweets from individuals who have just received their diagnosis and are about to start chemotherapy. In these cases, why would someone post such a personal tweet to a public audience that is potentially very large? Like many of the other situations presented in this book, Twitter, as a medium, is able to solicit timely personal information. An individual who has just received a diagnosis of a life-changing disease is most likely not going to sit down in the doctor's waiting room and write a blog post or fire off emails to everyone they know. However, tweeting only takes a minute and has become so routine for some people that their tweet about a cancer diagnosis may be tweeted almost quasi-unconsciously. In other words, it has become second nature – or perhaps routinized – for some individuals to tweet things that are both banal and profound in their lives. Additionally, the shock of the event may not have fully percolated, so that person's habitual routine continues (tweeting and all). Other individuals may have a desire to tell the world of this life-changing situation. Update cultures inherently encourage us to share. Alongside the erosion of public/private boundaries surrounding one's health, and the need for many individuals to affirm their identities (and the fact that they, as individual beings, are important), it is not surprising to see update cultures emerge in regards to health. Ultimately, for individuals to tweet that they have just received a cancer diagnosis and are fearful about chemotherapy only takes a minute, but the act "publishes" an intimate aspect of our lives. It concretizes our thoughts, and it draws our friends, family, and anyone who is interested into a potential dialogue about this part of our lives. This is part of Twitter's function as a micro-blog in that, like blogs, it is giving voice to its author. Additionally, this publishing of our innermost thoughts can be perceived by posters as self-affirming. In a world where communities are not tightly integrated and our voice may feel weak, tweets might be perceived by their authors as empowering. This is particularly felt if other Twitter users reply to these tweets.

Cancer Retweeted

Retweets play a powerful role in determining the impact of a tweet in terms of visibility within Twitter and beyond.[18] In the data collected for the study mentioned in the previous section, retweets behaved in a similar way. Tweets that were retweeted significantly snowballed into more retweets. This is interesting for several reasons. In the previous section, individual tweets soliciting support during chemotherapy were mentioned. However, these tweets usually have a small audience and are not retweeted (unless tweeted by celebrities or other users with large followings). The question this raises is just how far the voice of ordinary Twitter users can reach. In other words, what is the reach of tweets that inform of a cancer diagnosis or update on chemotherapy progress? It seems that these tweets succeed not only as part of a diary process, but they also fulfill our need to update our own "domain" on Twitter. Individuals who are tweeting about their health are not seeking to have their tweets become "viral." Rather, their audience is usually their immediate followers (what can be thought of as a "domain" within the larger Twitterverse). These domains are not islands, strictly speaking, but the dissemination of these health-related tweets is the exception rather than the rule.

However, some tweets do become viral. In the study mentioned in the previous section, five noticeable retweet events occurred (see figure 7.3 for an example of spikes in tweet frequency) that were thought to be important by the larger Twitter community. Though not visualized in figure 7.3, Aidan Reed, a five-year-old boy from Clearwater, Kansas, who was diagnosed with acute lymphoblastic leukemia (James 2010), was the subject of an earlier spike in late October 2010. Aidan enjoys drawing monsters, and his aunt, Mandi Ostein, came up with the idea for Aidan to sell his pictures online through etsy.com, an online marketplace for handmade and vintage goods, to help fund his medical treatment and the family's unforeseen expenses (James 2010). A tweet with a link to Aidan's etsy.com store was significantly retweeted. Ostein had expected to sell 60 prints by Thanksgiving of 2010, but ultimately sold 7,000 at $12 apiece (Cohen 2010). One of the most common iterations of the tweet was:

> Here's Aidan's blog (he's 5, has leukemia, is selling his monster drawings on Etsy to pay for his chemo). (http:// aid foraidan.wordpress.com/about/)

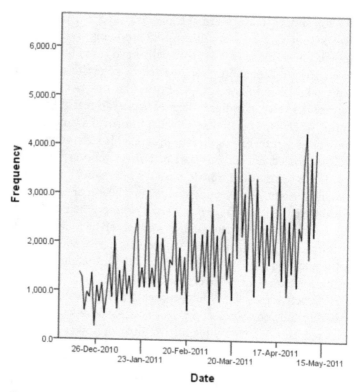

Figure 7.3   Frequency of tweets across all cancer-related keywords, December 2010–May 2011

On October 27, 2010, @abolishcancer, an established cancer charity group, retweeted this tweet[19] to their tens of thousands of followers, which resulted in the tweet traversing many subnetworks within Twitter and leading to a jump both in the "chemo" data set and in the aggregate cancer data set. The case of Aidan Reed reveals how a particular cancer story became picked up by influential Twitter users and ultimately caught the eye of @abolishcancer, which resulted in large-scale retweeting. This retweet surge led to ABC, CNN, and other traditional news media picking up the story, which in turn snowballed into more retweeting. This example highlights how Twitter's dissemination model facilitates the construction of "events" on the medium (and this parallels the emergence of viral videos on YouTube).

In 2011, a surge of lymphoma-related tweets was spurred by a Leukemia & Lymphoma Society charity triathlon event. In February 2011, tweets peaked when Hologic became the first company to obtain US Food and Drug Administration (FDA) approval for 3D breast tomosynthesis, a type of three-dimensional mammogram which could potentially detect certain breast cancers at an earlier stage than traditional mammography techniques. Similarly, in March 2011, tweets spiked regarding Bristol-Myers Squibb's experimental melanoma drug, Yervoy, whose clinical trials reported significant results in the treatment of patients with metastatic melanoma (Hobson 2011). A follow-on rise occurred in June 2011 when Yervoy's second-phase clinical trials were announced, reporting prolongation of life of patients with metastatic melanoma. Figure 7.3 illustrates spikes in the frequency of tweets during these events.

Interestingly, this reveals that the most prominent cancer-related events on Twitter are either charity-oriented or caused by perceived important drug discoveries. These findings reveal some of the ways in which cancer discourse exists on Twitter and what is considered important. The case of Aidan Reed also highlights the fact that Twitter has been important for individual cancer patients rather than exclusively to established cancer charities and drug companies (though the latter dominates major jumps and Aidan Reed is the exception rather than the rule). Examining these changes in tweet volume gives us insights not only into larger patterns of the relationship between health and Twitter, but also what events are considered most important to users. Specifically, only the event of Aidan Reed is "grassroots." The tweets regarding Reed started in a small domain and spread across Twitter as a whole, ultimately crossing over and catching the eye of mainstream media. Reed became a micro-celebrity on Twitter.

Indeed, there are various other cases of patients who have gained mainstream media attention (albeit, often fleeting) due to an unusual, attention-grabbing circumstance popularized on Twitter. A similar process occurs when tweets from citizen journalists are picked up by the mainstream media.[20]

The other spikes are attributable to events that had already caught the eye of the media (i.e., major charity events and drug discoveries). In these cases, activity on Twitter mirrors coverage by traditional media sources. In Reed's case, Twitter had real impact on his cancer experience. The interesting tension of Twitter is that there is a sea of tweets with cancer patients seeking support. Reed's case moved from semi-private domains to the radar of @abolishcancer, and then its reach exponentially increased. What this highlights is one of Twitter's unique abilities as a medium to make one a "star" within the community (i.e., a micro-celebrity). Are the legions of others whose tweets are not noticed left in the lurch? Not exactly. For if the posters get satisfaction and validation of their health situation by being noticed within their own domain, that is not only sufficient, but keeps them eager and willing to update their small circle of followers. In other words, people are not necessarily tweeting about their health to be noticed at the level of Reed, but desire to be noticed within their domain or to publish their own thoughts (e.g., as a diary).

Conclusion

Because health can often be a very intimate topic, an individual's decision to tweet such information is illustrative of several of the larger themes this book has been exploring. Namely, the case of health helps explain the shifting of public/private boundaries, tweets as part of an update culture, and Twitter as a means to publicize information to a wide audience. In the past, discussing one's insulin levels or being diagnosed with cancer was usually relegated to the private domain. Tweeting about such personal medical situations may *prima facie* seem downright shocking. However, it is emblematic of larger trends in which private health information is being volunteered publicly. A unique aspect of Twitter is the ease with which the medium allows individuals to tweet about their health. It is exponentially quicker to tweet rather than write a blog entry or other publication about having just been diagnosed with brain cancer. This time efficiency of Twitter should not be underestimated. It is a key reason why the medium is able to draw out such intimate, extemporaneous tweets from its users. Many of those tweeting would not write a blog entry from their doctor's waiting room about being anxious prior to a chemotherapy appointment, but do not hesitate to pick up their smartphone for 45 seconds and tweet about it. This perceived seamlessness is an important aspect of social communication in the Twitter age.

Another area this chapter has examined is Twitter's role in update cultures. Like Facebook, Twitter is built upon eliciting updates of everything from the minutiae of users' lives to the profound. These tweets appear side by side, fostering a unique tension between the banal and the profound. As society continues to become more individualized, our ability to socially update others in our community continues to become increasingly challenging. With fewer tight-knit communities (Putnam 2000), our desire to update people about our health has not decreased. However, this need has found an outlet in computer-mediated communication, including Twitter. The tweeting of health information develops into part of some individuals' socialization and becomes further cemented when others "update" via Twitter regarding their health.

Moreover, when friends, family, colleagues, and others reciprocally update on Twitter about their health, the culture of updating becomes further legitimized. This is crucial to users' continued perception of the social need to not only update, but to update at such a personal level. Furthermore, update cultures also offer participants an opportunity to monologue. Twitter provides them with a one-person audience, themselves, so they can write about their health – almost in a diary fashion – and the act of tweeting itself can be cathartic. Though the larger audience may not be felt (boyd and Marwick 2010) in these autobiographical exercises, the uniqueness of Twitter is the seamless permeability of the individual's intimate domain and the larger Twitterverse. For instance, strangers may find a tweet announcing a lymphoma diagnosis and send a tweet of support to that Twitter user. It is due to its ability to reduce social exclusion that Rajani et al. (2011) claim that Twitter may potentially be "good for one's health."

This chapter has also examined how retweets can demarcate health events on Twitter that are considered important. Research mentioned in the chapter highlights some of the events that resulted in surges of Twitter traffic around a particular cancer-related tweet. Though a tweet from a single user who does not have many followers (i.e., a normal Twitter user) can become noticed by the larger Twitterverse, this is of course the exception rather than the rule. In fact, in the research presented in this chapter that examined cancer-related tweets, only one case, that of Aidan Kelly, the five-year-old diagnosed with leukemia selling monster drawings on Etsy, can be considered grassroots (i.e., gaining attention via organic growth in Twitter itself rather than from prior media coverage). The most heavily retweeted cancer-related tweets concern major drug discoveries such as new treatments that have experienced promising results in clinical trials. What is interesting is that these are "events" which had already garnered the attention of traditional broadcast media, and Twitter ends up re-emphasizing and rebroadcasting these stories. What is unique about the medium is what happens if someone's tweet is picked from the crowd and a celebrity directs a tweet with encouragement to fight hard in the cancer battle, or CNN contacts the person for an interview.

Clearly, these are exceptional circumstances. Albeit rare, the sheer fact that a small number of users become micro-celebrities on Twitter and gain mainstream media attention can be considered one reason why people tweet. In the same way, though the vast majority of musicians posting videos on YouTube do not get scouted by major record labels, Justin Bieber did. The internet in general has ameliorated some of the barriers of entry to the celebrity world by enabling individuals to first attain a celebrity status online before crossing over to mainstream success (Gamson 2011). For this reason, some musicians keep uploading videos, hoping that the next one will make them a YouTube celebrity (Strangelove 2010). The same holds true for some who tweet about their health. Some hope the crippling health bills their treatment has brought will catch the attention of someone like Oprah and a check will be sent in the mail. This is based on a hope that ordinary people can become extraordinary via Twitter. Again, as long as the dream of such celebrity intervention is kept alive, the sheer rarity of such events remains insignificant for some who tweet about their health.

This chapter has also explored the ways in which Twitter may be affecting the relationship between and amongst doctors and patients. Individuals are using the medium to create support communities and to interact with doctors more directly. Doctors and medical researchers are using the medium to interact with each other and to specifically target patients to involve them in targeted clinical trials or in other research. Though the use of Twitter within cancer communities mentioned in this chapter signals important shifts in social communication regarding health, the use of social media by health institutions and individual doctors remains, by most measures, minimal. Though physicians underutilize Twitter, the public adoption of social media in terms of health-related topics has become much more common. This signals shifts in who has authority and expertise in health. In these Twitter-based health communities, other patients and their family members are viewed as authority figures whose medical advice is considered valuable. Like the shifts in journalistic practice highlighted in chapter 4, these changes mark potential shifts in health practices.

Though some populations (especially marginalized ones) remain on the wrong side of the digital divide, other vulnerable populations such as younger people are increasing their use of social media, and Twitter has an enormous potential to target this population on issues such as sexual health (Freeman et al. 2015), tobacco cessation (Prochaska et al. 2012), and human papillomavirus vaccination education (Dunn et al. 2015). In the USA, Twitter and other e-health interventions are seen as useful modes to engage African Americans, a demographic area that continues to experience differential health access (Chisolm and Sarkar 2015). Vance et al. (2009: 135) add that individual physicians have the potential to make significant impacts on large groups through Twitter by simple action recommendations, such as reminding people to wear their daily sunscreen. It is this ability of Twitter to have a larger reach that is attractive to some medical professionals. Joel Toph, a nephrologist in Detroit, believes that "out of any other way that I could get to talk to people about nephrology, this [Twitter] is the widest audience" (cited in Victorian 2010: 17). However, this reach also extends the dissemination of negative health messages. For instance, Prier et al. (2011) find that Twitter is routinely used by bars, clubs, and restaurants to promote tobacco use at their establishments. As a communications medium, it is a value-independent messenger.

Bette Midler ✓   👤 Follow ⌄
@BetteMidler

Kim Kardashian tweeted a nude selfie today. If
Kim wants us to see a part of her we've never
seen,
she's gonna have to swallow the camera.

RETWEETS   LIKES
137,909   223,070   

10:47 AM - 7 Mar 2016

↰ 5.9K   ♺ 138K   ♥ 223K

@BetteMidler[1]

Twitter has become heavily associated with celebrity culture
and gossip. One of the aspects of Twitter that made it popular amongst everyday users was the perception that they could
engage in the everyday lives of celebrity figures, including
politicians, pop-music stars, and the Hollywood A-list. The
ability to seamlessly and instantaneously post a message to
a celebrity is part of the uniqueness of Twitter. Whether one
receives a response or not, the communicative act itself is
important to the posting user. However, more of the draw of
Twitter in this context is the ability to follow in the moment
the lives of celebrities, as the tweet from Bette Midler above
highlights. The voyeurism that Twitter provides, knowing
what a celebrity had for breakfast, perhaps their politics, or a
salacious image, has made the medium attractive to the many
people who are interested in aspects of popular and celebrity
culture. Added to this is the fact that celebrities themselves
are posting things real-time and far faster than is reported by
traditional media.

CHAPTER EIGHT

Celebrities and Branding

The importance of celebrities on Twitter cannot be overstated. Though some celebrities have opted for a ghost Twitter account (Marwick and boyd 2011), others such as Katy Perry have viewed the medium as an important platform for directly engaging with their fans (Hughes 2014). Donald Trump has famously made clear that he himself is the one tweeting under @realDonaldTrump. Indeed, popular culture and entertainment journalists see Twitter as a go-to in terms of picking up candid commentary from celebrity personalities themselves (Andrews 2013: 37). Twitter simultaneously facilitates celebrity gaffes via "overly active tweeting" and reduces them by providing "more control over whether and when they get a voice in public, which topics are addressed, and how public issues are framed" (Christensen et al. 2016: 101). This also highlights the role of Twitter as a celebrity/pop-culture watchdog, wherein everyday people are able to check if a celebrity has stepped out of line. For example, Madonna was accused by some of being racist on social media (Robinson 2015). Both the banal and the profound tweets produced by celebrities go under the public microscope. As an aside, this also raises the issue of the blurring of the public and the private, which celebrities have always tended to do. Reality television has led to reality social media and the distinction between the two has become ever more blurred as celebrities tweet in on a diverse range of topics at the turn of a dime, including their daily ups and downs, and even selfies (Jerslev and Mortensen 2016).

Kim Kardashian (@KimKardashian), who was once paid $10,000 per tweet by the American fast-food restaurant Carl's

Jr (Bowen 2013) and notoriously posted twerking videos on Twitter,[2] went silent on the medium for three months after she was robbed at gunpoint in Paris in October 2016, with $10 million of jewelry stolen (Amatulli 2016). Such was the gravity of the situation that the star felt she had to stop tweeting. The irony is that police attributed the robbery to Kardashian's openness on social media about her life, including close-up photos of her jewelry (Ryan 2016).[3]

Clearly, the study of celebrity culture today has to include some discussion of Twitter or it is fundamentally incomplete. It is to this extent that the medium plays a significant role in celebrity culture across a variety of domains far beyond Hollywood, where celebrities and Twitter were historically linked. In the case of the 2016 US presidential elections, reality entertainment and politics converged in many ways and Twitter became the first port of call for both Hillary Clinton and Donald Trump to take jabs at each other.

Celebrity Engagement

Celebrity culture has been profoundly shaped by Twitter's @-mention. Though other social media platforms such as Facebook have facilitated interactions with celebrities, Twitter has arguably done the most to enable everyday people to connect with celebrities by making easy the traditional "hurdle of contacting and communicating with the celebrity" (Leets et al. 1995: 105). By "connect," I mean follow what they are doing, but also being able to communicate directly with them through @-mentions. This is different from comments posted on a public fan page or YouTube video. The celebrity (themselves) or via their ghost tweeter sometimes responds to everyday users, creating a perceived close connection. For example, Kim Kardashian regularly receives those requests and does respond to some users. Figure 8.1 illustrates one of these requests.[4] In many ways, it is perhaps irrelevant whether the actual celebrity responded, as a perceived closeness is

Emma
@kimyonceee

👤+ Follow   ∨

@KimKardashian it's my birthday today! I would love it so much if you tweeted me!

RETWEETS   LIKE
2   1

6:19 PM - 16 Feb 2017

↩   ⟲ 2   ♥ 1

Figure 8.1   Tweet to Kim Kardashian requesting a birthday reply

constructed through the act of tweeting. Horton and Wohl (1956; original emphasis) classically argued that electronic mediation fostered a "seeming face-to-face relationship between spectator and performer [,] a *para-social relationship.*" Moreover, Twitter is definitely part of para-social processes.

The act of receiving a response is particularly meaningful as fans have always understood that "the chance of reciprocity is still known to be very unlikely" (Leets et al. 1995: 105). Ghostwriters have always existed, being in the employ of minor-to-major celebrities and public figures. When people write to a legislator and receive a response, generally it is someone in the office who has prepared that letter and signed it. This was often true with fan mail in the past, where teams were tasked with responding to bags of such mail. Obtaining committed fans is generally more challenging than retaining them. In addition, fans can become even more committed to the celebrity by receiving a response. Celebrity-studies literature exploring Twitter has argued that the platform has influenced the dynamics of fan culture and has helped support the rise of "micro-celebrities," who have "friends or followers as a fan base" (Marwick and boyd 2011: 141). In terms of the former, Marwick and boyd (2011: 155–6) found that "Twitter does, to some extent, bring famous people and fans 'closer' together, but it does not equalize their status."

In the past, celebrity relationships were "constrained by the availability, approachability, and responsiveness of the target person" (Leets et al. 1995: 104). Writing a fan letter to Dwayne Johnson or Lady Gaga from Indonesia would historically have been cost- and time-prohibitive, and unlikely even to garner a response. But a tweet to them is free and it generally takes less than a minute for fans to fire one off. Celebrities and their ghost tweeters have the same low cost in terms of time and effort. And, as Marwick and boyd (2011: 150) argue, "Receiving a message from a highly followed individual is a status symbol in itself."

Unsurprisingly, the low stakes involved with tweeting a celebrity have increased the volume of @-mentions they receive. It is likely that some celebrities have turned to automated responses to their fans, using bots that read tweets sent to the celebrity, with a set of rules that decide how the bots respond back to the fan. If the content is questionable, these tweets may then be directed to the celebrity's staff in order to respond individually, or they are ignored; in the past, many letters to celebrities went unanswered.

A larger point that celebrity connections in Twitter highlight is that the platform fosters perceived closeness between celebrities and everyday people. In a personal example, my elementary-school daughter, during the 2016 US presidential election, told me that one of her school friends had tweeted @HillaryClinton and received a response back and was thrilled. Her friend went around school telling everyone that Hillary Clinton herself had responded to her and she was so overjoyed to receive this message from Hillary Clinton. Of course, this is a child. However, empirical work on celebrities and Twitter also indicates that even retweeting celebrity tweets "enhances fans' feeling of social presence" (Kim and Song 2016: 574). In addition, "when celebrities share their life and directly communicate about theses [sic] experiences, fans tend to feel as if those celebrities were socially present in their life" (Kim and Song 2016: 574). Being in the physical presence of a celebrity, as a musician comes offstage, or running into a Hollywood actor in a restaurant, leaves fans with a palpable, even physically measurable, closeness. Or, as Ferris (2001: 26) argues, "When a fan comes face-to-face with a celebrity, worlds collide and dichotomies collapse." Though a tweet may not elicit the same reaction, that type of closeness does occur. Seeing a famous cricketer or football player up close and having a conversation with them is, of course, qualitatively different from having one of your tweets favorited by them or getting a brief mention saying thanks. However, it is part of the spectrum of celebrity interactions. Indeed, for some, the Twitter interaction may be more valuable as it allows for easy sharing of that interaction, perhaps instantly boosting that user's status in their peer group. Ultimately, Twitter has become part of our interactions with celebrities and has contributed to a perception of us being close to them.

The Case of Anthony Weiner

Celebrity sex scandals have also been recurrent on Twitter. One of the more infamous ones is the case of former Democratic US Congressman Anthony Weiner, who sent a lewd photo of himself via Twitter to student Genette Cordova in 2011 (Parker and Barbaro 2011). His Twitter infamy began in May 2011 when a picture of a man's bulging crotch appeared on Weiner's Twitter feed (May 27, 2011) and he claimed his profile had been hacked (May 30, 2011). A week later, on June 6, 2011, he admitted that the picture was his and that he had sent it (Parker and Barbaro 2011). A couple of years later, on June 13, 2014, he favorited a tweet stating: "Tinder will now be the ultimate sext machine,"[5] though he claimed he accidentally hit the "star thing" (i.e., the "Favorite" icon) (Politi 2014). After the public humiliation of "Weinergate," he turned to private sexting via iMessage and other more closed platforms. However, in 2015, a sext that had his sleeping child next to him surfaced publicly (Rosenberg and Golding 2016). Indeed, during the exchange, he had worried that he accidentally publicly tweeted the image. As a result of being caught in his third sext scandal, he finally deleted his Twitter account in 2016 (Spargo and Robinson 2016). And when Weiner's sexting scandal emails became part of the investigation of Hillary Clinton's emails during the 2016 US presidential election, the incident was quickly labeled "Dickileaks" on Twitter, on other social media, and in the mainstream press (Smith 2016). The collective "Weinergate" incidents illustrate that liking, posting, and retweeting by celebrities is not only being carefully watched, but also that the ease of tweeting itself lends itself to accidental public posting of content intended to be within private Direct Messages (DM). This case therefore also underscores how Twitter simultaneously fosters intensely public and private social communication, whether intentional or not. This is qualitatively different from Facebook, for example, where one's feed generally has some level of privacy, whereas one's Twitter feed is, by design, completely open.

The Case of Stephen Fry

Celebrities have shaped Twitter since its early years. One celebrity who has been prominently associated with the medium is British actor and comedian Stephen Fry (@stephenfry), who joined Twitter in July 2008 and has tweeted nearly 22,000 times over eight years and has amassed 12.3 million followers. He is the tenth most followed celebrity in the UK (Landi 2016). Stephen Fry has supported various social movements on Twitter over the years. The Pakistan Floods case study in chapter 5 observes how he was one of the most mentioned users on Twitter during the floods. In November 2016, he supported banning the ivory trade in the UK with the tweet: "There's STILL an ivory trade in the UK?! Insane but true. Do sign the petition to ban such wickedness http://bit.ly/2cceQ4K #JoinTheHerd,"[6] which was retweeted

Stephen Fry ✓
@stephenfry

Will all you sanctimonious fuckers fuck the fuck off Jenny Beavan is a friend and joshing is legitimate. Christ I want to leave the planet

14/02/2016, 21:59

771 RETWEETS **2,263** LIKES

↩   ⟲   ♥   •••

Figure 8.2   Stephen Fry's "I want to leave the planet" tweet

over 1,500 times and liked over 1,600 times. Over 100 comment responses were elicited by the tweet, generating discussion over historical ivory as well as new elephant poaching. Fry's tweet encouraged followers to sign a UK parliamentary petition (Reuters 2016). After eight years on the platform, Fry decided to quit Twitter due to the "baglady" incident. At the 2016 British Academy of Film and Television Arts (BAFTA) awards, the United Kingdom's premier film and television awards ceremony, Fry, in his role as host, presented an award to the costume designer Jenny Beavan, while stating "Only one of the great cinematic costume designers would come to an awards ceremony dressed as a bag lady" (Lee 2016).

After #baglady went viral on Twitter, Fry was attacked on the platform by thousands of users. Unbeknownst to most Twitter users, the two are friends and Beavan took no offense. Regardless, dialogue ensued about casual sexism and pressure for women to conform to fashion norms. This incident led to Fry deactivating his profile and remarking that Twitter was no longer an enjoyable place as "too many people have peed in the pond," contrasting the mainstream status of the platform today versus it being a "pool in a magical glade in an enchanted forest" in its infancy (Thomas 2016). Fry spent five months off the platform, rejoining in August 2016 with a post on his blog titled "Switched On" (Fry 2016). His post reflects a deep commitment to Twitter, writing: "Twitter can still reward with its marvellous uses as a bulletin board and information exchange. Had anyone suggested that such a service might exist ten or fifteen years ago I would never have believed them" (Fry 2016). He adds in his post that he is acting in a CBS television comedy series, and will be posting updates on his Twitter feed about it. What is revealed by the #baglady incident, at least for specific observations about Twitter and celebrities, is that: (1) the medium is viewed as a critical aspect of their brands, enabling a communication channel with fans and the public at large; (2) celebrities are instantly held accountable on the platform, as Twitter provides a back-channel so that if a celebrity makes a gaffe or perceived gaffe, Twitter users are already commenting; (3) though the celebrity may not "enjoy" a Twitter backlash, users certainly delight in aspects of celebrity critique on the platform, an extension of celebrity "bashing" that happened more privately in the past; and (4) Twitter is seen by users as providing a means for their opinions to matter, what some have evaluated as a potential "public sphere" (Colleoni et al. 2014). So despite Fry's explosive and now-deleted tweet, stating that he "want[s] to leave the planet"[7] after the #baglady backlash (Lee 2016) (see figure 8.2), he re-entered Twitter by posting a photo of "charming crudités" that he had backstage "@latelateshow."[8] The ability to switch from a profound, seething commentary on the pollution of the "Twitter pond" to a banal crudité tweet illustrates a partial lack of Twitter memory as well. Users have moved on and #baglady is ancient history when measured in Twitter time.

Twitter and Advertising

From the smallest business to the largest multinational corporations, Twitter hashtags have been deployed for campaigns, sweepstakes promotions, and a host of other marketing and promotional campaigns. Previously, it was debated whether Twitter adopted adequate monetization strategies that involve sponsored/paid-for tweets and promoted hashtags. As the internet and social media more generally have become aggressively monetized, users are now increasingly used to the presence of sponsored content on social media platforms. Twitter seems to have minimized the amount of advertising through sponsored tweets and hashtags compared to other social media platforms such as Facebook, where ads and image-based advertising are much more prevalent. This is likely tied to Twitter's unsponsored approach to platform development. For example, when public proposals for lifting the 140-character cap on tweets have been forwarded, groups of users made clear that the character limit was part of what they felt was "unique" about the platform.[9] There is a certain belief that Twitter's attraction lies in its simplicity and brevity as well as its absence of excessive advertising. A study on millennials and Twitter advertising concluded that nearly half of their respondents "find Twitter ads irritating and refrain from clicking on them" (Murillo et al. 2016: 450).

Twitter has also become an important platform for branding and brand reputation. Even before the rise of so-called Web 2.0 (multimedia, interactive internet services), customers would take to social platforms to post experiences of brands succeeding or letting them down. Well-known early examples include an incident where a musician accused United Airlines of breaking his guitar and not offering compensation, which resulted in him creating a YouTube video titled "United Breaks Guitars," which was posted on July 6, 2009, and went viral with over 16 million views.[10] The various versions of the video of Dr David Dao in April, 2017, being dragged off United Flight 3411 went viral even faster. A Domino's Pizza employee in the USA filmed another employee putting cheese in his nose before placing the tainted ingredients on food, and posted the video on YouTube on April 13, 2009,[11] leading to a formal apology video posted on YouTube by the Domino's Pizza president at the time.[12] Twitter became an avenue to comment on the Domino's incident and has been a key platform since to name and shame companies.

Specifically, many now perceive Twitter as an important platform for customer empowerment. Indeed, Twitter has become a first point of contact for corporate accountability. Contemporary consumers are not hesitant to tweet when someone discovers something wrong with a food product they have purchased, a service they expected, or any other business-related goods and services. Their discontent and content have been transformed into 140-character tweets.

It is for this reason that companies have taken to employing firms to study sentiment and other analytics on Twitter around particular hashtags or products relevant to them. In various ways, this has augmented or even in some cases replaced traditional methods of consumer polling, where one is able to go to Twitter and see how an ad campaign or a particular product or a business is doing based on computerized analysis of tweets containing those keywords. In addition, companies have taken to using analytics platforms such as Crimson Hexagon (2017) that have unique relationships with Twitter, in order to have access to feeds of tweets that they are able to process real-time or near real-time to see how their brand, product, or advertising campaign is performing. If they see sentiment tracking as positive or negative, they can quickly intervene. Twitter has therefore become a customer service platform. For example, airlines launched Twitter accounts that are designed to help if you found yourself delayed and did not know what to do. A customer is able to tweet the airline and they can try to assist you. Often, this process is much faster than picking up the phone and waiting quite a while to speak with a customer services agent. A key difference here is that Twitter can be used to simultaneously deal with individual concerns around the company and to aggregate group-level behavior for data analytics (e.g., Simone

Guercini et al.'s 2014 study of customer tweets relevant to airlines). In other words, Twitter simultaneously allows companies to interact with individual customers, sometimes even getting feedback in terms of segmented focus groups, and in other situations is looking to aggregate customers, which is the case with sentiment analysis and topic modeling that are derived from group-level data around hashtags or terms associated with their products (Ghiassi et al. 2013). In addition, as Twitter is public, one of the very interesting aspects of this is that brands can also perform these analytics on their competitors, giving them new forms of business intelligence that they did not have easy access to in the past. Therefore, in addition to conducting sentiment analysis, machine learning, or other methods of analysis which they may use on their own products, services, and brands, Twitter may help give them unique insights into their specific market. It is partially for this reason that data-science education panels have become integrated into conferences such as the American Academy of Advertising (e.g. Li et al. 2014).

Twitter has played a role in transforming the relations between consumers and organizations. It would be easy to make an over-generalization in terms of Twitter increasing the accountability that companies have toward consumers. This can, of course, be the case in some situations where users turn to Twitter to express dissatisfaction around a product and are able to effect change, collectively acting as a consumer movement. For some organizations, Twitter is not seen as inherently having an effect on their customer base. However, with highly prominent cases, such as when Nordstrom was attacked by Donald Trump on Twitter in February 2017 for dropping his daughter, Ivanka Trump's, clothing and accessory line (D'Innocenzio and Condon 2017), this position is likely to be an increasingly minority one.

That said, there are differences in the demographics of Twitter users. As has been discussed previously in this book, there are biases in terms of what types of users Twitter tends to have. In this sense, what happens on Twitter may stay on Twitter. Put another way, for some brands and services more than others, what is being said on Twitter may not be as important, depending on target markets. When the first edition of this book was published, when Twitter represented a place for digital elites that Stephen Fry lamented the loss of, this was perhaps more the case. Today, it is much harder to argue that what happens on Twitter stays on Twitter, given how public the platform has become. Rather than being the stomping grounds for young people who had the social capital and interest to be involved in the medium, hashtags are not such a mysterious thing, nor is a tweet. If nothing else, 71-year-old President Donald Trump's love of Twitter has ended this era of Twitter as elite and rebranded it as a place for everyday people's voices to be heard without the intervention of elites. His tweets (rather than press conferences) are regularly quoted on news programs, in newspaper articles, and on radio programs. Just as one can be fired by a single tweet, much can also be done to benefit or damage a brand or company through just one tweet.

The Case of American Express

American Express started early on in terms of using Twitter to allow its customers to be able to tweet directly to them if they had an issue with one of their financial services, and the customer service agent tried to help through @-mentions (see figure 8.3).[13] Another company, @AskAmex, was launched in August 2009 and the organization has actively used Twitter for almost a decade. American Express deployed the #AMEX hashtag as well as @AmexOffers (launched in February 2012). The latter activates discounts at particular retailers if users tweet with hashtags listed by @AmexOffers (see figure 8.4).[14]

Twitter users who are American Express customers link their Twitter account with their credit card in order to be

zzzz @Tryrauhl · 1h
@AskAmex when registering card for contact less payments through app does it charge a test £1?

↩ 1   ↻   ♥   · · ·

Ask Amex ✓   ⬤ Follow
@AskAmex

@tryrauhl Good Afternoon. Google may charge a pre authorization charge. Please let me know if you have any other q's. Enjoy your day! ^R

11:28 AM · 13 Dec 2016

↩   ↻   ♥   · · ·

Figure 8.3   @AskAmex tweet response to a customer.

able to do this. Some customers just post the required hashtag, while others go far beyond this. For example, in the case of #Amex1800Flowers, users posted about who they were buying flowers for, while others posted Bible verses[15] or @loco_motive's "#Amex1800Flowers because I need a cheap Valentine's Day gift."[16] This was a surprise for me. Given that these tweets are unlikely to be retweeted or even read, they nonetheless hold importance for users in terms of documenting what retailer they are going to use the American Express offer with and what they are going to purchase with the discount. This fits the advertising literature, which argues that social advertising leaves the "branded message open to multiple interpretations" (Coker, Smith, and Altobello 2015: 170). Most would expect the minimum amount of characters to be posted or even some customers to be put off by this, as their friends and family would be "spammed" or, at the very least, exposed to their consumer preferences.

However, many social media users have become attuned to seeing this type of "noise" come through on their feeds and understand that this type of electronic word of mouth (eWOM) (Daugherty and Hoffman 2014) is a necessary product/part of Twitter. This is much like the promoted tweets that appear on their streams, and, as previous work has shown, many Twitter users are not angered by this type of explicit

Figure 8.4   @AmexOffers confirmation tweet to a customer.

advertising (Murillo et al. 2016). Therefore, as these tweets come up in people's feeds, American Express has socially advertised its brand to Twitter users, without having to go the more top-down route of promoting a tweet or sponsoring a hashtag. The subtlety of the marketing as originating from a Twitter user rather than American Express seems to have market value. The marketing literature argues that this type of electronic word of mouth (eWOM) has a higher chance of having an effect on consumers (Daugherty and Hoffman 2014). Consumers may be more open to this sort of soft advertising coming from friends and family, rather than from an external source.

In addition, one of the interesting aspects of social media more broadly in terms of advertising has been to place ads within the native wrapper of the social content. With this, the original tweet created by American Express, for example, is part of the reply a user makes, or a retweet. Ultimately, a tweet that has been propagated by a social campaign looks like original content produced by an individual Twitter user. These types of campaigns have had tremendous payoff for American Express specifically. After 30,000 tweets around Small Business Saturday and 1 million Facebook likes, American Express found that 40 percent of the general public was aware of Small Business Saturday and they estimate

JenniferGrose Design
@jgrosedesign   Follow

Today is #smallbusinessaturday so thought I'd
share this cute sticker from @crafty_wonder
that was given to me #ShopLocal #Craft
#stationery

Figure 8.5   American Express' #SmallBusinessSaturday
inspired tweet by @jgrosedesign; reproduced with permission
from Jennifer Grose and @craftywonderland

that revenues increased by 28 percent (Paniagua and Sapena
2014).

Ultimately, a tweet that appears on your feed that is
actually sponsored/promoted in some way has the endorsement of a user you are following. In some respects, this has
been Twitter's attempt to not be labeled by users as "selling out." They have been able, in some sense, to retain a
more grassroots/bottom-up feel as "native content" than
other platforms (most notably, Facebook). Some American
Express hashtags such as #SmallBizSat, #ShopSmall, and
#SmallBusinessSaturday disseminated widely as grassroots
movements dedicated to promoting shopping locally picked it
up and they created their own content (see figure 8.5).[17]

The power of this transformation, however, is linked to the

Tweet Activity

Impressions	311
Total engagements	24
Media engagements	19
Profile clicks	3
Likes	1
Link clicks	1

Figure 8.6   Personal analytics for tweets

brand capital of American Express. For this reason, despite highly visible partnerships such as that with American Express, Twitter faces challenges in terms of monetization. As research specific to American Express and Twitter has found, not all advertising efforts on Twitter are equal (Adamopoulos and Todri 2014). Rather, as Adamopoulos and Todri (2014: 8) argue, "promotional events on social media are more effective for brands that already have a large user base, since they can more effectively propagate their messages; this might contribute to a 'rich get richer' effect on social media." This is a fundamentally important point as American Express already had a very well-known brand and large user-base. The platform has faced financial troubles over the years, perhaps partly due to its soft approach to promoted advertising and the lack of sophisticated tools to monitor the effect of Twitter ads on sales (Marshall and Koh 2015). Twitter has launched new metrics tools within its standard interface that allow one to track the "success" of a tweet in terms of impressions and engagement. The tools offer additional, paid methods to promote one's tweet (see figure 8.6).[18] However, Twitter's approach to monetization has been fairly unaggressive, drawing cheers from its committed users and jeers from Wall Street.

Conclusion

For many, Twitter has become synonymous with celebrity culture. As such, the medium has been labeled a trivial space where the banal aspects of celebrity life are provided real-time to the public. However, this chapter has argued that we need much more nuanced readings of celebrities and Twitter. Perhaps more than any platform, Twitter has made interactions with celebrities seamless. The effort to @-mention a celebrity is an extremely low-stakes affair. It takes hardly any effort at all to direct a tweet to Kim Kardashian, asking her to tweet back when it is your birthday. As this chapter has discussed, whether that user receives a reply or not to their birthday tweet request, they have interacted with Kim Kardashian, which in itself is likely to be important to that user. Just as writing a fan letter in the past to a celebrity you followed meant something to you, the act of tweeting provides new avenues for this to happen. Moreover, as tweets have streamlined the process of getting in touch and receiving a response from the celebrity, they have also increased the traffic that celebrities are receiving from their fans. For some celebrities, social media may be a net positive, allowing, as Marwick (2013: 206) argues, a unique avenue for "strategically revealing insider information" to fans. For others, they may feel that this is a case of information overload. We perhaps might see a greater number of celebrities using bots or other automated mechanisms to respond to some of the social media traffic coming their way.

This chapter also explored specific cases where celebrities committed gaffes or perceived transgressions and were attacked on Twitter, a platform for which they themselves have great affection. The case of Stephen Fry and the #baglady incident is a clear example of this. This chapter discussed how Stephen Fry witnessed the public Twitter backlash over a comment he made at the British Academy of Film and Television Arts (BAFTA) awards ceremony and ultimately ended up deactivating his Twitter profile, though he rejoined Twitter five months later. Another important aspect of Twitter and celebrities that this chapter investigated was that around celebrity malfeasance or inappropriate conduct. The case of Anthony Weiner, who sexted publicly on Twitter, is used as a case study. Specifically, his public sharing of a sext on Twitter led to a public scandal. Weiner initially claimed that his Twitter account had been hacked, but later confessed to tweeting the image in question. This case additionally highlights the fact that celebrities are also using Twitter as a platform for private communication (i.e., direct messages). However, the blurring between private and public on Twitter, especially highlighted by the routine action of tweeting versus direct messaging, has led to some cases where celebrities are posting content that was intended to be private to their public Twitter feeds. Though they may try to delete this content, once it is posted on Twitter, it is likely that someone out there has already archived the tweet, as the #baglady case with Stephen Fry underscores. This raises an important point – that of the role of Twitter as a watchdog for celebrities as well as brands.

In the case of brands, Twitter has been used to report instances where consumers are satisfied or dissatisfied with a brand – ranging from goods, services, or reputation. As seen in chapter 6, which explored social movements, the investments by Wells Fargo with the Dakota Access Pipeline (DAPL) project led to a public outcry on Twitter and had some impact on the perception of Wells Fargo by Twitter users. In this case, some argue that the decision of Seattle to withdraw a $3 billion financing project from Wells Fargo was partially attributable to activism by #NoDAPL activists. This chapter has explored the ways in which Twitter has been used by brands and the importance of Twitter not only to brand reputation, but also to new forms of advertising. The case of American Express, which has employed Twitter for customer service, promotional offers (i.e., "AMEX offers"), and the

#SmallBusinessSaturday events in which small businesses are promoted, has been discussed in detail. Part of this discussion also explored the power of social advertising or social eWOM (electronic word of mouth). In the case of Twitter, content that is retweeted, @-mentioned, or commented upon may look like original content from users, but is actually a product of engagement with advertising content. This chapter explored particular instances of American Express content being picked up by "shop local" movements and transformed into new forms of advertising content that are perceived by other Twitter users as organic and not direct forms of advertising. These forms of social advertising may be quite powerful. However, as this chapter has also discussed, this has not led to substantial monetization by Twitter. Indeed, the platform has been beleaguered by monetization troubles. Rather than taking more explicit and direct approaches to advertising, such as the styles of targeted advertising employed by Facebook, the medium has engaged in softer and more indirect approaches to advertising, a fact that has pleased dedicated Twitter users. However, this has led to continued challenges for the platform in terms of adopting large-scale advertising strategies, which may threaten its future commercial success.

The Verbal Artisan
@VERBALARTISAN

SOCIETY IS CRAZY!!! PEOPLE ASK TO BE
STALKED THESE DAYS... follow me on
twitter... follow me on twitter....FOLLOW
twitter.com/theverbalartis...

9:59 AM - 29 Nov 2011

@VERBALARTISAN[1] (https://twitter.com/
verbalartisan)

The tweet above is commenting on the idea that people use
Twitter as a means for self-promotion (or, in the words of this
tweeter, they "ask to be stalked"). As this book has explored,
critics of Twitter have emphasized this egocentric side of
the medium. However, placing primacy on more egocentric
tweets is at the expense of the fact that many tweets on Twitter
are also highly communal. It is this irony of individual/
communal (and banal/profound) tweets side by side that
makes Twitter a particularly interesting object of analysis.
Similarly, a user could be tweeting about a sandwich one
minute and @-mentioning the Pope (@Pontifex)[2] the next.
This chapter brings together the diverse range of theory and
case studies raised throughout the book to draw broad conclusions about social communication in the Twitter age.

CHAPTER NINE

Conclusion

Though a relatively young communications medium, Twitter has shaped many aspects of our social, political, and economic lives. This book has sought to begin a critical conversation not just about Twitter, but also about social media and the "update cultures" they support. Specifically, it has been argued that a nuanced approach to understanding Twitter reveals that the medium is part of a larger historical trend toward update cultures, social norms that encourage us to share more in the public sphere (from intimately private aspects of one's life such as a cancer diagnosis to very public events such as an earthquake tremor or celebrity breakup). The Twitterverse as a whole contains vast arrays of complex, highly intermeshed networks, which reveal a highly efficient awareness system which powers Twitter's update culture. As Twitter has been studied here ultimately as a network, it is fitting to present many of the ideas discussed as a network. Figure 9.1 illustrates how this book has connected a wide array of themes that span a variety of disciplines in order to understand the nuances of Twitter. Many of the key themes discussed, such as update cultures, "ambient" news, Twitter as an awareness system, and the medium's ability to foster engaged communities, are illustrated as central in figure 9.1. My hope is that this diagram can help readers connect the dots between theory and practice, public and private, and historical and modern that the book has navigated. To bring together some of these diverse themes, this chapter re-examines Twitter through three frames: (1) history and theory; (2) voice and influence; and (3) aware communities. The aim is not only to provide some discernible conclusions about Twitter, but also to help spur further discussion of Twitter.

History and Theory

[N]o matter how much technology reduces the intellectual and social isolation of people, their metaphysical isolation is little affected. (McLuhan 1952: 189)

Marshall McLuhan's work has shaped the study of emergent communication technologies profoundly. His analysis of radio and television continues to be valuable to modern understandings of internet technologies. To provide broader conclusions on social communication in the Twitter age, I will refer to a couple of McLuhan's ideas that comment on technology and community, technology and communicative reach, and technology and celebrities. It is easy to lose sight of the political, social, and economic nuances of social media. In the context of Twitter, McLuhan is helpful in framing an argument that the medium may be increasing our intellectual and social integration globally but, at a micro-social level, it does not inherently integrate us with our local social climate (neighbors, local community, etc.). In other words, Twitter aids us in more tightly integrated globalized communication, McLuhan's (1967) "global village," but may not be helping local community structures. But does tweeting integrate us more with our local community? For instance, can we tweet "Thinking about going to dinner tonight, anyone want to join?"[3] and, in the process, reduce our social isolation? Theoretically, yes. However, answering in the affirmative to these questions supposes that people will tweet in these ways rather than about celebrity gossip or news headlines, for example.

Questions like these are important and have been covered throughout this book via both theory and practice. What is clear is that social communication is highly shaped by changes in technology and Twitter is no exception. McLuhan (1952:

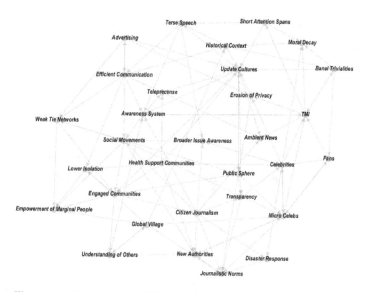

Figure 9.1   Interactions of themes discussed in this book

189) observes that in the age of communication by "unassisted human voice," reach was highly localized, but with the advent of the written word, "its range in time and space was [. . .] given enormous expansion." I have argued that social communication in the Twitter age continues this expansion along the spectrum that originated with early writing. If email moved us exponentially up the spectrum, communicating via Twitter and similar social media represents another enormous expansion of the spectrum in terms of instantaneous, global, and multiplexed communication. Rather than being locked in a binary analysis of Twitter (e.g., it has strengthened communities/weakened communities), a more productive approach is to view the Twitter age as part of a historical continuum.

This book has explored this continuum by focusing on the telegraph and its reception in the eighteenth and nineteenth centuries. Like Twitter, the telegraph had scores of critics who feared its terseness and believed the medium would kill off letter writing. The telegraph's supporters saw its global reach and immediacy of communicating messages as an epochal shift in global connectedness. Its opponents saw the telegraph as the bringer of moral decay. This book has argued that Twitter has faced both similar praise and criticism. However, the two technologies are different in many ways. Twitter, unlike the telegraph, is multicast and incorporates a social network (followers and following). Twitter also draws from the structure of social networking technologies like Facebook. Unlike the telegraph, Twitter is public (in terms of tweets), audio-visual, and free to use. In the eighteenth century, messages were not sent "down the wire" by ordinary people several times a day. Rather, telegraph messages were used more sparingly. Tweets, however, do not require a trip to the telegraph operator and can be sent at any time and from any place. Unlike the infrequent telegraph message, tweets can produce a quasi- "stream of consciousness," even in the middle of the night. In addition, when tweets flow rapidly between people, there is a feeling by users that their communication is no longer mediated. The immediacy of tweets generates a sense of "being there" with one's interlocutors (this idea of "telepresence" is discussed in chapter 3).

Voice and Influence

Another question this book has explored concerns whose voices rise above the flood of tweets. I have discussed how "celebrities" exert disproportionate influence on the shape of discourse in Twitter (see chapters 5 and 8). McLuhan (1952: 195) explores the construction of celebrity status and concludes that "the intimacy and immediacy of the flexible television camera and screen are much less favorable to the star system than the movie camera and its giant screen onto which are poured such dreams as money can buy." The question McLuhan raises is between media rather than within a single medium. So, is the "intimacy and immediacy" of Twitter "less favorable to the star system" of television and film? If anything, this is a straw man. Bar the occasional exception, the most followed users on Twitter are celebrities because of their fame outside of Twitter (rather than their fame being "homegrown" on Twitter). At the time of writing, the top 10 most followed individual users in ascending order are Katy Perry, Justin Bieber, Barack Obama, Taylor Swift, Rihanna, Ellen DeGeneres, Lady Gaga, Justin Timberlake, Britney Spears, and Cristiano Ronaldo (@twitaholic 2017). The top 100 list reads much the same. Barring former US President Barack Obama, a dystopic reading would see this as affirmation of Kierkegaard's claim that modernity is an age of indolence (see chapter 3). However, I have argued here that one's "banal" activity on Twitter (like following celebrity gossip) is as much a part of many people's identity as discussing current events. Indeed, it may be even more important to them. By ignoring this, we risk applying an elite bias to understanding Twitter. In addition, Twitter has gone from a niche social media platform to a mainstream one. This can be seen through changes in terms of what the most used hashtags on the platform are. The top five hashtags in 2010 were #rememberwhen, #slapyourself, #confessiontime, #thingsimiss, and #ohjustlikeme (Twitter 2010). Fast forward six years and the mainstreaming of Twitter is immediately evident with the top hashtags as: #Rio2016, #Election2016, #PokemonGo, #Euro2016, #Oscars, #Brexit, #BlackLivesMatter, #Trump, #RIP, and #GameofThrones (Kottasova 2016). Similarly, ordinary people interact with politicians and political parties as part of the course of an election or as everyday constituents. This phenomenon is no longer restricted to affluent countries.

Twitter is, of course, a corporate business. In its initial stages, it was focused on user growth. More recently, it has struggled to monetize. Its advertising models have raised controversy amongst Twitter users. One question which periodically crops up on Twitter is whether promoted tweets and trending topics (which are paid advertising services) reshape discourse on Twitter. Empirically, the effect is not highly discernible. None of the top Twitter hashtags is "promoted" and Twitter admits its current ad products are not working as expected and the company is facing very real financial issues. Its revenue grew by a mere 1 percent in the fourth quarter of 2016, leading to headlines such as "Twitter Needs More Than Just Donald Trump to Survive" (Ingram 2017). The historical statistics from Twitter (Twitter 2010) reveal that even when the promoted tweet products were highly marketed, "organic" topics were the most popular. Given the continuing power and reach of organic topics, this book has considered to what extent ordinary people have voice and influence on Twitter. The inclusion of #BlackLivesMatter in the 2016 top hashtag list gives additional credence to aspects of this argument. This question has been explored through the role of citizen journalists (see chapter 4), patients as health authorities (see chapter 7), consumers as watchdogs (see chapter 8), and everyday people as activists (see chapter 6). In many cases, celebrities and traditional media have overwhelming voice and influence (see chapters 4, 5, and 8). However, in other cases such as health communities, individual patients can be viewed as authorities whose voice Twitter has helped make legitimate (see chapter 7).

"Aware" Communities

In this book, the aim has been to explore the larger implications of Twitter for modern social, political, and economic life. Part of this exploration has involved examining the ways in which Twitter is both individualistic and communal. Barry Wellman, whose work has extensively covered the social implications of the internet and the rise of a more networked society (Wellman 1999; Wellman and Haythornthwaite 2002), remarked (in reference to the role of GPS navigation systems) that the technology is framed as "me-centric" as opposed to the society-centric focus that reading a physical map gives us (i.e., a greater context of our surroundings).[4] In a me-centric world, the focus is on you/your life/things from your vantage point, and is myopically oriented to "the moment." From Wellman's point of view,[5] it can also illustrate where your life is going (in terms of your momentum), whereas a society-centric view places primacy on your role in society as part of a collection of people. Though it appears that Twitter is me-centric, this binary does not seem to describe Twitter as well as it does GPS, the reason being that Twitter, as discussed, can help maintain communities (especially ad hoc ones) that resemble more society-centric formations, such as the cancer support groups (discussed in chapter 7) and communities in the aftermath of a disaster (discussed in chapter 5). The binary is useful in highlighting how Twitter can be viewed from two oppositional perspectives. Moreover, our social lives are not constructed from a mutually exclusive relationship between me-centric and society-centric. Rather, many of our daily activities straddle both. Twitter follows suit and is simultaneously individualistic and communal (as well as banal and profound). Furthermore, Twitter's (real/perceived) role in major news events (ranging from the downing of US Airways Flight 1549 to the 2011 "Arab Spring" movements and the 2016 Kaikoura earthquake in New Zealand) is framed as society-centric. The fact that Twitter has become mainstream through these events continues to change its demography and the ways in which the medium is used. Though social communication in the Twitter age may seem me-centric, there is more happening than meets the eye. One glance at the stream of tweets after a disaster provides evidence of society-centric awareness systems such as the "ambient" news environment discussed in chapter 4. Though I have argued that Twitter should not be viewed as a toppler of governments, perhaps, at another level, tweeting together can introduce us to new people and new ideas locally and globally. It may be making us aware of broader issues and engaging us with non-homophilic communities. At 140 characters at a time, tweeters support a complex update culture which, in many ways, represents a thriving – albeit disjointed – group capable of both the banal and the profound, sometimes simultaneously.

Twitter as Mainstream, yet Unique

Twitter maintains a unique position in contemporary social, political, and economic life. The combination of the medium's brevity and simplicity and mass diffusion has brought together a set of characteristics that has made it attractive. This is the case not only for individual people who broadcast thoughts, feelings, and ideas, but also for politicians, celebrities, and other prominent people who do the same. Twitter is simultaneously a very public and private space in that much of the communication that exists on the platform is never really heard by anyone except the person tweeting or a couple of other people. The vast majority of tweets theoretically have a large reach, but are only really being seen by a small group. At the same time, there are tweets circulating by more prominent people or opinion leaders in particular domains (from particular occupational domains to hobby/interest areas) that command a much greater influence on the platform. This is of course true with social communication more generally and social media more broadly. In other words, social communication is always stratified. However, the openness of Twitter in terms of being able to engage with anyone through an @-mention continues to be one of the unique aspects of Twitter that have captured the public imagination. Another simultaneous characteristic of Twitter is that many tweets are not inherently produced to be consumed by others. Having studied Twitter for nearly a decade, it has become clear to me that many also see value in writing things down and posting them on Twitter, much like they regarded diaries in the past (Murthy forthcoming). One of the interesting aspects of Twitter, not initially realized by scholars, is that not everyone on Twitter wants to be heard. Indeed, it is tempting for some to paint broad brushstrokes, labeling the platform as riddled with attention seekers. However, we should be careful in making totalizing arguments like this. In many ways, this could hardly be farther from the truth. Twitter has many individuals not crying out or chatting all the time, but using the medium to keep their finger on the pulse of what is relevant to them. Other users do, of course, choose to communicate many details about their lives on a daily basis.

That said, the proliferation of the Internet of Things (IoT) has made it easier for those regularly wanting to produce content about their lives. Specifically, in the case of fitness trackers, it is very easy to have your device automatically tweet updates about how far you have run, the number of steps you have taken during the day, how many calories you have burned, or where you have cycled to. These automatic postings do not have to originate from IoT devices, but could be coming from automatic posting of the weather in your area, Spotify favorites, recipes used, or items purchased from Amazon. In this way, Twitter has become part of a larger sharing culture (see Meikle 2016, for a fuller discussion). This is not something new, but harks back to long-standing trends of human communication. After all, we are social animals who want to share with others what is happening to us. People have shared Polaroids in the past with friends, sent clippings of news stories they found were interesting, and written letters. The difference with Twitter is that the volume of this has increased many times, as well as the speed at which it is happening. And our diverse responses to platforms such as Twitter can in part be attributable to the increases in this volume and speed, which we still have not fully understood in terms of its impact on our lives. Like previous electronic communication technologies, Twitter is compressing space and time. Moreover, as Luke (1997: 103) argues, "Each new technology and discourse of modernity fabricates its own complex of technoregions to be conquered and mastered" and we are still in the early stages of social communication in the Twitter age. Though Twitter is a fast-moving target and one that is challenging, there is now more need than ever to understand it.

The Future

Twitter is a very active medium and presents a wide range of possible areas to study. This book has started the conversation rather than concluding it. For example, one area not explored here is censorship, a subject that has been invoked with reference to newsgroups, websites, blogs, and many other internet spaces. Twitter has had an explicit "tweets must flow" policy since 2011, which was penned by co-founder Biz Stone (Stone 2011). And the limits of the platform have been historically tested. Take the case of Peter Daou's (@peterdaou) tweet in August 2011: "Unbelievable: Is Twitter REALLY allowing #reasonstobeatyourgirlfriend to be a trending topic??!"[6] Twitter activists responded to the #reasonstobeatyourgirlfriend with the hashtags #violenceisnotfunny and #14oreasonsdvisnotajoke (led by @feministing). The latter hashtag was picked up by prominent Twitter users, including @nationalnow (the US-based National Organization of Women) and @Fem2pto, who used this hashtag to counter tweets encouraging domestic violence. Despite this response, a significant number of users asked for the hashtag to be censored. Cases like this have been plentiful on Twitter over the years. But the surge of the so-called alt-right white nationalist movement on Twitter during the 2016 US presidential election led to the company rethinking parts of the "tweets must flow" policy. They banned prominent members of the movement such as Charles Johnson "for soliciting donations to 'take out' a Black Lives Matter activist" (Schreckinger 2017). Moreover, in February 2017, Twitter launched a "safe search" feature which was intended to help combat abusive speech (Kuchler 2017). However, when Twitter tried to curb abuse done through the listing notification feature, they grossly misunderstood the situation and had to roll back the change after a mere two hours as users leveraged notifications to identify abusers (Newton 2017). This incident highlights the tension between Twitter's American free-speech ideals and differing legal restrictions on speech worldwide – an issue not restricted to Saudi Arabia and China, but also in European countries such as Germany. Twitter's highly variable corporate footprint outside the USA also has the potential to land the medium in legal disputes over hate speech and other "problematic content."

Clearly, Twitter has political, social, and economic effects, and the multitude of specific cases could never be fully captured in a book like this. Ultimately, it is a communications medium and its perception and use are socially constructed. Issues ranging from bullying to excessive intrusions of privacy are important to understanding Twitter and, indeed, its future. However, the medium has also fostered innovative social formations built on extensive weak-tie networks, which have updated the world during disasters or helped solve problems through crowdsourced collective intelligence. Like every "new" communications medium, Twitter will be eclipsed at some point in the future. The American Library of Congress is archiving tweets and one day historians will study selections of the enormous corpus of text generated by the Twitterverse. For better or for worse, one thing is clear: Twitter has shaped modern social communication.

Gerry Acuña
@GerryAcuna

🙎⁺ Follow   ⌄

That's the end of that

6:59 PM - 4 Apr 2017 from Earlimart, CA

↩   ↺   ♥

Notes

PREFACE

1 See <https://twitter.com/jack/status/20>.
2 See <https://twitter.com/biz/status/40>.
3 The "screenshot-driven" perspective (see Bonneau, C. (May 2015), "Pursuing the legacy of Aaron Swartz, one tweet at a time. A screenshot-driven essay," M@n@gement 18: 363–9) sees the method of examining screenshots of tweets one at a time as allowing one to "make tangible and visible actions that are often conducted in the form of behind-the-scenes work that is usually not accessible to people outside these situations." Screenshots of tweets with no embedded images are treated as "public domain by the licence of agreement between Twitter members and Twitter" (see Crook, T., *The UK Media Law Pocketbook*, Routledge, 2013, p. 156). Per Polity Press policy, tweets with posted images are only included if explicit permission was granted by the Twitter user posting the image.

CHAPTER 1 WHAT IS TWITTER?

1 Other sites include Blellow, Jaiku, Plurk, and Foursquare.
2 In practice, the question is not indicative of the responses, as they can and do encompass anything of interest to the user, from what one is doing to commenting on an issue (Michaud, cited in Honeycutt and Herring 2009: 1).
3 As long as the user has not restricted access to their tweets. A minority of users make their tweets "protected," a status by which only approved "followers" of their tweets have access to them. In this case, a Twitter-based "conversation" could only occur with permitted followers.
4 See <http://dl.acm.org/citation.cfm?id=2890088>, p. 576.
5 Biz Stone is also a Twitter co-founder.

6 See: <https://twitter.com/lauriehandler/status/80347952807303 1681>.

7 Some of these services are now defunct. Friendfeed was acquired by Facebook. Jaiku was purchased by Google. Squeelr has since shut down.

8 Except for the small minority of users who make their Twitter profiles private.

9 Twitter has been labeled a microblog technology due to the medium's combination of "text messaging with the instant messaging cultures of the PC and Internet, as well as blogging and social networking" (Goggin 2011: 125). Microblogging services, like Twitter, are one type of social media.

10 However, the types of content afforded by each medium generally differ. Instagram, for example, is preferred by many users for fashion-related content.

11 For example, Serena Beakhurst, a 14-year-old girl from London, went missing in January 2011 and tweets about her case were retweeted by celebrities, which raised the profile of the case. Ultimately, the London Metropolitan Police found Serena.

12 Personal interview.

13 At: <https://twitter.com/JayseDavid/status/8512236629760040 96>.

CHAPTER 2 CONTEXTUALIZING TWITTER

1 The advent of internet-based technologies has often been understood through the "global village" (Hanson 2007; Jefferis 2002; Levinson 2001; Wellman 1999).

CHAPTER 3 THEORIZING TWITTER

1 At: <https://twitter.com/NatashaT_R/status/137273653527195648>.

2 Tying this back to Goffman, these changes in social communication are part of "ego" and "personal feelings," and are critical to understanding Twitter and, especially, its role in self-production.

3 Bakhtin and Holquist (1981) refer to this as a "dialogic community."

4 Furthermore, we should not underestimate the startling ability of states to pull the plug, as occurred in Egypt in 2011.

5 An ad campaign in the UK run by BMI (British Midland Airways)

has billboards proclaiming "Skype is good, but it can't give you a hug." BMI's billboards, albeit purely for marketing purposes, serve as a direct challenge to telepresence and a call for users to privilege physical face-to-face contact over mediated communication.

6 The ability to fly off here and there is not possible for everyone. For example, marginalized asylum-seekers and other underprivileged migrants reading the BMI billboards (see note 5) in London have no other choice than mediated communication. Therefore, privileging face-to-face communication over mediated communication in cases such as these is itself stratified by socioeconomic factors.

7 See "Quote tweet" in the Glossary. Quote tweets embed a tweet from another user into a new tweet, allowing the retweeting user to add original text rather than a straightforward retweet.

8 However, this assumes that the response exchanges can be paired into "dialogic units," as Goffman (1981: 6) refers to them.

9 At: <https://twitter.com/DRUDGE_REPORT/status/8523841274 20579841>.

10 Additionally, the diminishing of the illocutionary force of tweets may be accelerated when non-native English speakers enter the predominantly English Twitterverse. But, paradoxically, Twitter may be increasing illocutionary force for non-native speakers of the global lingua franca who enter into this English-dominated media space because it may require less English-language competency.

Chapter 4   Twitter and Journalism

1 At: <https://twitter.com/reykai/status/5200756062>.

2 At: <https://twitter.com/Enrique_Acevedo/status/867243747008 012289>.

3 At: <https://twitter.com/i/web/status/7784517470438154626>.

4 See chapter 6.

5 At: <http://twitpic.com/135xa>.

6 At: <https://twitter.com/dupree_/status/1025231955>.

7 At: <https://twitter.com/ashokjjr/status/1026419764>.

8 At: <https://twitter.com/dina/status/1026416468>.

9 An example of one request from the *New York Post* is: <https://twitter.com/yaldamn/status/851397008896258050>.

10 At: <https://mobile.twitter.com/yaldamn/status/851397008896 258050>.

11 A group they term "Living in the Business World."
12 A group they term "Reliving the College Days."
13 Furthermore, far from being concerned about tweeting, these households are more focused on getting food on the table. This situation has been amplified by the current economic recession.
14 At: <<http://www.frontlinesms.com/>.
15 Of course, Twitter and text messaging are not mutually exclusive. Indeed, far from it.
16 At: <http://yfrog.com/kh807bmj>
17 At: <https://twitter.com/hugorifkind/status/8017845822573813 76>; Rifkind's tweet was subsequently deleted.
18 At: <https://twitter.com/sarahkendzior/status/80180549899128 8320>.
19 For example, Morozov (2009) argues that the "Iranian Twitter revolution" was itself a construction of the American media.

Chapter 5 Twitter and Disasters

1 At: <https://twitter.com/vickkysoni/status/7990344743904296 97>.
2 At: <https://twitter.com/ZeherAkash/status/79903171141373131328>.
3 The Sri Lankan government's land grab of prime coastal property for hotel development, rather than returning the land to the villagers who had lived on it for generations, makes this painfully clear in the aftermath of the 2004 Indian Ocean tsunami (Cohen 2011).
4 He adds that 90 percent of loan applications from inner-city South Central Los Angeles were refused (Steinberg 2000: 178).
5 These would be the online equivalent of what the sociologist Émile Durkheim (1964) refers to as communities with "organic" forms of solidarity.
6 When they are given a podium in cyberspace, it becomes even more tempting to equate this with a high level of agency amongst disaster victims. Furthermore, access to these technologies is highly stratified in "developing" nation-states (Hoffman 2004).
7 These "representations" are, following de Certeau, understood not as absolute representations. Rather, a key significance of them is the way in which they are consumed.
8 Online donations to 2004 Indian Ocean tsunami relief agencies were unprecedented. The American wing of the NGO Action Against Hunger raised over $400,000 online in the first 10 days

after the tsunami, an amount just short of the organization's total 2004 donations (Aitchison, cited in Glasius et al. 2005: 7).

9 At: <https://www.youtube.com/watch?v=bP1UMqJuW1I>.

10 At: <https://www.facebook.com/nepalphotoproject/>.

11 See Leach's (2005) critique of the reporting of the 2004 Indian Ocean tsunami.

12 Trending topics appear in a box within the profile pages of all Twitter users. Additionally, given this placement within Twitter as well as search engine results, users are known to be guided to trending topics (Abrol and Khan 2010). See chapter 1 for a further discussion on the importance of trending topics.

13 There were 300 Twitter users selected from this sample for further study (the 100 users with the most tweets, the 100 most at-mentioned users, and 100 randomly selected users).

14 But it also reveals that Western users were the ones who enabled Pakistan to become a trending topic, rather than users based in Pakistan (the USA had the highest frequency of tweets; almost double that of Pakistani Twitter users).

15 At: <https://twitter.com/wyclef/status/7707325967>.

16 At: <https://twitter.com/aplusk/status/15761318365221 6832>.

17 At: <https://twitter.com/danieljgillies/status/79944968214563 6356>.

18 At: <https://twitter.com/NewshubBreaking/status/79828508504 4711424>.

19 Ibid.

20 At: <https://www.youtube.com/watch?v=7Yoik3MmKgI> and <https://www.youtube.com/watch?v=LCXv9lhlIwU>.

21 At: <https://twitter.com/EQCNZ/status/797772171112157184>.

22 At: <https://twitter.com/NZcivildefence/status/79783384516896 7680>.

23 At: <https://twitter.com/SkyNews/status/79814080241324 0320>.

24 At: <https://twitter.com/JKCorden/status/7978283528117575 68>.

25 At: <https://twitter.com/RCArmitage/status/7978196698099 50720>.

Chapter 6   Twitter and Activism

1 At: <https://twitter.com/Timcast/status/1408465956116889 60>.

2 At an average of 200 characters and the 95th percentile at 250 characters (Davies and Barber 1973).

3 Of course, this depends on what criteria are applied to defining "Arab Spring" countries.

4 At: <https://twitter.com/TrayneshaCole/status/80624567718550 7328>.

5 Full discussions of SMOs exist elsewhere (Earl 2015).

6 At: <https://twitter.com/RuthHHopkins/status/804570003785 846784>.

7 At: <https://twitter.com/SpeakerRyan/status/8055628929218314 24>.

8 Excepting the fact that governments detained and arrested some individuals based on Twitter activity.

9 However, other expatriate Twitter activists, including @oxfordgirl, feared reprisals on family in MENA countries.

CHAPTER 7   TWITTER AND HEALTH

1 At: <https://twitter.com/_Tattycoram_/status/1412552840384512 00>.

2 At: <https://twitter.com/dperkins28/status/8486756931561144 32>.

3 At: <https://twitter.com/_Katleho_/status/8547748092087787 53>.

4 At: <https://twitter.com/vnnv__/status/855195067643863040>.

5 This is part of a larger trend that gained critical mass from the turn of the twentieth century: by 2009, 61 percent of adult Americans looked online for health information (Fox and Jones 2009: 2). Of these "e-patients," 41 percent "have read someone else's commentary or experience about health or medical issues on an online news group, website, or blog" (ibid.: 3). Additionally, 15 percent of e-patients "have posted comments, queries, or information about health or medical matters" (ibid.: 17). Though the last percentage may seem small, this sharing of personal health information on social networking sites represented a starting point that paved the way for Twitter to be used in health contexts. Moreover, the use of social media among older internet users (aged 65 and older) also grew from a mere 2 percent in 2005 to 35 percent by 2015 (Perrin 2015: 3).

6 At: <https://twitter.com/bswhealth_NTX/status/567484870494 928896>.

7 At: <https://twitter.com/bswhealth_NTX/status/567493662804 697089>.

8 At: <https://twitter.com/bswhealth_NTX/status/567496839784439808>.

9 At: <https://twitter.com/HealthyBoston/status/804060164336873473>.

10 At: <http://twitter.com/ALSUntangled>.

11 See chapters 4–5.

12 See chapter 3 for a discussion of social capital.

13 Cancer survivors are a group considered "lost in transition" in terms of healthcare support (Hewitt et al. 2006). Twitter may be providing them with a solution to this situation.

14 At: <https://twitter.com/Dozyhead/status/21944796979>.

15 At: <https://twitter.com/DrAnasYounes/status/21954348261>

16 All tweets containing five cancer-related keywords – "chemo," "lymphoma," "mammogram," "melanoma," and "cancer survivor" – were collected from December 15, 2010, to May 12, 2011.

17 The data confirm this.

18 See chapters 1–3.

19 At: <https://twitter.com/abolishcancer/status/28912463027>.

20 See chapter 4 for a fuller discussion.

CHAPTER 8 CELEBRITIES AND BRANDING

1 At: <https://twitter.com/BetteMidler/status/70691409356787302 4>.

2 For example, see: <https://twitter.com/KimKardashian/status/767010808979070977>.

3 At: <https://twitter.com/KimKardashian/status/781590523656212480/>.

4 At: <https://twitter.com/kimyonceee/status/832368899244978176>.

5 At: <https://twitter.com/KFILE/status/477299992671948800>.

6 At: <https://twitter.com/stephenfry/status/797444433264320512/>.

7 Stephen Fry had already deleted his "I want to leave the planet" tweet. It was at <https://twitter.com/stephenfry/status/698989876725878784>. It is archived at: <http://web.archive.org/web/20160214235817/https://twitter.com/stephenfry/status/698989876725878784>.

8 At: <https://twitter.com/stephenfry/status/807012156071759873>.

9 See, e.g.: <https://twitter.com/benthompson/status/6392176445 25088769>.
10 At: <https://www.youtube.com/watch?v=5YGc4zOqozo>.
11 At: <https://www.youtube.com/watch?v=OhBmWxQpedI>.
12 At: <https://www.youtube.com/watch?v=dem6eA7-A2I>.
13 At: <https://twitter.com/AskAmex/status/8087550701163806 72>.
14 At: <https://twitter.com/AmexOffers/status/8298014603428659 31>.
15 At: <https://twitter.com/MacAdamOquendo/status/82686706 0869365765>.
16 At: <https://twitter.com/loco_motive/status/8268271269051760 64>.
17 At: <https://twitter.com/jgrosedesign/status/8227708297506283 52>.
18 Based on this tweet: <https://twitter.com/dhirajmurthy/status/83 2294431508213760>.

CHAPTER 9 CONCLUSION

1 At: <https://twitter.com/VERBALARTISAN/status/1415 77119359709184>. Though in the public domain, permission from @VERBALARTISAN was granted to reproduce this screenshot.
2 Who, it should be noted, has over 10 million followers, a record first reached by @ladygaga.
3 At: <https://twitter.com/run_andrew_run/status/77488208472 047616>.
4 Email sent to the email list of the Communication and Information Technology section of the American Sociological Association (CITASA) by Barry Wellman on July 9, 2011.
5 Email sent to the email list of the Communication and Information Technology section of the American Sociological Association (CITASA) by Barry Wellman on July 9, 2011.
6 At: <https://twitter.com/peterdaou/status/97642435060039 680>.

Glossary

@-mention	Abbreviated as @ or referred to as a "mention," within Twitter this provides a means for users to direct tweets to specific user(s); discussions on Twitter often leverage @-mentions in order for speaker and recipient to be easily identifiable (e.g., "@realDonaldTrump Make America Great Again!")
bulltwit	bullshit tweets; tweets that are deemed to be fake, unsubstantiated, or not worth paying attention to
direct message	this refers to a private tweet between two individuals; direct messages (often abbreviated as DM) are like an email or instant message which is not published publicly to one's followers
DM	see "direct message"
dtweet	tweet sent while intoxicated; a contraction of "drunken tweet"
Explore	A section of the Twitter website and app which serves as a portal for displaying popular content from the platform; Explore displays both trending hashtags (see "trending topics") and popular news content (see "Moments")
fail whale	when Twitter has been over capacity (especially during major world events), a picture of a whale is displayed and this image has become known as the "fail whale"

FF	see "Follow Friday"
follow	this indicates that one has elected to "subscribe" to the tweets of another user to be displayed in their timeline (see "timeline")
Follow Friday	on Fridays, Twitter users use the hashtag (#FF) to suggest Twitter users to follow
follower	a user who has elected to follow you (see "follow"); a list of followers including a total number of followers is listed on a user's profile page
following	this refers to users one follows (see "follow")
hashtag	this refers to subject classifiers within tweets; by using # before any text, a user can identify their tweet with a larger conversation topic (e.g., #Brexit)
lists	groups of Twitter users can be associated with a list which any Twitter user can curate; lists are public and span everything from professional groups to lists of musical groups
mistweet	accidental tweet; particularly important when content is accidentally publicly tweeted rather than sent via Direct Message (DM) (see "direct message")
Moments	a "news" aggregation feature, now integrated in the Explore tab (see "Explore"); Moments uses a proprietary algorithm to display what Twitter considers to be the most relevant popular content for a user; categories such as Sports, News, and Entertainment can be selected; it is used by some users as a news portal, given its continuous updating
profile	the equivalent of a "homepage" on Twitter; a user's biographical information, profile picture, published tweets, followers, and following are displayed

promoted	trending topics (see "trending topics") are placed at the top of the trending topic list or tweets are placed at the top of search results for a fee paid to Twitter
PRT	please retweet; this encourages followers to retweet one's tweet
quote tweet	a sub-function of retweet (see "retweet") which allows users to fully quote/embed a tweet with a new tweet of their own; in other words, this function is used to retweet with comments
reply tweet	a tweet which replies to another Twitter user(s) directly via an at-mention (see "at-mention")
retweet	this is the term given to the act of forwarding tweets written by others; a retweet (often abbreviated as RT) is viewable by one's followers; retweets can also comment on tweets using the quote function (see "quote tweet")
RT	see "retweet"
timeline	a list of all tweets which are displayed real-time; one's own timeline displays one's tweets as well as tweets by others
TMB	tweet me back; requests a response back from followers or other recipients of the tweet
TMI	Too Much Information, used to refer to levels of information disclosure perceived as high or excessive
trending topics	Twitter maintains lists of hashtags which are the most popular hashtags at the time; these are prominently visible on the site
twaddict	a colloquial expression referring to an individual who is perceived as addicted to Twitter (synonymous with "tweetaholic")
twalking	tweeting while walking; can also lead to mistweets (see "mistweet" entry)

tweeps	this term is derived from the colloquial word "peeps," which refers to one's friends or "peoples." On Twitter, this has been extended to refer to one's Twitter friends (i.e., one's followers on Twitter)
tweet	messages on Twitter; tweets are restricted to, as of November 2017, 280 characters and are usually publicly visible to anyone regardless of whether they have a Twitter account
tweeter	a Twitter user
twilliterate	a colloquial term referring to those who are unfamiliar with Twitter; it was made particularly popular through a viral YouTube video called "The Twitter Song"
twitiquette	Twitter etiquette
Twitterati	an elite set of Twitter users; this more often refers to celebrity Twitter users who are highly active in the medium (e.g., Katy Perry, Rihanna, Justin Bieber, and Stephen Fry)
twitter-crastination	a colloquial expression referring to the use of Twitter as a procrastination tool
Twitterer	see "tweeter"
twitterpated	a colloquial expression referring to being overwhelmed by tweets
Twitterverse	the entire user community of Twitter; generalizations about the Twitter population often invoke this term
twug	a Twitter hug which can be used in many contexts ranging from between friends to within support communities on Twitter

References

@twitaholic 2017 "The Twitaholic.com Top 100 Twitterholics based on followers," available at: <http://twitaholic.com/>.

Abbey-Lambertz, K. 2016 "White man accused of killing black teen who bumped into him," *The Huffington Post* (November 23); at: <http://www.huffingtonpost.com/entry/james-means-william-pulliam-racist-killing_us_5835ea6de4b000af95edad9e>.

Abrol, S. and Khan, L. 2010 "TWinner: understanding news queries with geo-content using Twitter," *Proceedings of the 6th Workshop on Geographic Information Retrieval*, Zurich, Switzerland: ACM.

Adamopoulos, P. and Todri, V. 2014 *Social Media Analytics: The Effectiveness of Promotional Events on Brand User Base in Social Media.* Paper presented at the ICIS 2014, Auckland, New Zealand.

Adkins, B. A. and Nasarczyk, J. 2009 "Asynchronicity and the 'time envelope' of online annotation: the case of the photosharing website, Flickr," *Australian Journal of Communication* 35(3): 115–40.

Adorno, T. W. and Bernstein, J. M. 1991 *The Culture Industry: Selected Essays on Mass Culture*, London: Routledge.

Allen, R. C. 1992 *Channels of Discourse, Reassembled: Television and Contemporary Criticism*, 2nd edn, Chapel Hill, NC: University of North Carolina Press.

ALSUntangled 2015 "ALSUntangled: introducing the table of evidence," *Amyotrophic Lateral Sclerosis and Frontotemporal Degeneration* 16(1–2): 142–5.

ALSUntangled 2016 *Completed Reviews*; available at: <http://www.alsuntangled.com/completed.html>.

Amatulli, J. 2016 "One of Kim Kardashian's stolen necklaces found on Paris sidewalk," *The Huffington Post* (October 10); available at: <http://www.huffingtonpost.com/entry/kim-kardashian-robbery-necklace-found_us_57fbf307e4b0b6a43034bbfb>.

Anderson, M. 2015 *Technology Device Ownership: 2015*; available at: <http://www.pewinternet.org/2015/10/29/technology-device-ownership-2015/>.

Andrews, P. 2013 *Sports Journalism: A Practical Introduction* (2nd edn), Thousand Oaks, CA: Sage Publications.

Arrabal-Sánchez, G. and De-Aguilera-Moyano, M. 2016 "Communicating in 140 characters. How journalists in Spain use Twitter," *Comunicar* (46): 9–17.

Associated Press of Pakistan 2010 "1,802 confirmed dead in floods: Kaira," *Associated Press of Pakistan*, Islamabad: Associated Press of Pakistan.

Attai, D. J., Cowher, M. S., Al-Hamadani, M., Schoger, J. M., Staley, A. C., and Landercasper, J. 2015 "Twitter social media is an effective tool for breast cancer patient education and support: patient-reported outcomes by survey," *Journal of Medical Internet Research* 17(7): e188.

Austin, M. 2011 *Useful Fictions: Evolution, Anxiety, and the Origins of Literature*, Lincoln, NB: University of Nebraska Press.

Australian Broadcasting Corporation News. 2016 "New Zealand earthquake: Tsunami hits after magnitude-7.8 quake strikes near Christchurch," *Australian Broadcasting Corporation* (November 14); available at: <http://www.abc.net.au/news/2016-11-13/new-zealand-earthquake-hits-near-christchurch-generating-tsunami/8021922>.

Ayoo, P. O. 2009 "Reflections on the digital divide and its implications for the internationalization of higher education in a developing region: The Case of East Africa," *Higher Education Policy* 22(3): 30–18.

Bakhtin, M. M. and Holquist, M. 1981 *The Dialogic Imagination: Four Essays*, Austin, TX: University of Texas Press.

Barabási, A.-L. 2003 *Linked: How Everything is Connected to Everything Else and What it Means for Business, Science, and Everyday Life*, New York: Plume.

Barnard, S. R. 2016 "'Tweet or be sacked': Twitter and the new elements of journalistic practice," *Journalism* 17(2): 190–207.

Barton, A. 1969 *Communities in Disaster: A Sociological Analysis of Collective Stress Situations*, Garden City, NY: Doubleday & Company, Inc.

Bassett, M. T. 2015 "#BlackLivesMatter – a challenge to the medical and public health communities," *New England Journal of Medicine* 372(12): 1085–7.

Bates, F. L. and Peacock, W. G. 1987 "Disasters and social change," in R. R. Dynes, B. D. Marchi, and C. Pelanda (eds), *Sociology of Disasters: Contribution of Sociology to Disaster Research*, Milan: Franco Angeli Libri.

Baudelaire, C. 1965 "The modern public and photography," part 2 of "The salon of 1859," in J. Mayne (ed.), *Art in Paris, 1845–1862*, London: Phaidon Publishers; distributed by New York Graphic Society Publishers, Greenwich.

Bauman, Z. 2000 *Liquid Modernity*, Cambridge, UK: Polity.

Baym, N. K. 2015 *Personal Connections in the Digital Age* (2nd edn), Cambridge; Malden, MA: Polity.

BBC News 2008 "As it happened: Mumbai attacks 27 November," BBC News.

Beaumont, C. 2008 "Mumbai attacks: Twitter and Flickr used to break news," *The Telegraph*, London: Telegraph Media Group Ltd; available at: <http://www.telegraph.co.uk/news/worldnews/asia/india/3530640/Mumbai-attacks-Twitter-and-Flickr-used-to-breaknews-Bombay-India.html>.

Beaumont, C. 2009 "New York plane crash: Twitter breaks the news, again," *The Telegraph*, London: Telegraph Media Group Ltd; available at: <http://www.telegraph.co.uk/technology/twitter/4269765/NewYork-plane-crash-Twitter-breaks-the-news-again.html>.

Beaumont, P. 2011 "Friends, followers and countrymen: The uprisings in Libya, Tunisia and Egypt have been called 'Twitter revolutions' – but can social networking overthrow a government? Peter Beaumont reports from the Middle East on how activists are really using the web," *Guardian*, February 25, 2011, p. 4, London: Guardian Newspapers Limited.

Bedlack, R. and Hardiman, O. 2009 "ALSUntangled (ALSU): a scientific approach to Off-Label Treatment Options for People with ALS Using Tweets and Twitters," *Amyotrophic Lateral Sclerosis* 10(3): 129–30.

Benedictus, L. 2010 "Twitter's old hat if you've used The Notificator," *Guardian*, June 15, 2010, London: Guardian News and Media Limited; available at: <http://www.guardian.co.uk/technology/2010/jun/15/the-notificator-precursor-of-twitter>.

Benn, T. 2011 "The flowers of the Arab spring grow from buds of free information," *New Statesman* 140(5048): 12.

Bennett, W. L. and Toft, A. 2009 "Identity, technology, and narratives: transnational activism and social networks," in A. Chadwick and P. N. Howard (eds), *Routledge Handbook of Internet Politics*, London and New York: Routledge, pp. 246–60.

Berman, M. 1982 *All That is Solid Melts into Air: The Experience of Modernity*, New York: Simon and Schuster.

Bianco, J. S. 2009 "Social networking and cloud computing: precarious affordances for the 'prosumer'," *Women's Studies Quarterly* 37(1&2): 303–12.

Bianculli, D. 1992 *Teleliteracy: Taking Television Seriously*, New York: Continuum.

Black, I. 2011 "Death of Bin Laden: analysis: al-Qaida's influence slips from marginal to almost irrelevant in light of Arab Spring: uprisings bypassed forces of militant Islamism Twitter and Facebook had more effect than 'martyrs'," *Guardian*, May 3, 2011, p. 16, London: Guardian Newspapers Limited.

Blair, W. 1915 *I Hear a Little Twitter and a Song. Words by G. Plass*, Cincinnati: J. Church Co.

Blank, G. 2016 "The digital divide among Twitter users and its implications for social research," *Social Science Computer Review*; doi:10.1177/0894439316671698.

Blau, J. 2006 "Talk Is cheap," *IEEE Spectrum* 43(10): 14–16.

Bliven, B. 1924 "How radio is remaking our world," *20th Century Magazine* 108: 149.

Bloom, D. 2016 "New Zealand earthquake: stranded cows rescued," *CNN.com*; available at: <http://www.cnn.com/2016/11/14/asia/new-zealand-stranded-cows-trnd/>.

Boaz, J. 1802 *A Few Particulars Respecting Mr. Boaz's Patent Telegraph*, London: Unknown.

Bolger, N., Davis, A., and Rafaeli, E. 2003 "Diary methods: capturing life as it is lived," *Annual Review of Psychology* 54(1): 579–616.

Bonilla, Y. and Rosa, J. 2015 "# Ferguson: digital protest, hashtag ethnography, and the racial politics of social media in the United States," *American Ethnologist* 42(1): 4–17.

Bonneau, C. 2015 "Pursuing the legacy of Aaron Swartz, one tweet at a time. A screenshot-driven essay," *M@ n@ gement* 18(5): 363–9.

Boon, S. and Sinclair, C. 2009 "A world I don't inhabit: disquiet and identity in Second Life and Facebook," *Educational Media International* 46(2): 99–110.

Borchers, C. 2017 "The real cost of Trump's 'fake news' accusations," *The Washington Post* (April 18); available at: <https://www.washingtonpost.com/news/the-fix/wp/2017/04/18/the-real-cost-of-trumps-fake-news-accusations/? utm_term=.6529f83454e0>.

Bourdieu, P. 1984 *Distinction: A Social Critique of the Judgement of Taste*, Cambridge, MA: Harvard University Press.

Bowen, S. A. 2013 "Using classic social media cases to distill ethical guidelines for digital engagement," *Journal of Mass Media Ethics* 28(2): 119–33.

boyd, d. m. and Ellison, N. B. 2008 "Social network sites: definition, history, and scholarship," *Journal of Computer-Mediated Communication* 13(1): 210–30.

boyd, d. and Marwick, A. E. 2010 "I tweet honestly, I tweet passion-ately: Twitter users, context collapse, and the imagined audience," *New Media & Society* 13(1): 114–33.

boyd, d. m., Golder, S., and Lotan, G. 2010 "Tweet, tweet, retweet: conversational aspects of retweeting on Twitter," *2010 43rd Hawaii International Conference on System Sciences*, Koloa, Kauai, Hawaii.

Bracken, C. C. and Skalski, P. D. 2009 *Immersed in Media: Telepresence in Everyday Life*, New York: Routledge.

Brindley, D. 2015 "How one Korean taco truck launched an $800 million industry," *National Geographic*; available at: <http://ngm. nationalgeographic.com/2015/07/food-trucks/brindley-text>.

Bruns, A. 2005 *Gatewatching: Collaborative Online News Production*, New York: P. Lang.

Bruns, A. and Burgess, J. E. 2011 "New methodologies for research-ing news discussion on Twitter," in *The Future of Journalism*, 8–9 September 2011, Cardiff: Cardiff University (unpublished); available at: <http://eprints.qut.edu.au/46330/>.

Bryant, J. and Miron, D. 2004 "Theory and research in mass commu-nication," *Journal of Communication* 54(4): 662–704.

Bull, M. 2005 "No dead air! The iPod and the culture of mobile listen-ing," *Leisure Studies* 24(4): 343–55.

Burgess, J. and Green, J. 2009 *YouTube: Online Video and Participatory Culture*, Cambridge, UK, and Malden, MA: Polity.

Burns, A. 2010 "Oblique strategies for ambient journalism," *M/C Journal* 13(2).

Butcher, L. 2009 "How Twitter is transforming the cancer care com-munity," *Oncology Times* 31(21): 36–9.

Butcher, L. 2010a "Oncologists using Twitter to advance cancer knowl-edge," *Oncology Times*: 32(1): 8–10.

Butcher, L. 2010b "Profiles in oncology social media: Naoto T. Ueno, MD, PhD – @teamoncology," *Oncology Times* 32(13): 38–9.

Butler, J. G. 2010 *Television Style*, New York: Routledge.

Callcott, J. G. 1863 *The First Twitter of Spring. Part Song, Written by W. S. Passmore*, London: Foster & King.

Castells, M. 1996 *The Rise of the Network Society*, Cambridge, MA, and Oxford: Blackwell.

Castells, M. 2000 "Materials for an exploratory theory of the network society," *British Journal of Sociology* 51(1): 5–24.

CBS 2011 "Wael Ghonim and Egypt's new age revolution" *60 Minutes*, USA.

Celik, H., Lagro-Janssen, T., Klinge, I., van der Weijden, T., and Widdershoven, G. 2009 "Maintaining gender sensitivity in the family practice: facilitators and barriers," *Journal of Evaluation in Clinical Practice* 15(6): 1220–25.

Cha, M., Haddadi, H., Benevenuto, F., and Gummadi, K. 2010 "Measuring user influence in Twitter: the million follower fallacy," *Fourth International AAAI Conference on Weblogs and Social Media*, George Washington University.

Chatterji, M. 2016 "Tremors in Delhi, Gurgaon after 4.4 magnitude earthquake today in Haryana," *NDTV* (November 17); available at: <http://www.ndtv.com/delhi-news/huge-earthquake-tremors-felt-in-delhi-1626442>.

Chib, A., van Velthoven, M. H., and Car, J. 2015 "mHealth adoption in low-resource environments: a review of the use of mobile healthcare in developing countries," *Journal of Health Communication* 20(1): 4–34.

Chisolm, D. J. and Sarkar, M. 2015 "E-health use in African American internet users: can new tools address old disparities?" *Telemedicine and e-Health* 21(3): 163–9.

Chou, W.-y. S., Hunt, Y., Beckjord, E. B., Moser, R., and Hesse, B. 2009 "Social media use in the United States: implications for health communication," *Journal of Medical Internet Research* 11(4): 48.

Christensen, C. 2011 "Twitter revolutions? Addressing social media and dissent," *The Communication Review* 14(3): 155–7.

Christensen, C., Bruns, A., Enli, G., Skogerbo, E., and Larsson, A. 2016 *The Routledge Companion to Social Media and Politics*. London: Sage.

Chung, D. S. 2008 "Interactive features of online newspapers: identifying patterns and predicting use of engaged readers," *Journal of Computer-Mediated Communication* 13(3): 658–79.

Cisneros, J. D. and Nakayama, T. K. 2015 "New media, old racisms: Twitter, Miss America, and cultural logics of race," *Journal of International and Intercultural Communication* 8(2): 108–27.

Clapperton, G. 2009 *This is Social Media: How to Tweet, Post, Link and Blog Your Way to Business Success*, Chichester, UK: Capstone.

Clark, A. 2003 *Natural-born Cyborgs: Why Minds and Technologies are Made to Merge*, New York: Oxford University Press.

Clarke, L. 2004 "Using disaster to see society," *Contemporary Sociology* 33(2): 137–9.

Clayfield, M. 2012 "Tweet the press: how social media is changing the way journalists do their jobs," *Metro Magazine: Media and Education Magazine* (171): 92–7.

Cohen, E. 2010 "Aidan's art helps pay for his own cancer care," *CNN Health*, December 3, 2010, Atlanta, GA: CNN.

Cohen, E. 2011 "Tourism and land grab in the aftermath of the Indian Ocean tsunami," *Scandinavian Journal of Hospitality and Tourism* 11(3): 224–36.

Coker, K. K., Smith, D. S., and Altobello, S. A. 2015 "Buzzing with disclosure of social shopping rewards," *Journal of Research in Interactive Marketing* 9(3): 170–89.

Coleman, J. S. 1988 "Social capital in the creation of human capital," *American Journal of Sociology* 94(S1): S95–S120.

Colleoni, E., Rozza, A., and Arvidsson, A. 2014 "Echo chamber or public sphere? Predicting political orientation and measuring political homophily in Twitter using big data," *Journal of Communication*, 64(2): 317–32.

Comninos, A. 2011 "Twitter revolutions and cyber crackdowns: user generated content and social networking in the Arab Spring and beyond," Association for Progressive Communications (APC); available at: <http://www.apc.org/en/system/files/AlexComninos_MobileInternet.pdf>.

Connor-Linton, J. 1999 "Competing communicative styles and crosstalk: a multi-feature analysis," *Language in Society* 28(01): 25–56.

Cottle, S. 2011 "Media and the Arab uprisings of 2011: research notes," *Journalism* 12(5): 647–59.

Courier Mail 2008 "Terrorists turn technology into weapon of war in Mumbai" *Courier Mail*, Queensland: Queensland Newspapers; available at: <http://www.couriermail.com.au/news/world/terrorists-and-technology/story-e6freop6-111111811178210>.

Cravens, J. D., Whiting, J. B., and Aamar, R. O. 2015 "Why I stayed/left: an analysis of voices of intimate partner violence on social media," *Contemporary Family Therapy* 37(4): 372–85.

Crawford, K. 2009 "Following you: disciplines of listening in social media," *Continuum: Journal of Media & Cultural Studies* 23(4): 525–35.

Crimson Hexagon 2017 *Our Thoughts on the Twitter Official Partner Program*; at: <https://www.crimsonhexagon.com/blog/platform/our-thoughts-on-the-twitter-official-partner-program/>.

Crook, T. 2013 *The UK Media Law Pocketbook*, Abingdon: Routledge.

Cropp, M. (Writer) and R. N. Zealand (Director) 2016 "Twitter turns ten(ish) today" (radio), *Morning Report*, Radio New Zealand, March 21, 2016; available at: <http://www.radionz.co.nz/news/national/299507/twitter-turns-ten-ish-today>.

Dailey, D. and Starbird, K. 2016 "Addressing the information needs of crisis-affected communities: the interplay of legacy media and social media in a rural disaster," in M. Lloyd and L. A. Friedland (eds), *The Communication Crisis in America, and How to Fix It.* New York: Palgrave Macmillan US, pp. 285–303.

Daugherty, T. and Hoffman, E. 2014 "eWOM and the importance of capturing consumer attention within social media," *Journal of Marketing Communications* 20(1–2): 82–102.

Davies, D. W. and Barber, D. L. A. 1973 *Communication Networks for Computers,* London and New York: John Wiley.

Dayan, D. 1998 "Particularistic media and diasporic communications," in T. Liebes, J. Curran, and E. Katz (eds), *Media, Ritual, and Identity,* London and New York: Routledge.

De Choudhury, M., Sundaram, H., John, A., Seligmann, D. D., and Kelliher, A. 2010 "'Birds of a feather': does user homophily impact information diffusion in social media?"; available at: <http://arxiv.org/abs/1006.1702>.

Delanty, G. 2006 "The cosmopolitan imagination: critical cosmopolitanism and social theory," *The British Journal of Sociology* 57(1): 25–47.

Dent, J. D. 1795 *The Telegraph, or, a New Way of Knowing Things: A Comic Piece, as Performed at the Theatre Royal, Covent Garden, with Universal Applause,* London: J. Downes & Co.

Derks, D., Bos, A. E. R., and von Grumbkow, J. 2008 "Emoticons in computer-mediated communication: social motives and social context," *CyberPsychology & Behavior* 11(1): 99–101.

DeVoe, K. M. 2009 "Bursts of information: microblogging," *Reference Librarian* 50(2): 212–14.

Dewan, A., Grinberg, E., and O'Sullivan, D. 2016 "New Zealand: dozens of aftershocks follow deadly earthquake," *CNN* (November 14); available at: <http://www.cnn.com/2016/11/13/asia/new-zealand-earthquake/>.

DiMaggio, P., Hargittai, E., Neuman, W. R., and Robinson, J. P. 2001 "Social implications of the Internet," *Annual Review of Sociology* 27(1): 307–36.

DiMicco, J. M. and Millen, D. R. 2007 "Identity management: multiple presentations of self in Facebook," *Proceedings of the 2007 International ACM Conference on Supporting Group Work,* Sanibel Island, Florida, USA: ACM.

D'Innocenzio, A., and Condon, B. 2017 "Donald Trump's latest Twitter battle with Nordstrom fuels concerns about White House conflicts of interest," *The Independent* (February 9); available at: <http://www.independent.co.uk/news/world/americas/donald-trump-twitter-

nordstrom-ivanka-luxury-brand-dropped-white-conflict-interests-us-president-a7570626.html>.

Dobransky, K. and Hargittai, E. 2016 "Unrealized potential: exploring the digital disability divide," *Poetics* 58: 18–28.

Dolnick, S. 2008 "Bloggers provide raw view of Mumbai attacks: dramatic siege threw user-generated corner of the Internet into high gear," Redmond, WA: msnbc.com.

Dreher, H. M. 2009 "Twittering about anything, everything, and even health," *Holistic Nursing Practice* 23(4): 217–21.

Dreyfus, H. L. 2009 *On the Internet*, 2nd edn, London: Routledge.

Dunn, A. 2011 "The Arab Spring: revolution and shifting geopolitics – unplugging a nation: state media strategy during Egypt's January 25 uprising," *The Fletcher Forum of World Affairs Journal* 35(2): 15–24.

Dunn, A. G., Leask, J., Zhou, X., Mandl, K. D., and Coiera, E. 2015 "Associations between exposure to and expression of negative opinions about human papillomavirus vaccines on social media: an observational study," *Journal of Medical Internet Research* 17(6); available at: <http://www.jmir.org/2015/6/e144/>.

Durant, A. 2010 *Meaning in the Media: Discourse, Controversy and Debate*, Cambridge, UK: Cambridge University Press.

Durkheim, É. 1964 *The Division of Labor in Society*, New York: Free Press of Glencoe.

Earl, J. (2015). "The future of social movement organizations: the waning dominance of SMOs online," *American Behavioral Scientist* 59(1): 35–52.

Ebner, M. and Schiefner, M. 2008 "Microblogging – more than fun?," *Proceedings of IADIS Mobile Learning Conference 2008*: 155–9.

Edwards, S. B. and Harris, D. 2016 *Black Lives Matter*, Minneapolis, MN: ABDO.

Egan, M. 2017 "Seattle to cut ties with Wells Fargo over Dakota access pipeline," *CNN* (February 8); available at: <http://money.cnn.com/2017/02/08/investing/seattle-wells-fargo-dakota-access-pipeline/>.

Ellcessor, E. 2010 "Bridging disability divides," *Information, Communication & Society* 13(3): 289–308.

Ellerman, E. 2007 "The Internet in context," in J. Gackenbach (ed.), *Psychology and the Internet: Intrapersonal, Interpersonal, and Transpersonal Implications*, 2nd edn, Amsterdam and Boston, MA: Elsevier/Academic Press.

Elliott, C. 2014 "Why an article on Lisa Bonchek Adams was removed from the Guardian site," *Guardian* (January 16); available at:

<https://www.theguardian.com/commentisfree/2014/jan/16/why-article-lisa-bonchek-adams-removed>.

Emmett, A. 2008 "Networking news," *American Journalism Review* 30(6): 40–43.

Enteen, J. B. 2010 *Virtual English: Queer Internets and Digital Creolization*, New York and London: Routledge.

Esfandiari, G. 2010 "The Twitter devolution," *Foreign Policy*, June 7; available at: <http://www.foreignpolicy.com/articles/2010/06/07/the_twitter_revolution_that_wasnt>.

Fahrenthold, D. A. 2016 "How a Univision anchor found the missing $10,000 portrait that Trump bought with his charity's money," *The Washington Post*; available at: <https://www.washingtonpost.com/news/post-politics/wp/2016/09/21/how-a-univision-anchor-found-the-missing-10000-portrait-that-trump-bought-with-his-charitys-money/?hpid=hp_special-topic-chain_trumpportrait 630pm>.

Fandy, M. 1999 "CyberResistance: Saudi opposition between globalization and localization," *Comparative Studies in Society and History* 41(1): 124–47.

Farber, D. 2011 "P. J. Crowley's Twitter diplomacy" *CNN.com WorldWatch*, Atlanta, GA: CNN.

Farhi, P. 2016 "#Biased? Reporters on Twitter don't hold back about Trump," *The Washington Post* (October 27); available at: <https://www.washingtonpost.com/lifestyle/style/biased-reporters-on-twitter-dont-hold-back-about-trump/2016/10/26/a1002ce4-9b9c-11e6-9980-50913d68eacb_story.html>.

Fatima, I., Halder, S., Saleem, M. A., Batool, R., Fahim, M., Lee, Y.-K., and Lee, S. 2015 "Smart CDSS: integration of social media and interaction engine (SMIE) in healthcare for chronic disease patients," *Multimedia Tools and Applications* 74(14): 5109–29.

Fearn-Banks, K. 2010 *Crisis Communications: A Casebook Approach*, 4th edn, New York: Routledge.

Ferris, K. O. 2001 "Through a glass, darkly: the dynamics of fan–celebrity encounters," *Symbolic Interaction* 24(1): 25–47.

Firger, J. 2015 "Hospital live tweets heart transplant surgery," *CBS News* (February 17); available at: <http://www.cbsnews.com/news/hospital-live-tweets-heart-transplant-surgery/>.

Fischer, C. S. 1992 *America Calling: A Social History of the Telephone to 1940*, Berkeley, CA: University of California Press.

Fischer, H. W. 1998 *Response to Disaster: Fact Versus Fiction & Its Perpetuation: the Sociology of Disaster*, 2nd edn, Lanham, MD: University Press of America.

Forster, E. M. [1909] 1997 *The Machine Stops and Other Stories*, London: André Deutsch.

Fox, S. and Jones, S. 2009 "The social life of health information," *Pew Internet & American Life Project*, Washington, DC: Pew Research Center.

Freeman, B., Potente, S., Rock, V., and McIver, J. 2015 "Social media campaigns that make a difference: what can public health learn from the corporate sector and other social change marketers," *Public Health Research & Practice* 25(2): e2521517; available at: <http://www. phrp.com.au/issues/march-2015-volume-25-issue-2/social-media-campaigns-make-difference-can-public-health-learn-corporate-sec tor-social-change-marketers/>.

Friemel, T. N. 2016 "The digital divide has grown old: determinants of a digital divide among seniors," *New Media & Society* 18(2): 313–31.

Fry, S. 2016 *Switched On*; available at: <http://www.stephenfry. com/2016/08/switched-on/>.

Gadamer, H.-G., Weinsheimer, J., and Marshall, D. G. 2004 *Truth and Method*, 2nd edn, London and New York: Continuum.

Gallagher, R. J., Reagan, A. J., Danforth, C. M., and Dodds, P. S. 2016 "Divergent discourse between protests and counter-protests: #BlackLivesMatter and#AllLivesMatter"; available at: <https://arxiv. org/abs/1606.06820>.

Gamson, J. 2011 "The unwatched life is not worth living: the elevation of the ordinary in celebrity culture," *PMLA* 126(4): 1061–9.

García de Torres, E. and Hermida, A. 2017. "The social reporter in action: an analysis of the practice and discourse of Andy Carvin," *Journalism Practice* 11(2–3): 177–94.

Gauthier, B. 2016 "Ivanka Trump allegedly responded to Donald's creepy comments in 2006: 'If he wasn't my father, I would spray him with Mace'," *Salon* (November 25); available at: <http://www. salon.com/2016/11/25/ivanka-trump-allegedly-responded-to-don alds-creepy-comments-in-2006-if-he-wasnt-my-father-i-would-spray-him-with-mace/>.

Geere, D. 2011 "Twitter spread misinformation faster than truth in UK riots," *Wired* magazine; available at: <http://www.wired.co.uk/ news/archive/2011-08/09/twitter-misinformation-riots>.

Gerbaudo, P. 2012 *Tweets and the Streets: Social Media and Contemporary Activism*. London: Pluto.

Ghiassi, M., Skinner, J., and Zimbra, D. 2013 "Twitter brand senti-ment analysis: a hybrid system using n-gram analysis and dynamic artificial neural network," *Expert Systems with Applications* 40(16): 6266–82.

Ghosh, S., Seshagiri, S., and Ponnada, A. 2016 *Exploring Regional User Experience for Designing Ultra Low Cost Smart Phones. Paper presented at the Proceedings of the 2016 CHI Conference Extended Abstracts on Human Factors in Computing Systems*, Santa Clara, California, USA.

Gibbs, M., Meese, J., Arnold, M., Nansen, B., and Carter, M. 2015 "#Funeral and Instagram: death, social media, and platform vernacular," *Information, Communication and Society* 18(3): 255–68.

Gigliotti, C. 1999 "The ethical life of the digital aesthetic," in P. Lunenfeld (ed.), *The Digital Dialectic: New Essays on New Media*, Cambridge, MA: MIT Press, pp. 46–63.

Gilder, G. 1994 "Life after television, updated," *Forbes ASAP*; available at: <http://www.seas.upenn.edu/~gaj1/tvgg.html>.

Gitlin, T. 2011 "Sandmonkey: 'too stupid to govern us'," *Dissent* 58(3): 5–7.

Gladwell, M. 2010 "Small change," *New Yorker* 86(30): 42–9.

Glasius, M., Kaldor, M., and Anheier, H. 2005 "Introduction," in M. Glasius, M. Kaldor, and H. Anheier (eds), *Global Civil Society 2005/06*, London: Sage.

Goffman, E. 1959 *The Presentation of Self in Everyday Life*, Garden City, NY: Doubleday.

Goffman, E. 1981 *Forms of Talk*, Oxford: Blackwell.

Goffman, E. 1983 "The interaction order: American Sociological Association, 1982 presidential address," *American Sociological Review* 48(1): 1–17.

Goggin, G. 2011 *Global Mobile Media*, Abingdon, Oxon, and New York: Routledge.

Goodman, M. K., and Barnes, C. 2011 "Star/poverty space: the making of the 'development celebrity'," *Celebrity Studies* 2(1): 69–85.

Goolsby, R. 2009 "Lifting elephants: Twitter and blogging in global perspective," *Social Computing and Behavioral Modeling*, New York: Springer; available at: <http://dx.doi.org/10.1007/978-1-44190056-2_2>.

Gould, M. 2013 *The Social Media Gospel: Sharing the Good News in New Ways*. Collegeville, MN: Liturgical Press.

Granovetter, M. S. 1973 "The strength of weak ties," *American Journal of Sociology* 78(6): 1360–80.

Green, N. 1889 "Are telegraph rates too high?," *The North American Review* 149(396): 569–79.

Griffis, H. M. et al. 2014 "Use of social media across US hospitals: descriptive analysis of adoption and utilization," *Journal of Medical Internet Resources* 16(11): e264.

Gruzd, A. 2016 *Netlytic: Software for Automated Text and Social Network Analysis*; available at: <https://netlytic.org/>.

GSMA Intelligence 2016 *The Mobile Economy 2016*; available at: <https://www.gsmaintelligence.com/research/?file=97928efe09cd ba2864cdcf1ad1a2f58canddownload>.

Guattari, F. 1995 *Chaosmosis*, Bloomington, IN: Indiana University Press.

Hadar, L. T. 2011a "Start the Twitter revolution without me," Cato Institute Blog, vol. 2011; available at: <http://www.cato.org/publica tions/commentary/start-twitter-revolution-without-me>.

Hadar, L. T. 2011b "This is a struggle for power, not Arab Spring," *The Business Times*, Singapore: Singapore Press Holdings.

Hansen, D. L., Shneiderman, B., and Smith, M. 2010 "Visualizing threaded conversation networks: mining message boards and email lists for actionable insights," in A. An, P. Lingras, S. Petty, and R. Huang (eds), *Active Media Technology*, vol. 6335, Berlin/ Heidelberg: Springer.

Hanson, J. 2007 *24/7: How Cell Phones and the Internet Change the Way We Live, Work, and Play*, Westport, CT: Praeger.

Hargittai, E. 2006 "Hurdles to information seeking: spelling and typo- graphical mistakes during users' online behavior," *Journal of the Association for Information Systems* 7(1): 52–67.

Hargittai, E. and Jennrich, K. 2016 "The online participation divide," in M. Lloyd and L. A. Friedland (eds), *The Communication Crisis in America, and How to Fix It*. New York: Palgrave Macmillan US, pp. 199–213.

Hargittai, E. and Litt, E. 2011 "The tweet smell of celebrity success: explaining variation in Twitter adoption among a diverse group of young adults," *New Media & Society* 13(5): 824–42.

Harp, J. 2016 "Strictly vs The Apprentice! Ed Balls throws down a dance challenge to Lord Sugar after 'drunk giraffe' insult," *Digital Spy* (November 2); available at: <http://www.digitalspy.com/tv/ strictly-come-dancing/news/a812955/strictly-vs-the-apprentice-ed- balls-and-lord-sugar-dance-off/>.

Hartley, J. 1999 *Uses of Television*, London and New York: Routledge.

Harvey, D. 1989 *The Condition of Postmodernity: An Enquiry into the Origins of Cultural Change*, Oxford: Blackwell.

Haseeb, K. E.-D. 2011 "On the Arab 'Democratic Spring': lessons derived," *Contemporary Arab Affairs* 4(2): 113–22.

Hassanpour, N. 2011 "Media disruption exacerbates revolutionary unrest: evidence from Mubarak's natural experiment," *APSA 2011 Annual Meeting Paper*.

Hawn, C. 2009 "Take two aspirin and tweet me in the morning: how Twitter, Facebook, and other social media are reshaping health care," *Health Affairs* 28(2): 361–8.

Hayashi, F. and Klee, E. 2003 "Technology adoption and consumer payments: evidence from survey data," *Review of Network Economics* 2(2): Article 8.

Hayes, A. S., Singer, J. B., and Ceppos, J. 2007 "Shifting roles, enduring values: the credible journalist in a digital age," *Journal of Mass Media Ethics* 22(4): 262–79.

Heaivilin, N., Gerbert, B., Page, J. E., and Gibbs, J. L. 2011 "Public health surveillance of dental pain via Twitter," *Journal of Dental Research* 90(9): 1047–51.

Heidegger, M. 1977 *The Question Concerning Technology, and Other Essays*, New York: Garland Publishers.

Helsper, E. J. and Reisdorf, B. C. 2016 "The emergence of a 'digital underclass' in Great Britain and Sweden: changing reasons for digital exclusion," *New Media & Society*; online first article available at: <http://journals.sagepub.com/doi/abs/10.1177/1461444816634676>.

Hermida, A. 2010a "From TV to Twitter: how ambient news became ambient journalism," *Media/Culture Journal* 13(2); available at: <http://papers.ssrn.com/sol3/papers.cfm?abstract_id=1732603>.

Hermida, A. 2010b "Twittering the news," *Journalism Practice* 4(3): 297–308.

Herring, S. C. 2001 "Computer-mediated discourse," in D. Schiffrin, D. Tannen, and H. E. Hamilton (eds), *The Handbook of Discourse Analysis*, Oxford: Blackwell, pp. 612–34.

Herron, P. D. (2015) "Opportunities and ethical challenges for the practice of medicine in the digital era," *Current Reviews in Musculoskeletal Medicine* 8(2): 113–17.

Hewitt, M. E., Ganz, P. A., Institute of Medicine (U.S.), and American Society of Clinical Oncology (U.S.), 2006 *From Cancer Patient to Cancer Survivor: Lost in Transition: An American Society of Clinical Oncology and Institute of Medicine Symposium*, Washington, DC: National Academies Press.

Hewlett, S. (writer) 2016 "How a tweet about Trump spread 'fake' news," *BBC Radio 4 The Media Show*. London: British Broadcasting Corporation.

Himelboim, I., McCreery, S., and Smith, M. 2013 "Birds of a feather tweet together: integrating network and content analyses to examine cross-ideology exposure on Twitter," *Journal of Computer-Mediated Communication* 18(2): 40–60.

Hobbs, W. R., Burke, M., Christakis, N. A., and Fowler, J. H. 2016 "Online social integration is associated with reduced mortality risk," *Proceedings of the National Academy of Sciences* 113(46): 12980–4.

Hobson, J. 2008 "Digital whiteness, primitive blackness," *Feminist Media Studies* 8(2): 111–26, London: Routledge.

Hobson, K. 2011 "A.M. Vitals: Bristol-Myers Squibb's melanoma drug improves survival," *Wall Street Journal Blogs*, New York: Dow Jones & Co; available at: <http://blogs.wsj.com/health/2011/03/22/a-mvitals-bristol-myers-squibbs-melanoma-drug-improves-survival/>.

Hoffman, B. 2004 *The Politics of the Internet in Third World Development: Challenges in Contrasting Regimes with Case Studies of Costa Rica and Cuba*, New York: Routledge.

Hogan, B. 2010 "The presentation of self in the age of social media: distinguishing performances and exhibitions online," *Bulletin of Science, Technology & Society* 30(6): 377–86.

Honeycutt, C. and Herring, S. 2009 "Beyond microblogging: conversation and collaboration via Twitter," *HICSS '09. 42nd Hawaii International Conference on System Sciences*.

Horton, D. and Richard Wohl, R. 1956 "Mass communication and para-social interaction: observations on intimacy at a distance," *Psychiatry* 19(3): 215–29.

Hounshell, B. 2011a "A guide to the foreign policy Twitterati," *Foreign Policy* 187: 22.

Hounshell, B. 2011b "The revolution will be tweeted," *Foreign Policy* 187: 20–21.

Houston, J. B. et al. 2015 "Social media and disasters: a functional framework for social media use in disaster planning, response, and research," *Disasters* 39(1): 1–22.

Hughes, A. L. and Palen, L. 2009 "Twitter adoption and use in mass convergence and emergency events," *6th International ISCRAM Conference*, Gothenburg, Sweden.

Hughes, A. L., Palen, L., Sutton, J., Liu, S. B., and Vieweg, S. 2008 "'Site-seeing' in disaster: an examination of on-line social convergence," *5th International ISCRAM Conference*, Washington, DC.

Hughes, N. 2014 "10 celebs that actually run their own Twitter account. *The Huffington Post* (January 28); available at: <http://www.huffingtonpost.com/fueled/10-celebs-that-celebrity-twitter_b_4676062.html>.

Huyssen, A. 2000 "Present pasts: media, politics, amnesia," *Public Culture* 12(1): 21–38.

Idle, N. and Nunns, A. 2011 *Tweets from Tahrir: Egypt's Revolution as it Unfolded, in the Words of the People Who Made it*, New York: OR Books.

Imtiaz, S. Y., Khan, M. A., and Shakir, M. 2015 "Telecom sector of Pakistan: potential, challenges and business opportunities," *Telematics and Informatics* 32(2): 254–8.

Ingram, M. 2017 "Twitter needs more than just Donald Trump to survive," *Fortune* (February 9); available at: <http://fortune.com/2017/02/09/twitter-growth-trump/>.

International Telecommunication Union 2010 *Fixed Broadband Subscriptions*, available at: <http://www.itu.int/ITU-D/ict/statistics/>.

International Telecommunications Union 2011 *Key Global Telecom Indicators for the World Telecommunication Service Sector*, Geneva, Switzerland: International Telecommunications Union.

International Telecommunications Union 2015 *Measuring the Information Society Report 2015*, Geneva, Switzerland; available at: <https://www.itu.int/en/ITU-D/Statistics/Documents/publications/misr2015/MISR2015-w5.pdf>.

International Telecommunications Union 2016 *World Telecommunication/ICT Development Report and database, and World Bank estimates*; available at: <http://databank.worldbank.org/data/reports.aspx?source=2andseries=IT.NET.USER.P2andcountry=>.

Irish Times, The 2010 "Anger builds as disaster affects three million," August 4, 2010, p. 8, *The Irish Times*, Dublin: Irish Times.

James, Susan Donaldson 2010 "Little boy battles cancer with monsters," ABC World News with Diane Sawyer (November 11), available at: <http://abcnews.go.com/Health/CancerPreventionAndTreatment/aid-aidan-sells-4000-monster-drawings-boy-leukemia/story?id=12113304>.

Java, A., Xiaodan, S., Finin, T., and Tseng, B. 2007 "Why we twitter: understanding microblogging usage and communities," *Proceedings of the 9th WebKDD and 1st SNA-KDD 2007 Workshop on Web Mining and Social Network Analysis*, San Jose, California: ACM.

Jefferis, D. 2002 *Internet: Electronic Global Village*, New York: Crabtree.

Jerslev, A. and Mortensen, M. 2016 "What is the self in the celebrity selfie? Celebrification, phatic communication and performativity," *Celebrity Studies* 7(2): 249–63.

Jiang, S. and Beaudoin, C. E. 2016 "Health literacy and the internet: an exploratory study on the 2013 HINTS survey," *Computers in Human Behavior* 58: 240–8.

Jue, A. L., Marr, J. A., and Kassotakis, M. E. 2010 *Social Media at Work:*

How Networking Tools Propel Organizational Performance, 1st edn, San Francisco, CA: Jossey-Bass.

Jurgenson, N. 2012 "Augmented collectives: revolution, occupation, protest, riots, flash mobs at the intersection of atoms and bits" *Eastern Sociological Society Annual Meeting*, New York.

Kahn, J. G., Yang, J. S., and Kahn, J. S. 2010 "'Mobile' health needs and opportunities in developing countries," *Health Affairs* 29(2): 254–61.

Kalyanam, J., Velupillai, S., Doan, S., Conway, M., and Lanckriet, G. 2015 *Facts and Fabrications about Ebola: A Twitter Based Study*; available at: <https://arxiv.org/abs/1508.02079>.

Katz, E. and Lazarsfeld, P. F. 1955 *Personal Influence: The Part Played by People in the Flow of Mass Communications*, Glencoe, IL: Free Press.

Keen, A. 2010 "Reinventing the Luddite: an interview with Andrew Keen," *Futurist* 44(2): 35–6, Bethesda, MD: World Future Society.

Kelley, T. 2011 "Environmental health insights into the 2011 Tōhoku Japan earthquake disaster," *Environmental Health Insights* 2011: 21.

Kenny, C. 2016 "'You can't hug Skype': Irish mammies on their emigrant children," *The Irish Times* (June 10); available at: <http://www.irishtimes.com/life-and-style/abroad/generation-emigration/you-can-t-hug-skype-irish-mammies-on-their-emigrant-children-1.2679755>.

KHOU.com 2016 "USGS: 5.0-magnitude earthquake rattles Oklahoma" (November 7); available at: <http://www.khou.com/news/nation-now/50-quake-rocks-oklahoma-felt-states-away/348920320>.

Kierkegaard, S. and Dru, A. 1962 *The Present Age and Of the Difference between a Genius and an Apostle*. Translated and with an introduction by Alexander Dru, London and Glasgow: Collins.

Kim, J. and Song, H. 2016 "Celebrity's self-disclosure on Twitter and parasocial relationships: a mediating role of social presence," *Computers in Human Behavior* 62: 570–7.

Kireyev, K., Palen, L., and Anderson, K. 2009 "Applications of topics models to analysis of disaster-related Twitter data," *NIPS Workshop on Applications for Topic Models: Text and Beyond*, La Jolla, CA: Neural Information Processing Systems Foundation.

Kirkpatrick, D. and Preston, J. 2011 "Google executive who was jailed said he was part of Facebook campaign in Egypt," *New York Times*, February 7, 2011, New York: New York Times.

Knorr Cetina, K. 2009 "The synthetic situation: interactionism for a global world," *Symbolic Interaction* 32(1): 61–87.

Kohut, A. et al. 2011 *Global Digital Communication: Texting, Social Networking Popular Worldwide*: Pew Research Centre.

Kolko, B. E., Nakamura, L., and Rodman, G. B. 2000 *Race in Cyberspace*, New York: Routledge.

Kottasova, I. 2016 "The top hashtag of the year had nothing to do with Donald Trump," *CNN.com* (December 6); available at: <http://money.cnn.com/2016/12/06/technology/twitter-top-events-hashtags-2016/index.html>.

Krowchuk, H. V. 2010 "Should social media be used to communicate with patients?," *MCN The American Journal of Maternal/Child Nursing* 35(1): 6–7.

Kubetin, S. K. 2011 "A lesson in taking social media to the medical level," *Internal Medicine News* 44(7): 75.

Kuchler, H. 2017 "Twitter steps up efforts to combat abuse as user growth slows," *The Financial Times* (February 7); available at: <https://www.ft.com/content/47f33e38-ed46-11e6-930f-061b01e23655>.

Kwak, H., Lee, C., Park, H. and Moon, S. 2010 "What is Twitter, a social network or a news media?," *Proceedings of the 19th International Conference on World Wide Web*, Raleigh, North Carolina: ACM.

Landi, M. 2016 "What was the most-talked about Twitter moment of the year? Biggest trends of 2016 revealed," *Daily Mirror* (December 6); available at: <http://www.mirror.co.uk/news/uk-news/what-most-talked-twitter-moment-9399754>.

Lariscy, R. W., Avery, E. J., Sweetser, K. D., and Howes, P. 2009 "An examination of the role of online social media in journalists' source mix," *Public Relations Review* 35(3): 314–16.

Larson, L. C. 2010 "Digital readers: the next chapter in e-book reading and response," *The Reading Teacher* 64(1): 15–22.

Larsson Anders, O. and Hallvard, M. 2015 "Bots or journalists? News sharing on Twitter," *Communications* 40: 361.

Lasorsa, D. L., Lewis, S. C., and Holton, A. E. 2011 "Normalizing Twitter," *Journalism Studies* 13(1): 19–36.

Last, J. V. 2009 "Tweeting while Tehran burns," *Current* 515: 9–10.

Leach, S. L. 2005 "How to tell story of the dead without offending the living," *Christian Science Monitor* 97(38): 11.

Lee, B. 2016 "Stephen Fry hits back at criticism of Baftas 'bag lady' joke: 'She got it. Derrr'," *Guardian*; available at: <https://www.the-guardian.com/film/2016/feb/14/stephen-fry-hits-back-at-criticism-of-baftas-bag-lady-joke-she-got-it-derrr>.

Leets, L., De Becker, G., and Giles, H. 1995 "Fans: exploring expressed motivations for contacting celebrities," *Journal of Language and Social Psychology* 14(1–2): 102–23.

Lenhart, A., Purcell, K., Smith, A., and Zickuhr, K. 2010 "Social media & mobile internet use among teens and young adults," *Pew Internet & American Life Project*, Washington, DC: Pew Research Center.

Leo, J. 2009 "Citizen journo Janis Krums twitters amazing Hudson plane crash photo from ferry," *Los Angeles Times*, Los Angeles: Los Angeles Times Group: available at: <http://qa.travel.latimes.com/daily-deal-blog/index.php/citizen-journo-janis-3851/>.

Levinson, P. 2001 *Digital McLuhan: A Guide to the Information Millennium*, London and New York: Routledge.

Li, H., Nelsen, M. R., Huh, J., and Gangadharbatla, H. 2014 *Preconference Session: Big Data for Advertising Research and Education*. Paper presented at the American Academy of Advertising Conference Proceedings (Online).

Liang, B. A. and Mackey, T. 2011 "Direct-to-consumer advertising with interactive Internet media," *JAMA: The Journal of the American Medical Association* 305(8): 824–5.

Licoppe, C. 2004 "'Connected' presence: the emergence of a new repertoire for managing social relationships in a changing communication technoscape," *Environment and Planning D: Society and Space* 22(1): 135–56.

Liebmann, M. 1996 *Arts Approaches to Conflict*, London: Jessica Kingsley Publishers.

Ling, C. L. M., Pan, S. L., Ractham, P., and Kaewkitipong, L. 2015 "ICT-enabled community empowerment in crisis response: social media in Thailand flooding 2011," *Journal of the Association for Information Systems* 16(3): 174–212.

Liu, Y., Mei, Q., Hanauer, D. A., Zheng, K., and Lee, J. M. 2016 "Use of social media in the diabetes community: an exploratory analysis of diabetes-related tweets," *JMIR Diabetes* 1(2): e4.

Livingstone, S. 2008 "Taking risky opportunities in youthful content creation: teenagers' use of social networking sites for intimacy, privacy and self-expression," *New Media Society* 10(3): 393–411.

Livingstone, S. and Helsper, E. 2007 "Gradations in digital inclusion: children, young people and the digital divide," *New Media Society* 9(4): 671–96.

Loeb, S. et al. 2015 "Updated survey of social media use by members of the American Urological Association," *Urology Practice* 2(3): 138–43.

Loft, J. B. 2005 "Understanding community weblogs" unpublished PhD thesis, South Dakota State University.

Longley, P. A., Adnan, M., and Lansley, G. 2015 "The geotemporal demographics of Twitter usage," *Environment and Planning A*, 47(2): 465–84.

Lotan, G., Graeff, E., Ananny, M., Gaffney, D., Pearce, I., and boyd, d. 2011 "The revolutions were tweeted: information flows during the 2011 Tunisian and Egyptian revolutions," *International Journal of Communication* 5: 1375–1405.

Lüfkens, M. 2016 *2015 Burson-Marsteller Twiplomacy Report*; available at: <http://twiplomacy.com/blog/twiplomacy-study-2016/>.

Luke, T. W. 1997 "New world order or neo-world orders: power, politics and ideology in informationalizing glocalities," in M. Featherstone, S. Lash, and R. Robertson (eds), *Global Modernities*. London; Thousand Oaks, CA: Sage Publications, pp. 91–107.

Luke, T. W. 2017 "Overtures for the triumph of the Tweet: white power music and the Alt-Right in 2016," *New Political Science* 39(2): 277–82.

Lyles, C. R., López, A., Pasick, R., and Sarkar, U. 2013 "'5 mins of uncomfyness is better than dealing with cancer 4 a lifetime': an exploratory qualitative analysis of cervical and breast cancer screening dialogue on Twitter," *Journal of Cancer Education* 28(1): 127–33.

McAulay, L. 2007 "Unintended consequences of computer-mediated communications," *Behaviour & Information Technology* 26(5): 385–98.

McCartney, M. 2011 "Panic about nuclear apocalypse overshadows Japan's real plight," *BMJ* 342: d1845; available at: <http://www.bmj.com/content/342/bmj.d1845.full>.

McCulloch, R. 2009 "The man who changed twitter," *Third Sector Lab*: Third Sector Lab; available at: <http://thirdsectorlab.co.uk/?p=27>.

McLuhan, H. M. 1952 "Technology and Political Change," *International Journal* 7(3): 189–95.

McLuhan, M. 1962 *The Gutenberg Galaxy: The Making of Typographic Man*, Toronto: University of Toronto Press.

McLuhan, M. and Fiore, Q. 1967 *The Medium is the Message*, New York: Random House.

McLuhan, M. and Fiore, Q. 1968 *War and Peace in the Global Village: An Inventory of Some of the Current Spastic Situations that Could be Eliminated by More Feedforward*, 1st edn, New York: McGraw-Hill.

McNab, C. 2009 "What social media offers to health professionals and citizens," *Bulletin of the World Health Organization* 87: 566.

McPherson, M., Smith-Lovin, L., and Cook, J. M. 2001 "Birds of a feather: homophily in social networks," *Annual Review of Sociology* 27(1): 415–44.

McTernan, J. 2016 "Donald Trump is giving a master class in how to use Twitter" (December 21); available at: <http://www.cnn.com/2016/12/21/opinions/trump-twitter-mcternan-opinion/>.

Maheshwari, S. 2016 "How fake news goes viral: a case study, *The New York Times*; available at: <http://www.nytimes.com/2016/11/20/business/media/how-fake-news-spreads.html?_r=0>.

Manfredi, C., Kaiser, K., Matthews, A. K., and Johnson, T. P. 2010 "Are racial differences in patient–physician cancer communication and information explained by background, predisposing, and enabling factors?," *Journal of Health Communication* 15(3): 272–92.

Manjoo, F. 2008 *True Enough: Learning to Live in a Post-Fact Society*, Hoboken, NJ: John Wiley and Sons.

Manovich, L. 2001 *The Language of New Media*, Cambridge, MA, and London: MIT Press.

Marshall, J. and Koh, Y. 2015 "The problem with Twitter ads," *The Wall Street Journal* (April 30); available at: <https://www.wsj.com/articles/the-problem-with-twitter-adsthe-problem-with-twitter-ads-1430438275>.

Marwick, A. E. 2013 *Status Update: Celebrity, Publicity, and Branding in the Social Media Age*. New Haven, CT: Yale University Press.

Marwick, A., and boyd, d. 2011 "To see and be seen: celebrity practice on Twitter," *Convergence* 17(2): 139–58.

Mascheroni, G. and Ólafsson, K. 2015 "The mobile internet: access, use, opportunities and divides among European children," *New Media & Society* 18(8): 1657–79.

Meeder, B., Tam, J., Kelley, P. G., and Cranor, L. F. 2010 "RT@ IWantPrivacy: widespread violation of privacy settings in the Twitter social network." In Web 2.0 Privacy and Security Workshop, IEEE Symposium on Security and Privacy.

Meikle, G. 2016 *Social Media: Communication, Sharing and Visibility*. New York and Abingdon, Oxford: Routledge.

Menchik, D. A. and Tian, X. 2008 "Putting social context into text: the semiotics of e-mail interaction," *American Journal of Sociology* 114(2): 332–70.

Meyer, K. M. and Tang, T. 2015 "#SocialJournalism: local news media on Twitter," *International Journal on Media Management* 17(4): 241–57.

Minsky, M. 1980 "Telepresence," *OMNI* magazine: 45–51.

Misopoulos, F., Mitic, M., Kapoulas, A., and Karapiperis, C. 2014 "Uncovering customer service experiences with Twitter: the case of airline industry," *Management Decision* 52(4): 705–23.

Mocanu, D. et al. 2013 "The twitter of babel: mapping world languages through microblogging platforms," PLoS ONE 8(4): e61981.

Modern Mechanix and Inventions magazine 1935 "Robot messenger displays person-to-person notes in public," *Modern Mechanix and Inventions* magazine: 80.

Molla, R. 2016 "Social studies: Twitter vs. Facebook," *Bloomberg* (February 12); available at: <https://www.bloomberg.com/gadfly/articles/2016-02-12/social-studies-comparing-twitter-with-facebook-in-charts>.

Moore, A. 2011 "Imperial hubris of the war on terror," *Lateline*, Australia: Australian Broadcasting Corporation.

Moore, J., Ford, P., Lynch, S., Delaney, M., and Montlake, S. 2011 "Social media day: did Twitter and Facebook really build a global revolution?," *Christian Science Monitor*; available at: <http://www.csmonitor.com/World/Global-Issues/2011/0630/Social-media-Did-Twitter-and-Facebook-really-build-a-global-revolution>.

Moore, M. 2009 "'Dalai Lama' Twitter account suspended after exposed as fake," *The Telegraph*, London: Telegraph Media Group Ltd; available at: <http://www.telegraph.co.uk/news/newstopics/howaboutthat/4577342/Dalai-Lama-Twitter-account-suspended-after-exposed-as-fake.html>.

Morán, A. L., Rodríguez-Covili, J., Mejia, D., Favela, J., Ochoa, S., Kolfschoten, G., Herrmann, T., and Lukosch, S. 2010 "Supporting informal interaction in a hospital through impromptu social networking," *Collaboration and Technology*, vol. 6257, Berlin: Springer, pp. 305–20.

Morozov, E. 2009 "Iran: Downside to the 'Twitter Revolution'," *Dissent* 56(4): 10–14.

Morozov, E. 2011 *The Net Delusion: The Dark Side of Internet Freedom*, 1st edn, New York: Public Affairs.

Morris, T. 2009 *All a Twitter: A Personal and Professional Guide to Social Networking with Twitter*, Indianapolis, IN: Que.

Motadel, D. 2011 "Waves of revolution," *History Today* 61(4): 3–4.

Mowlana, H. 1979 "Technology versus tradition: communication in the Iranian Revolution," *Journal of Communication* 29(3): 107–12.

Mroue, B. 2011 "Syria Facebook, YouTube ban lifted: reports," *The Huffington Post*; available at: <http://www.huffingtonpost.com/2011/02/08/syria-facebook-youtube-ba_n_820273.html>.

Murdock, G. 1993 "Communications and the constitution of modernity," *Media, Culture and Society* 15(4): 521–39.

Murillo, E., Merino, M., and Núñez, A. 2016 "The advertising value of

Twitter ads: a study among Mexican millennials," *Revista Brasileira de Gestão de Negócios* 18(61): 436–56.

Murthy, D. 2010 "Muslim punks online: a diasporic Pakistani music subculture on the Internet," *South Asian Popular Culture* 8(2): 181–94.

Murthy, D. 2011 "Twitter: microphone for the masses?," *Media, Culture & Society* 33(5): 779–89.

Murthy, D. 2012 "Towards a sociological understanding of social media: theorizing Twitter," *Sociology* 46(6): 1059-73.

Murthy, D. 2013 "New media and natural disasters: blogs and the 2004 Indian Ocean tsunami," *Information, Communication & Society* 16(7): 1176–92.

Murthy, D. 2015 "Twitter and elections: are tweets, predictive, reactive, or a form of buzz?" *Information, Communication & Society* 18(7): 816–31.

Murthy, D. Forthcoming "Comparative Process-Oriented Research Using Social Media and Historical Text," *Sociological Research Online*.

Murthy, D. and Eldredge, M. 2016 "Who tweets about cancer? An analysis of cancer-related tweets in the USA," *Digital Health* 2; available at: <http://journals.sagepub.com/doi/abs/10.1177/20552 07616657670>.

Murthy, D. and Gross, A. J. 2017 "Social media processes in disasters: implications of emergent technology use," *Social Science Research* 63: 356–70.

Nadiri, M. I. and Nandi, B. 2015 "Modern communication technology and its economic impact: a survey of research findings," *Communications & Strategies* 100: 125.

Nakamura, L. 2002 *Cybertypes: Race, Ethnicity, and Identity on the Internet*, New York: Routledge.

Nelson, R. E. 1989 "The strength of strong ties: social networks and intergroup conflict in organizations," *The Academy of Management Journal* 32(2): 377–401.

Newton, C. 2017 "Twitter rolls back a change designed to counter abuse after complaints it encouraged abuse," *The Verge* (February 13); available at: <https://www.theverge.com/2017/2/13/14603822/ twitter-rolls-back-a-change-designed-to-counter-abuse-after-com plaints-it-encouraged-abuse>.

Newton, C. 2017a "Twitter is rolling out 280-character tweets around the world," *The Verge*; available at: <https://www.theverge. com/2017/11/7/16616076/twitter-280-characters-global-rollout>.

Niedzviecki, H. 2009 *The Peep Diaries: How We're Learning to Love*

Watching Ourselves and Our Neighbors, San Francisco, CA: City Lights Books.

Nosko, A., Wood, E., and Molema, S. 2010 "All about me: disclosure in online social networking profiles: The case of FACEBOOK," *Computers in Human Behavior* 26(3): 406–18.

O'Dell, J. 2011 "How Egyptians used Twitter during the January crisis," New York City: Mashable.com; available at: <http://mash able. com/2011/02/01/egypt-twitter-infographic/>.

Olmstead, K. and Atkinson, M. 2015 *Apps Permissions in the Google Play Store*, Washington DC; available at: <http://www.pewinternet. org/2015/11/10/apps-permissions-in-the-google-play-store/>.

Orsini, M. 2010 "Social media: how home health care agencies can join the chorus of empowered voices," *Home Health Care Management & Practice* 22(3): 213–17.

Otto, M. A. 2011 "Social media facilitate medical communication: experts debate risks and benefits of engaging in Twitter, Facebook, texting, and blogs," *Internal Medicine News* 44(2): 55.

Oyeyemi, S. O., Gabarron, E., and Wynn, R. 2014 "Ebola, Twitter, and misinformation: a dangerous combination?" *BMJ: British Medical Journal* 349; doi:10.1136/bmj.g6178.

Palen, L. 2008 "Online social media in crisis events," *EDUCAUSE Quarterly* 31(3): 76–8.

Palen, L., Starbird, K., Vieweg, S., and Hughes, A. 2010 "Twitter-based information distribution during the 2009 Red River Valley flood threat," *Bulletin of the American Society for Information Science and Technology* 36(5): 13–17.

Palser, B. 2009 "Amateur content's star turn," *American Journalism Review* 31(4): 42–3.

Panahi, S., Watson, J., and Partridge, H. 2014 "Social media and physicians: exploring the benefits and challenges," *Health Informatics Journal* 22(2): 99–112.

Paniagua, J. and Sapena, J. 2014 "Business performance and social media: love or hate?" *Business horizons* 57(6): 719–28.

Papacharissi, Z. and Oliveira, M. d. F. 2011 "The rhythms of news storytelling on Twitter: coverage of the January 25th Egyptian uprising on Twitter," *World Association for Public Opinion Research Conference*, Amsterdam.

Papacharissi, Z. and Oliveira, M. d. F. 2012 "Affective news and networked publics: the rhythms of news storytelling on #Egypt," *Journal of Communication* 62(2): 266–82.

Parker, A. and Barbaro, M. 2011 "In reckless fashion, rapid online pursuits of political admirers," *The New York Times* (June 8); available at: <http://www.nytimes.com/2011/06/09/nyregion/weiners-pat tern-turning-political-admirers-into-online-pursuits.html>.

Parker, T. (Writer) 2013 "Let go, let gov," *South Park*: Comedy Central; available at: < http://www.imdb.com/title/tt2492922/>.

Parker, T. (Writer) 2016 "The damned," *South Park*: Comedy Central; available at: <http://www.imdb.com/title/tt5218396/>.

Payne, R. 2014 "Frictionless sharing and digital promiscuity," *Communication and Critical/Cultural Studies* 11(2): 85–102.

Perrin, A. 2015 *Social Media Usage*. Pew Research Center; available at: <http://www.pewinternet.org/files/2015/10/PI_2015-10-08_Social-Networking-Usage-2005-2015_FINAL.pdf>.

Petronzio, M. 2016 "How young Native Americans built and sustained the #NoDAPL movement," *Mashable.com*; available at: <http://mashable.com/2016/12/07/standing-rock-nodapl-youth/-e_.KHLP pDqqd>.

Pfeifle, M. 2009 "A Nobel Peace Prize for Twitter?," *Christian Science Monitor* (July 6): 9. Available at: <http://www.csmonitor.com/com mentary/opinion/2009/0706/p09s02-coop.html>.

Philpott, D. 2001 *Revolutions in Sovereignty: How Ideas Shaped Modern International Relations*, Princeton, NJ: Princeton University Press.

Piwek, L. and Joinson, A. 2016 "'What do they snapchat about?' Patterns of use in time-limited instant messaging service," *Computers in Human Behavior* 54: 358–67.

Poell, T. and Borra, E. 2011 "Twitter, YouTube, and Flickr as platforms of alternative journalism: the social media account of the 2010 Toronto G20 protests," *Journalism*; available at: <http://jou.sage-pub.com/content/early/2011/12/14/1464884911431533.abstract>.

Poell, T. and Rajagopalan, S. 2015 "Connecting activists and journalists," *Journalism Studies* 16(5): 719–33.

Politi, D. 2014 "Anthony Weiner favorites 'ultimate sext machine' tweet, calls it an accident," *Slate.com* (June 15); available at: <http://www.slate.com/blogs/the_slatest/2014/06/15/anthony_weiner_favorites_ultimate_sext_machine_tweet.html>.

Poushter, J. 2016 *Smartphone Ownership and Internet Usage Continues to Climb in Emerging Economies*. Washington, DC; available at: <http://www.pewglobal.org/2016/02/22/smartphone-ownership-and-internet-usage-continues-to-climb-in-emerging-economies/>.

Prier, K. W., Smith, M. S., Giraud-Carrier, C., and Hanson, C. L. 2011 "Identifying health-related topics on twitter: an exploration of tobacco-related tweets as a test topic," *Proceedings of the 4th International Conference on Social Computing, Behavioral-Cultural Modeling and Prediction*, College Park, MD: Springer-Verlag.

Prince, S. H. 1920 "Catastrophe and social change: based upon a socio-logical study of the Halifax disaster," unpublished Ph.D. thesis, New York: Columbia University.

Prochaska, J. J., Pechmann, C., Kim, R., and Leonhardt, J. M. 2012 "Twitter= quitter? An analysis of Twitter quit smoking social networks," *Tobacco Control* 21(4): 447–9.

Puente, A. and Tan, C. C. 2015 *Survey of Smartphone-Based Police Monitoring Apps* (October 19–22). Paper presented at the 2015 IEEE 12th International Conference on Mobile Ad Hoc and Sensor Systems.

Putnam, R. D. 2000 *Bowling Alone: The Collapse and Revival of American Community*, New York: Simon & Schuster.

Rainie, L. and Wellman, B. 2012 *Networked: The New Social Operating System*, Cambridge, MA: MIT Press.

Rajani, R., Berman, D. S. and Rozanski, A. 2011 "Social networks – are they good for your health? The era of Facebook and Twitter," *QJM* 104(9): 819–20.

Raley, R. 2009 *Tactical Media*, Minneapolis, MN, and London: University of Minnesota Press.

Rebillard, F. and Touboul, A. 2010 "Promises unfulfilled? 'Journalism 2.0' user participation and editorial policy on newspaper websites," *Media Culture Society* 32(2): 323–34.

Reinardy, S., and Wanta, W. 2015 *The Essentials of Sports Reporting and Writing* (2nd edn), New York and Abingdon: Routledge.

Rettie, R. 2009 "Mobile phone communication: extending Goffman to mediated interaction," *Sociology* 43(3): 421–38.

Reuters 2016 "Vietnam authorities destroy ivory worth $7 million," *International Business Times* (November 12); available at: <http://www.ibtimes.co.in/vietnam-authorities-destroy-ivory-worth-7-million-703883>.

Rheingold, H. 1993 *The Virtual Community: Homesteading on the Electronic Frontier*, Reading, MA: Addison-Wesley.

Rickford, R. 2016 "Black lives matter: toward a modern practice of mass struggle," *New Labor Forum* 25(1): 34–42.

Riordan, Monica A. 2017 "Emojis as tools for emotion work: communicating affect in text messages," *Journal of Language and Social Psychology*; available at: <http://dx.doi.org/10.1177/0261927X17704238>.

Riordan, M. A. 2017 "Emojis as tools for emotion work: communicating affect in text messages," *Journal of Language and Social Psychology*; available at: <http://journals.sagepub.com/toc/jls/0/0>.

Ritzer, G., and Jurgenson, N. 2010 "Production, consumption, prosumption. The nature of capitalism in the age of the digital 'prosumer'," *Journal of Consumer Culture* 10(1): 13–36.

Riva, G. and Galimberti, C. 1998 "Computer-mediated communication: identity and social interaction in an electronic environment," *Genetic, Social and General Psychology Monographs* 124(4): 434–64.

Robertson, R. 1992 *Globalization: Social Theory and Global Culture*, London: Sage.

Robinson, P. 2015 "Madonna: how the control queen lost her touch when media went social," *Guardian* (January 5); available at: <https://www.theguardian.com/music/musicblog/2015/jan/05/madonna-control-queen-social-media-rebel-heart>.

Rochon, P. A., Mashari, A., Cohen, A., Misra, A., Laxer, D., Streiner, D. L., Clark, J. P., Dergal, J. M., and Gold, J. 2004 "The inclusion of minority groups in clinical trials: problems of under representation and under reporting of data," *Accountability in Research* 11(3–4): 215–23.

Rosen, J. 2011 "The 'Twitter can't topple dictators' article," in J. Rosen (ed.), *PressThink*, vol. 2011, New York: Jay Rosen; available at: <http://pressthink.org/2011/02/the-twitter-cant-topple-dictators-article/>.

Rosenberg, R. and Golding, B. 2016 "Anthony Weiner sexted busty brunette while his son was in bed with him," *New York Post* (August 28); available at: <http://nypost.com/2016/08/28/anthony-weiner-sexted-busty-brunette-while-his-son-was-in-bed-with-him/>.

Rosenthal, A. 2008 "Gerald M. Phillips as electronic tribal chief: socioforming cyberspace," in T. Adams and S. A. Smith (eds), *Electronic Tribes: The Virtual Worlds of Geeks, Gamers, Shamans, and Scammers*, 1st edn, Austin, TX: University of Texas Press, pp. 159–76.

Ryan, L. 2016 "Paris police blame social media for Kim Kardashian robbery," *The Cut*, New York magazine (October 5); available at: <https://www.thecut.com/2016/10/police-blame-kim-kardashians-social-media-for-robbery.html>.

Salama, V. 2012 "Covering Syria," *The International Journal of Press/Politics* 17(4): 516–26.

Salem, F. and Mourtada, R. 2011 "Civil movements: the impact of Facebook and Twitter," *Arab Social Media Report* 1(2): 1–29.

Saussure, F. de, Bally, C., Riedlinger, A., and Sechehaye, A. 1916 *Cours de linguistique generale*, Paris: Payot.

Schreckinger, B. 2017 "The Alt-Right comes to Washington," *Politico*; available at: <http://www.politico.com/magazine/story/2017/01/alt-right-trump-washington-dc-power-milo-214629>.

Sedrak, M. S., Cohen, R. B., Merchant, R. M., and Schapira, M. M.

2016 "Cancer communication in the social media age," *JAMA Oncology* 2(6): 822–3.

Seipel, B. 2016 "Ivanka Trump quoted in '06 as saying: 'If he wasn't my father, I would spray him with Mace'," *The Hill* (November 24); available at: <http://thehill.com/blogs/in-the-know/in-the-know/307502-ivanka-on-trumps-sexual-comments-about-her-if-he-wasnt-my>.

Shah, N. 2008 "From global village to global marketplace: metaphorical descriptions of the global Internet," *International Journal of Media and Cultural Politics* 4(1): 9–26.

Shehata, D., El-Hamalawy, H., and Lynch, M. 2011 "Youth movements and social media: their role and impact," From *Tahrir: Revolution or Democratic Transition Conference*, Cairo, Egypt.

Sheldon, A. 1991 "Giving voice to the poor," *Foreign Policy* (84): 93–106.

Shirky, C. 2010 *Cognitive Surplus: Creativity and Generosity in a Connected Age*, New York: Penguin Press.

Shklovski, I., Palen, L., and Sutton, J. 2008 "Finding community through information and communication technology in disaster response," *Proceedings of the 2008 ACM Conference on Computer Supported Cooperative Work*, San Diego, CA: ACM.

Siegel, A. and Tucker, J. 2016 "Here's what 29 million tweets can teach us about Brexit," *The Washington Post* (July 20); available at: <https://www.washingtonpost.com/news/monkey-cage/wp/2016/07/20/heres-what-29-million-tweets-can-teach-us-about-brexit/>.

Siegle, L. 2005 "Armchair warrior," *The Observer* magazine, March 6, 2005, p. 55.

Silver, C. 2017 "Twitter muses 280 character tweets, doubling down on the death of conversation"; available at: <https://www.forbes.com/sites/curtissilver/2017/09/27/twitter-muses-expanding-twet-character-limit-to-280-doubling-down-on-the-death-of-conversation/#45a3650124f9>.

Singh, H., Fox, S. A., Petersen, N. J., Shethia, A., and Street, R. L. 2009 "Older patients' enthusiasm to use electronic mail to communicate with their physicians: cross-sectional survey," *Journal of Medical Internet Research* 11(2): 13.

Sloan, L., Morgan, J., Burnap, P., and Williams, M. 2015 "Who tweets? Deriving the demographic characteristics of age, occupation and social class from Twitter user meta-data," *PLOS ONE* 10(3): e0115545.

Smith, A. 2016 "The New York Post cover on Clinton email bombshell is out – and it does not disappoint," *Business Insider* (October

28); available at: <http://www.businessinsider.com/new-york-post-weiner-clinton-emails-fbi-2016-10>.

Sohn, E. 2015 "Networking: hello, stranger," *Nature* 526(7575): 729–31.

Sorokin, P. A. 1943 *Man and Society in Calamity: The Effects of War, Revolution, Famine, Pestilence upon Human Mind, Behavior, Social Organization and Cultural Life*, New York: E.P. Dutton & Company, Inc.

Spargo, C. and Robinson, W. 2016 "Anthony Weiner deletes Twitter after he is caught sexting AGAIN while long-suffering wife Huma campaigns with Hillary: Former pol 'sent semi-nude pic while his son, four, was in bed with him'," *Daily Mail* (August 28); available at: <http://www.dailymail.co.uk/news/article-3762999/The-return-Carlos-Danger-Anthony-Weiner-sexted-brunette-son-bed-him.html>.

Spitzberg, B. H. 2006 "Preliminary development of a model and measure of computer-mediated communication (CMC) competence," *Journal of Computer-Mediated Communication* 11(2): 629–66.

Standage, T. 1998 *The Victorian Internet: The Remarkable Story of the Telegraph and the Nineteenth Century's On-line Pioneers*, New York: Walker and Co.

Steinberg, T. 2000 *Acts of God: The Unnatural History of Disasters in America*, New York: Oxford University Press.

Stephenson, R. and Anderson, P. S. 1997 "Disasters and the information technology revolution," *Disasters* 21(4): 305–34.

Stone, B. 2011 *The Tweets Must Flow*; available at: <https://blog.twitter.com/2011/the-tweets-must-flow>.

Strangelove, M. 2010 *Watching YouTube: Extraordinary Videos by Ordinary People*, Toronto and Buffalo, NY: University of Toronto Press.

Surowiecki, J. 2004 *The Wisdom of Crowds: Why the Many are Smarter than the Few and How Collective Wisdom Shapes Business, Economies, Societies, and Nations*, 1st edn, New York: Doubleday.

Swasy, A. 2016 *How Journalists Use Twitter: The Changing Landscape of U.S. Newsrooms*, Lanham, MD: Lexington Books.

Sysomos 2014 *Inside Twitter: An In-Depth Look Inside the Twitter World*, Toronto, Canada; available at: <http://sysomos.com/sites/default/files/Inside-Twitter-BySysomos.pdf>.

Szabo, L. 2012 "Breast cancer survivor group is a social movement," *USA Today* (October 23); available at: <http://www.usatoday.com/story/news/nation/2012/10/23/breast-cancer-group-support/1637633/>.

Terry, M. 2009 "Twittering healthcare: social media and medicine," *Telemedicine and e-Health* 15(6): 507–10.

Thaker, S. I., Nowacki, A. S., Mehta, N. B., and Edwards, A. R. 2011 "How U.S. hospitals use social media," *Annals of Internal Medicine* 154(10): 707–8.

Thandar, M. and Usanavasin, S. 2015 "Measuring opinion credibility in Twitter," in H. Unger, P. Meesad, and S. Boonkrong (eds), *Recent Advances in Information and Communication Technology 2015: Proceedings of the 11th International Conference on Computing and Information Technology (IC2IT)*, Cham: Springer International Publishing, pp. 205–14.

the edge 2010 "Celebs tweet their support for quake affected Canterbury," available at: <http://www.theedge.co.nz/Celebs-tweet-their-support-for-quake-affected-Canterbury/tabid/198/arti cleID/8619/Default.aspx>.

The List 2016 "Gregg Wallace fell in love with wife Anna on Twitter," *The List* (November 29); available at: <https://www.list.co.uk/article/86730-gregg-wallace-fell-in-love-with-wife-anna-on-twit ter/>.

Therborn, G. 2000 "At the birth of second century sociology: times of reflexivity, spaces of identity, and nodes of knowledge," *British Journal of Sociology* 51(1): 37– 57.

Thomas, K. 2016 "'I am absolutely not upset': costume designer Jenny Beavan insists she's still friends with Stephen Fry after BAFTAs 'bag lady' jibe," *Daily Mail* (February 17); available at: <http://www.dai lymail.co.uk/tvshowbiz/article-3450835/Costume-designer-Jenny-Beavan-friends-Stephen-Fry-BAFTAs-bag-lady-jibe.html>.

Time magazine 2011 "The 2011 TIME 100," *Time* magazine (May 2); available at: <http://www.time.com/time/specials/packages/arti cle/0,28804,2066367_2066369,00.html>.

Times, The 1796 "Yesterday a TELEGRAPH was erected over the Admiralty," *The Times*, vol. issue 3504, London: Times Newspapers Ltd.

Times, The 1900 "The Post Office (Letters to the Editor)," *The Times*, vol. issue 36250, London: Times Newspapers Ltd.

Tomlinson, H. 2011 "Online dissent has mobilised millions but found no leaders," *The Times*, 1st edn, London: Times Newspapers Ltd.

Toosi, N. 2011 "Young Pakistanis blog, tweet to push for change," MSNBC.com (June 16); available at: <http://www.msnbc.msn. com/ id/43424657/ns/technology_and_science-tech_and_gadgets/t/ young-pakistanis-blog-tweet-push-change/>.

Traveler24 2015 "10 Instagram pics showing the sorrow and hope of Nepal," *Traveler24.com* (May 14); available at: <http://m.traveller24.

news24.com/Traveller/News/10-Instagram-pics-showing-the-sorrow-and-hope-of-Nepal-20150514>.

Tucker, C. 2011 "Social media, texting play new role in response to disasters: Preparedness, communication targeted," *The Nation's Health* 41(4): 1, 18.

Tucker, M. E. 2015 "How a beauty queen with diabetes found her 'sugar linings'," *NPR* (July 30); available at: <http://www.npr.org/sections/health-shots/2015/07/30/427711228/how-a-beauty-queen-with-diabetes-found-her-sugar-linings>.

Tucker, P. 2009 "The dawn of the postliterate age," *Futurist* 43(6): 41–5.

Turner, G. 2010 *Ordinary People and the Media: The Demotic Turn*, London: Sage.

Twitter 2010 "2010 Year in review," available at: <http://yearinreview.twitter.com/trends/>.

Twitter.com 2010 "2010 trends on Twitter," Twitter.com, San Francisco, CA: Twitter Inc.

Twitter.com 2016a *Twitter Usage/Company Facts*; available at: <https://about.twitter.com/company>.

Twitter.com 2016b *Twitter's Supported Mobile Carriers*; available at: <https://support.twitter.com/articles/20170024>.

United Nations Department of Economic and Social Affairs 2010 *World Statistics Pocketbook*, New York: United Nations.

Vance, K., Howe, W., and Dellavalle, R. P. 2009 "Social Internet sites as a source of public health information," *Dermatologic Clinics* 27(2): 133–6.

Vice Staff 2016 "How doctors are using fecal transplants to treat deadly diseases," *Vice* (June 22); available at: <http://www.vice.com/read/vice-on-hbo-student-debt-fecal-transplant>.

Victorian, B. 2010 "Nephrologists using social media connect with far-flung colleagues, health care consumers," *Nephrology Times* 3(1): 1, 16–18.

Vitak, J., Zube, P., Smock, A., Carr, C. T., Ellison, N., and Lampe, C. 2011 "It's complicated: Facebook users' political participation in the 2008 election," *CyberPsychology, Behavior & Social Networking* 14(3): 107–14.

Wahl, A. 2006 "Red all over," *Canadian Business* 79(4): 53–4.

Wajcman, J. 2008 "Life in the fast lane? Towards a sociology of technology and time," *British Journal of Sociology* 59(1): 59–77.

Waldman, D. 1977 "Critical theory and film: Adorno and 'the culture industry' revisited," *New German Critique* (12): 39–60.

Walther, J. B. 1996 "Computer-mediated communication," *Communication Research* 23(1): 3–43.

Warf, B. 2011 "Myths, realities, and lessons of the Arab Spring," *The Arab World Geographer* 14(2): 166–8.

Watson, C. 2017 "Twitter users respond to 280-character limit – mostly in 140 characters," *Guardian*; available at: <https://www.theguardian.com/technology/2017/sep/28/twitter-users-respond-to-280-character-limit-mostly-in-140-characters>.

Watts, D. J. 2003 *Six Degrees: The Science of a Connected Age*, 1st edn, New York: Norton.

Weaver, M. 2010a "Special report: Iran: social media: the 'Twitter revolution' that never materialised," *Guardian*, June 10, 2010, p. 19, London: Guardian Newspapers Limited.

Weaver, M. 2010b "Twitter: Ahmadinejad's nemesis, online from Oxfordshire," *Guardian*, February 11, 2010, p. 17, London: Guardian Newspapers Limited.

Wei, R. 2016 "The mobile phone and political participation in Asia: theorizing the dynamics of personalized technologies and networked externality," in R. Wei (ed.), *Mobile Media, Political Participation, and Civic Activism in Asia: Private Chat to Public Communication*, Dordrecht: Springer Netherlands, pp. 1–15.

Weiner, J. 2015 "A personal reflection on social media in medicine: I stand, no wiser than before," *International Review of Psychiatry* 27(2): 155–60.

Wellman, B. 1999 *Networks in the Global Village: Life in Contemporary Communities*, Boulder, CO: Westview Press.

Wellman, B. and Haythornthwaite, C. (eds) 2002 *The Internet in Everyday Life*, Oxford: Blackwell.

Wells, C. et al. 2016 "How Trump drove coverage to the nomination: hybrid media campaigning," *Political Communication* 33(4): 669–76.

Wheatstone, R., Haworth, J., Kitching, C., and Walker, M. 2016 "New Zealand earthquake: recap after 7.8 magnitude quake killed 2 and more than 1600 aftershocks caused 'utter devastation'," *The Daily Mirror* (November 15); available at: <http://www.mirror.co.uk/news/world-news/new-zealand-tsunami-feared-live-9251551>.

Whittaker, E. and Kowalski, R. M. 2015 "Cyberbullying via social media," *Journal of School Violence* 14(1): 11–29.

Widmer, R. J. et al. 2016 "An academic healthcare Twitter account: the Mayo Clinic experience," *Cyberpsychology, Behavior, and Social Networking* 19(6): 360–6.

Williams, R. and Williams, E. 1990 *Television: Technology and Cultural Form*, 2nd edn, ed. Ederyn Williams. London: Routledge.

Witte, J. C. and Mannon, S. E. 2010 *The Internet and Social inequalities*, 1st edn, New York: Routledge.

World Bank, The 2010 "World development indicators," Washington, DC: The World Bank.

Xu, X. et al. 2015 "Advances in smartphone-based point-of-care diagnostics," *Proceedings of the IEEE* 103(2): 236–47.

Yan, Qu, Philip Fei Wu, and Xiaoqing Wang 2009 "Online community response to major disaster: a study of Tianya Forum in the 2008 Sichuan earthquake," paper presented at the 42nd *Hawaii International Conference on System Sciences*, pp. 1–11, January 2009, Waikoloa, Big Island, Hawaii.

Yin, J., Karimi, S., Lampert, A., Cameron, M., Robinson, B., and Power, R. 2015 *Using Social Media to Enhance Emergency Situation Awareness*; paper presented at the 24th International Conference on Artificial Intelligence, Buenos Aires, Argentina.

Yuan, Y. C. and Gay, G. 2006 "Homophily of network ties and bonding and bridging social capital in computer-mediated distributed teams," *Journal of Computer-Mediated Communication* 11(4): 1062–84.

Zee Media Bureau 2016 "4.2 magnitude earthquake hits Haryana, tremors felt in Delhi-NCR," *Zee News* (November 17); available at: <http://zeenews.india.com/news/india/4-2-magnitude-earthquake-hits-haryana-tremors-felt-in-delhi-ncr_1950491.html>.

Zhuo, X., Wellman, B., and Yu, J. 2011 "Egypt: the first Internet revolt?," *Peace Magazine* 27(3): 6–10.

Zickuhr, K. 2013 *Location Based Services*, Washington, DC; available at: <http://www.pewinternet.org/2013/09/12/location-based-servi ces/>.

Index

CPSIA information can be obtained
at www.ICGtesting.com
Printed in the USA
LVHW011753281118
598530LV00013B/390/P